"If some men are willing to pay for sex, and some women are willing to provide it at a price they consider fair, and if nobody is being taken advantage of or coerced, then why is it wrong? Maybe it's my entrepreneurial bias, but when each party has something the other wants, and they're able to make a deal, that constitutes a good and fair exchange.... It may not sound very romantic, but the fact is that sex is a commodity just like anything else. And like every other commodity, it operates on the law of supply and demand. All over the world, some people are in the position to sell, and others are interested in buying. It's ridiculous to make sex the one area of life where people who wish to are not allowed to make a living with their bodies. Our society has no qualms about a masseuse who is paid for touching people, or about laborers, or professional athletes or dancers, all of whom make a living with their bodies. Why should we make an exception for sex?"

"I really loved my business.... Had we been a large enterprise, such diverse areas as personnel, advertising, training, operations, and accounting would each have been handled by different departments. But here I was, without a standard college education—much less an MBA—operating a successful and complex business by following my instincts, utilizing my experiences, and keeping my eyes open."

"I just fell into it. I didn't think about me or the illegality. There was an empty market niche and I knew I could do it better than anyone else."
Sydney Biddle Barrows in *The Wall Street Journal*

MAYFLOWER MADAM

The Secret Life of Sydney Biddle Barrows

"A highly readable and engaging account ... Miss Barrows is quite upbeat about her distinguished lineage and, from the detail she provides, has just reason to be proud of the business acumen she brought to what too often is a haphazard and sleazy pandering." *King Features Syndicate*

"Miss Barrows seems to have a delicious and surprisingly mature sense of humor about it all."
Cincinnati Post

"There can be no doubt that Barrows knows her former business down to the last detail. Her instructions to her charges, as she describes them, are more elaborate than the service manual for a Mercedes-Benz and a lot more interesting."
The Washington Post Book World

Please turn the page for a sampling of tidbits from

MAYFLOWER MADAM

"I was very selective about whom we accepted. . . . I always paid close attention to types of girls: I knew, for example, that I could use only a certain number of tall brunettes. Tall busty blondes were another story, and I could always have used more of them."

"Having grown up in the age of panty hose, most of the girls had never actually worn stockings before. . . . 'A *real* lady,' I would explain with a hint of reproval, 'wears stockings no matter *how* hot it is.' "

"Now it's time for him to pay you, and a lot of men get embarrassed at this point. . . . However they give you the money, if it's cash, it's your responsibility to count it before you leave. . . . Before you leave, be sure to thank him for calling us, and tell him you had a lovely time. At this point, he may give you a tip, and if he does be sure to thank him."

MAYFLOWER MADAM

The Secret Life of Sydney Biddle Barrows

SYDNEY BIDDLE BARROWS
WITH WILLIAM NOVAK

IVY BOOKS • NEW YORK

For Risa,
who did everything—and more

Ivy Books
Published by Ballantine Books
Copyright © 1986 by Sydney Barrows and William Novak

Library of Congress Catalog Card Number: 86-10839

ISBN 0-8041-0150-7

This edition published by arrangement with Arbor House Publishing
Company, a division of The Hearst Corporation.

Manufactured in the United States of America

First Ivy Books Edition: July 1987

"I didn't set out to be madam. . . . Madaming is the sort of thing that happens to you—like getting a battlefield commission or becoming the Dean of Women at Stanford University."

Sally Stanford,
The Lady of the House

Preface

On *the evening* of October 11, 1984, at the age of thirty-two, I had to endure one of the most dreaded rituals a single woman in our society can undergo: I went on a blind date.

I was lucky, as Barry was both handsome and intelligent. Our first few minutes together were awkward, but once we had overcome our initial apprehensions, there was plenty to talk about. At first, we chatted about our work: he was in the business end of publishing, and I gave my usual cover story about operating a fashion accessories business. But within a few minutes, we discovered that his family had a farm right next to a country place owned by some of my relatives and that he knew my cousin Elodie and her daughter, Muffin.

He had called me a week earlier at the suggestion of my friend Susan, whom I had known from boarding school, and we had agreed to meet for dinner at Zinno, an Italian place in Greenwich Village. After a leisurely meal, Barry escorted me back to my apartment on the Upper West Side. At the door to my building, we said good night and talked about getting together again.

In the lobby, I stopped at my mailbox, where I was pleased to find two personal letters among the bills, magazines, and usual clutter of junk. As I headed toward the stairway, I heard Raul, the doorman, calling to me.

"Oh, Miss Barrows," he said in his heavy Spanish accent. "Some people were here looking for you."

"I'm sorry I missed them," I said mindlessly, trying to read one of my letters. "How many were there?"

"About ten," he replied.

Ten? That was odd. I folded the letter and stared at him. "Do you know who they were?" I asked.

"Police."

A shock went through me. "Oh, really?" I said, trying to maintain my poise. "What did they want?"

"They were looking for you. They went upstairs. When they saw you weren't there, they went away."

I stood there for a moment, trying to collect my thoughts. "Raul," I said softly, "please do me a favor. If the police come back, tell them you haven't seen me all night."

"Okay, Miss Barrows."

My heart was pounding as I flew up the stairs to my apartment. I jammed the key into the door and ran for the phone. Somehow, I managed to punch in the number of Cachet, the escort service I owned and operated. Eight rings, no answer. Biting my lip, I hung up and tried again, slower this time, hoping against hope that in my haste I had somehow dialed the wrong number. No such luck.

Why the hell don't they leave me alone? I thought. I didn't know exactly what was going on, but I knew it had to be serious. I wondered how long it would take us to recover this time.

I had no idea that the secret life I had been building up so carefully for the past five and a half years was about to come crashing down.

Chapter One

The annual meeting of the Society of Mayflower Descendants begins with a roll call of New England's first settlers. As each name from the *Mayflower*'s passenger list is announced, anyone in the room who is descended from that person stands up to be counted.

According to a tradition in my father's family, I could have stood for John Howland, an indentured servant who somehow managed to fall overboard just as the ship was about to reach Plymouth Rock. They fished him out with a hook, and he lived to tell the tale. But nobody in the family had been willing to undertake the rigorous research and paperwork necessary to make these things official, so I remained seated when Howland's name was called. Still, the idea that I might be descended from the guy who fell off the *Mayflower* has always had a certain appeal to me.

My mother's family, however, had documented our direct descent from Elder William Brewster, the minister who served as spiritual head of the brave little group that sailed into Plymouth Rock on November 21, 1620. He may not have been as colorful as John Howland, but I was proud to stand up for him.

Fifteen generations have passed since the Pilgrims landed, and along the way I managed to pick up an intriguing collection of ancestors on both sides of the family. On my mother's side, my great-great-great-grandfather was Peter Ballantine, who arrived in this country from Scotland in 1820 and founded the brewery that still bears his name. Like John Howland before him, he arrived on these shores a little wetter than he might have wished. When I was growing up, one of my great-uncles always liked to tell the story of how Peter Ballantine couldn't afford to pay the entry tax, so the captain of the ship helped him out by sending him off in a small boat under cover of darkness. The boat sank before it reached land, and Peter had to wade ashore. He was carrying the family Bible, which still bears the marks of his inauspicious arrival.

On my father's side I am a Biddle, which makes me a member of one of the first families of Philadelphia. The family patriarch was William Biddle, a London Quaker and shoemaker who settled in New Jersey in 1681. Back in England, he had served as a major in Cromwell's army, but after Cromwell's death and the restoration of the monarchy, he and a group of fellow Quakers were arrested and sent to Newgate Prison for deviating from the established church. So he must have been especially grateful for the opportunity to reach what his people regarded as the Promised Land.

Clement Biddle, William's great-grandson, was a friend of George Washington, who presented him with a dozen mahogany dining room chairs that are still in the family. Not much is known about Clement, but historians agree that he had a special fondness for cologne in his bath. From the way this trait was described by his contemporaries, I can only conclude that it must have been considered pretty racy in those days. It's fun to think that one of my own indulgences may have been carried across the centuries through the family genes.

Charles Biddle, another of William's descendants,

was a friend of Aaron Burr; and when Burr killed Hamilton in their famous duel, it was in Charles Biddle's Philadelphia home that he sought refuge. Edward, a brother of Charles, was supposed to sign the Declaration of Independence, but he was too sick to participate, so the show went on without him. Nicholas, a third brother, was the first American naval hero; he was killed when the British sank his ship.

If I could meet just one of my ancestors, it would be the other Nicholas Biddle, a nephew of the first. He was, among other things, a lawyer, poet, scientist, and journalist. In addition, he was known as an authority on art, horticulture, and ancient Greece. On the side, he edited *Port Folio*, America's first intellectual magazine.

From all accounts, Nicholas Biddle was a flamboyant character: gracious, self-confident, and a little condescending. He was also a sharp dresser, and his long hair hung about his face in silken curls. He built an elaborate country estate called Andalusia, on the banks of the Delaware, where he raised silkworms and rare grapes.

But it was as a banker that he became famous—and later infamous. In 1822, President James Monroe named him head of the Bank of the United States, which made Nicholas Biddle the second most powerful man in the nation. But when the bank failed in the panic of 1841, his reputation was ruined. As a child, I was told that the reason our branch of the Biddles had so little money was that after the failure of the bank, Nicholas had insisted on reimbursing his friends out of his own pocket.

After his disgrace, this man who had been virtually worshiped by his contemporaries was shunned by society. He was spoken of with contempt, and most of his old acquaintances would have nothing to do with him. But he responded with great courage and self-possession, and the phrase "calm as a summer morning" was coined after being used to describe Nicholas Biddle's measured response to the political and legal turmoil that swirled around him.

Although Nicholas was by far the best known and most interesting of the Biddles, I have some other fascinating ancestors, including Thomas Biddle, Nicholas's own brother, whose life ended prematurely in a duel with a congressman from Missouri. Following a bitter argument about Nicholas and the bank, the two antagonists fought each other on an island in the middle of the Mississippi. Thomas, who was nearsighted, requested that the contest be engaged with pistols at a distance of five feet, and as hundreds looked on, the two men promptly killed each other.

In our own century, there was Anthony Drexel Biddle, who maintained a collection of pet alligators. While in his sixties, he taught hand-to-hand combat to marines during World War II, and he was reported to have known more ways of killing a person than any man in history.

His son, Anthony Joseph Drexel Biddle, was ambassador to Poland when the war broke out, and he spent those years helping many innocent people escape the Nazis. In true Biddle fashion, he also managed to win the court-tennis championship of France along the way.

More recently, a group of four Biddle brothers left their mark on society: Francis served as attorney general under FDR (and later was one of the judges at the Nuremberg trials); George was a noted artist who was active in the WPA; Sydney, a prominent psychoanalyst, had studied with Anna Freud in Vienna; and Moncure was an investment banker and bibliophile.

When I was a child, however, the only Biddle who really mattered to me was Granny Sydney, my father's mother. She may not have made the history books, but her life has been a remarkable romp through the twentieth century. As a teenager, she was one of the very few people in Philadelphia who owned a car, and she and two girl-friends were the talk of the town after taking a motor trip with no adults to chaperone them. Later, she was one of the first Americans to ride in an airplane.

We used to visit her in Lancaster, Pennsylvania, where she and Bapaw lived in a big, rustic house at the top of a mountain. Granny had been a wildly popular debutante in her day, and I loved to look at the scrapbooks she kept from that period. She still had the invitation to every ball she attended, along with a record of what she wore and who was there. "I met Dan Barrows tonight," she wrote at one point, referring to her first husband, my father's father. And two parties later, "I danced with Dan Barrows three times." They were married within a few months.

She left him—I never learned why—while she was pregnant with their second child. She once told me that at the appointed time, she drove herself to the hospital, had the baby, and never even bothered to inform him! Later, she married Bapaw, a sweet and loving man, and they traveled the world together. As a child, I sat in awe as Granny told me about their trip to China—back in the days before that mysterious land was virtually closed to outsiders.

Bapaw died several years ago, and Granny is no longer very active. But she still has her memories, and my years of looking through her scrapbooks and listening to her stories made me aware that our lives are a compendium of our experiences—the places we've been to, the people we've met, the things we've done. With Granny Sydney as my role model, I decided that one of my goals in life was to be adventurous, to be open enough to take the occasional risk. For rich experiences lead to rich memories, and in the end, memories are all we have.

Dan Barrows also remarried, and when I was young he lived with his second wife in Edgemont, a magnificent estate on the Main Line in Philadelphia consisting of an enormous stone house, stables, and a carriage house. I was especially impressed by the driveway, which seemed to go on for miles. But the real attraction of Edgemont was a pony named Tonio that my grandfather had bought just for the grandchildren. Whenever my younger brother, Andrew, and I came to visit, George, my grandfather's valet, would take us riding.

Dinner at Edgemont was served by candlelight at a table half a mile long. We ate from fine china, closely attended by a couple who had spent their lives working for my grandparents. We never thought of them as servants, however, as they had long ago become part of the family.

On the eve of our visits to Edgemont, my parents were always afraid that Andrew and I would embarrass them with less-than-perfect table manners. But they needn't have worried, as their instructions were more than adequate. We were well-trained and obedient children, and we sat patiently through the many courses, used our finger bowls in the proper fashion, and handled ourselves like little grown-ups. Ever since those dinners, I've never had to worry about my table manners. When you were trained for Edgemont, you were trained for life.

Years later, Edgemont was sold and turned into a country club. It wasn't a difficult conversion. When I stopped by one day to see what had been done, it broke my heart to find a huge bar in the middle of the grand old living room, and wall-to-wall orange carpeting covering the beautiful old wooden floors where fine Oriental rugs used to lie.

I was always aware of my heritage, but only in the most general terms. Except for a few references to Nicholas Biddle, almost nobody ever mentioned the illustrious ancestors. Then again, nobody had to. I knew that I came from a privileged family whose history was intertwined with that of America. On visits to Edgemont, I would marvel at the beautiful antiques and priceless heirlooms, and I used to listen avidly to stories about how these objects had first come into the family. It all made me wish I had been born a hundred years earlier.

Even though some of my relatives lived in grandeur, our own circumstances were far more modest. Still, even in our house there were Oriental rugs and antiques, and I grew up with the idea that going to a store to buy furniture was something other people did. We ourselves had very little money, but we did enjoy some of the trappings of old wealth.

Not long ago, I came across a wonderful line by John Ciardi, the American poet, that sums up my family situation in one sentence. "Gentility," he wrote, "is what is left over from rich ancestors after the money is gone."

Chapter Two

I was born on January 14, 1952, in New Jersey, not far from Rumson, where my mother's parents lived. When I was four, my father left us to marry a woman who worked in his office. My mother was devastated. She would never talk about the divorce, which became a forbidden topic in our family. To this day, I still don't know the details. All I remember is that one day my mother told my younger brother and me that Daddy wouldn't be coming home anymore.

I idealized and adored my father and for years after the divorce blamed my mother for his absence. (I was really angry at *him*, of course, but he wasn't around, so I took it out on her.) I was also jealous of little Andrew, who was just a baby when Daddy left. Understandably, my mother paid him a lot more attention—or so it seemed. I felt left out, and I responded by being nasty to both of them.

I'm not proud of how I behaved, especially now that I realize how frightened and alone my mother must have felt. After all, she was only twenty-three when my father left. She had grown up in a house full of servants and had married this nice young man, and the four of us were supposed to live happily ever after. Instead, she found herself alone with two small children and all the drudgery of being a housewife. She coped as well as she could, and now that I realize what she went through, I really admire her.

My father moved to New York. For the next three years or so, he used to drive down to our house in Hopewell once or twice a month, on Saturday, to see Andrew and me. I lived for those weekends, and when I woke up on Saturday mornings I could barely contain my excitement. I'd be dressed at dawn and outside by seven, sitting on the steps and waiting anxiously for him to drive up, although he never arrived before ten. I wouldn't even come in for breakfast, so my mother used to carry it out on a tray.

By the time I was seven or eight, however, my father's visits had dwindled to the point that we had virtually no contact with him. He no longer called us for our birthdays or at Christmas, and instead of presents he sent checks. At first, my mother tried to protect us from the truth by buying gifts, wrapping them up, and telling us they came from Daddy. But eventually she stopped the charade and simply handed us the money.

I reacted to this hurt by withdrawing from everyone. Books became my chief companion, and I spent most of my time reading. At school I felt different from the other kids, who lived in "normal" households, with two parents at home. Once, in first grade, we had a discussion about our families. My father's new wife had recently had a baby girl, and although I had never seen her, I announced to the class that I had a brother and a sister.

Paul Cranston looked at me from across the room and said, "Sydney, you don't have a sister!"

"I do so," I replied.

"You do *not*! Then where is she?"

"She's a baby. She lives with my father and my stepmother in New York."

But in 1958, families were still *very* nuclear. The concept of a stepmother outside of a fairy tale was unfamiliar to the other kids, who probably thought I was making it up.

I ended up in tears in the teachers' lounge. My mother was summoned to school, where she was advised that Sydney wasn't coping well with the divorce and that I might benefit from "professional help."

My mother couldn't afford to send me to a child psychiatrist, but later, when we moved in with her parents, they paid for a "counselor," as therapists were called in those days. I hated him, and I was so hostile that the sessions didn't help at all. In fact, they made things worse, because in addition to everything else, I now had an embarrassing secret.

After my father left, I was very aware that we had no money for anything but the necessities. My mother received no alimony—probably because she didn't want it—so we survived on his child support payments of two hundred dollars a month. Even in the late 1950s, that sum could barely maintain a household with two small children, especially for a woman who had grown up in affluence. The only part-time work my mother could find was in a college bookstore, which didn't pay very much. After my father left, money was a constant problem.

Until I was nine, we lived in Hopewell, New Jersey, which was about an hour out of Princeton and about five minutes out of a Norman Rockwell painting. It was a small and idyllic little rural town where people left their homes unlocked and their keys in the car. It was also a marvelous place for kids, and I was devastated when my mother, finally tired of struggling along on her own, accepted her parents' offer to move in with them in Rumson, on the New Jersey shore.

My grandparents lived in a huge house and owned a beautiful store called the China and Glass Shop, which sold exquisite china and silver and an assortment of other luxurious items. The two of them always looked so elegant and aristocratic: he was tall and handsome, she was the epitome of a lady. Every morning, Estelle, the maid, would serve them an elaborate breakfast in bed on wicker trays.

What I remember most clearly about their house are the magnificent parties they gave in the huge living room. Estelle made me a little apron, and I would help her pass the hors d'oeuvres. Everybody would make a fuss over me and compliment my grandparents on "Sydney's lovely manners." I loved those parties, and I used to dream about the day when I, too, would be able to entertain in that fashion.

Apparently, "nobody" in Rumson went to public school, so I was enrolled in the fourth grade of Rumson Country Day School, where my mother and her two brothers had gone. The children there had known each other for years, not only from school, but from the yacht club and the beach club and the tennis club and the country club, to which their parents all belonged.

I had never sailed in my life. And nobody in our family ever owned a tennis racket.

On the first day of school, I couldn't wait for recess. Back in Hopewell, I had been a real pro at jumping rope, and now I was eager to show off my skills to my new classmates. Kids all over the country jumped rope, so at least we'd have *this* in common. But to my dismay, the girls at Rumson Country Day preferred a game called horsey, in which they ran around the field pretending to be horses. As I watched in amazement, they went through the various steps and jumps that their beloved animals knew so well. Many of these girls actually owned their own horses, which was something I couldn't imagine.

To make matters worse, I had a weak left eye, and the eye doctor decided that the only way to strengthen it was to have me wear an eyepatch over the right one. Here I was, in a brand-new school, already feeling different, and now looking different as well. I was sure nobody would want to be my friend.

In retrospect, the kids at my new school were probably no less friendly than children anywhere else would be to a new girl who suddenly showed up in the fourth grade. It would have helped, of course, had I been outgoing and warm, but I was too insecure and shy to make new friends. Instead of playing with the other kids, I spent most of my free time reading. Within a few years, I had managed to finish every children's book in the town library.

My reading habit was helped along by the fact that my mother was very strict about television. Andrew and I were allowed to watch only one hour a day—and only after we had finished our homework. We were also restricted to programs that met her approval. "The Mickey Mouse Club" and "Lassie" were okay, but almost everything else was not. "Dr. Kildare" was forbidden because I might learn about scary new diseases and develop psychosomatic symptoms. Alfred Hitchcock was off limits because I might get nightmares. In the eighth grade, I was the only one in the class whose mother wouldn't let her watch "The Man from U.N.C.L.E." because it had too much gratuitous violence. For most children of my generation, television was the great unifying bond, but in my case it was one more reminder of how different I was from the others.

I may have been lonely and unhappy inside, but on the outside I was quite the proper young lady who always did what she was told and tried to please the grown-ups. Still, as I reached adolescence, I began to fight more with my mother. Like most teenagers, I felt that my mother wanted to control me, and I resented her for it. She, in turn, told me I was selfish and inconsiderate. When it was time for me to go to high school, we both agreed that boarding school was a good idea. I chose Stoneleigh, a small school in Greenfield, Massachusetts, nestled in among the Berkshire Mountains. Granny Sydney and Bapaw took care of my tuition.

The summer before I went off to Stoneleigh was the happiest time of my life, because I had my first boyfriend. Like me, Geoff was a loner, although in his case it was because he was an only child whose overprotective parents didn't allow him to go places or do things on his own. They loved their son and were only trying to do what was best for him, but he felt smothered.

We were two lonely kids who fell in love, and I'm still surprised at how emotionally sturdy our relationship was. We used to spend hours talking together, and it was as much a friendship as a romance. We were always honest and direct with each other, and we're still good friends today. We also had our share of fun—going to the beach, riding in Geoff's sleek yellow speedboat, or driving to the boardwalk in Asbury Park.

Geoff's mother was the first truly elegant woman I had ever met. Her husband adored her and was always bringing her flowers and lavishing gifts of beautiful jewelry on her. She wore the latest designer fashions from Bonwit Teller, Saks, Bergdorf Goodman, and other glamorous New York shops. I had been subscribing to *Vogue* since I was twelve, and she always looked to me as if she had just stepped out of a page of that magazine.

My relationship with Geoff continued during my entire time at Stoneleigh. We wrote to each other daily, talked on the phone at least twice a week, and visited whenever we could—which wasn't very often, unfortunately.

Except for missing Geoff, I loved boarding school. Every girl had to select a sport, and I chose riding, which I adored and at which I became fairly skilled. Besides, I've never seen the point of competitive sports, preferring, I guess, to unleash my competitive instincts in the business world.

Being away from my mother was a tremendous relief—for her, I'm sure, as much as for me. And socially, Stoneleigh was a godsend. For the first time in my life I had my own little group of friends, and we had some good times. It was mostly the kind of innocuous mischief teenagers at a boarding school get into, such as spray-painting toilets gold or sprinkling Rice Krispies on the floor to warn of the housemother's approach.

During my first couple of years at Stoneleigh, these pranks were mild enough to keep me out of trouble. But by senior year my luck ran out, and I was disciplined for a few minor infractions. Although I didn't smoke, I was friendly with some girls who did, and at one point an ashtray I had carelessly stuffed into my desk drawer was discovered by the housemother. When I refused to name the other girls who had been involved, I was "posted" for two weeks, which meant that I couldn't leave the school grounds.

I was posted again a few weeks later after my best friend, Nancy Love, and I had served as a lookout for Maria, a girl on our floor who actually succeeded in sneaking a boy into her room. Sneaking him back out, however, proved to be rather more difficult, and Maria was threatened with expulsion unless she revealed the names of her two co-conspirators, which she promptly did.

Nancy and I were faced with the threat of a brief suspension, which certainly seemed preferable to being posted for weeks on end. Besides, since Nancy was from Connecticut and I was from New Jersey, we would both have to take the train into Manhattan on our way home. New York State had recently lowered the drinking age to eighteen, and the two of us eagerly looked forward to hoisting a few Mai Tais at Trader Vic's in the

Plaza Hotel. But when the school authorities got wind of our ill-concealed anticipation, they changed their minds and had us posted for two long months.

Around the same time, Geoff, who was now a freshman at Franklin and Marshall College in Lancaster, Pennsylvania, invited me to the college's winter carnival weekend. The featured band was Blood, Sweat and Tears, and to a restless high-school senior in an all-girl prep school, the weekend sounded impossibly exciting and glamorous. Posted or not, there was no way on earth I was going to miss it.

With the inspired assistance of Nancy, who by now was developing quite a reputation as an accomplice to Stoneleigh's criminal element, I succeeded in sneaking out to Lancaster. (Among other tricks, Nancy covered my tracks by climbing into my bed for bed check before scurrying back to her own room.) The winter carnival was everything I had dreamed of: I met Geoff's friends, toured the campus, and attended the concert. Naturally, we also took the opportunity to spend some time by ourselves at The Sauce House, the local hotel where my room was. We were still in love, and it was wonderful to be together again.

When I returned to Stoneleigh, both the housemother and the dean were waiting for me, and I was hauled down to the headmaster's office. They grilled me for hours about where I had been, and although I told them virtually the entire story, they wouldn't let up in their questions. In addition to their hostility, I had to put up with the smarmy innuendos of the headmaster's son, who took it upon himself to sit in on the proceedings although he had no business being there. When I admitted that yes, my boyfriend had been staying with me at The Sauce House, he sneered, "The Sauce House? *That* sounds appropriate!"

I had had it with this guy. I looked him straight in the

eye and said, "Fuck you." That ended our little meeting, for I was expelled on the spot. As I left, the girls were cheering me from the windows.

I had certainly never said "fuck you" to anyone before, and being expelled from school was the first really serious thing that ever happened to me.

My mother took it very well. She knew that I probably felt worse about it than she did and that nothing would be gained by disciplining me further. I wasn't in contact with my father, but he was in no position to be critical, having been kicked out of St. George's boarding school twenty-five years earlier.

I still had a few months of high school to complete. The local public high school was beset with racial tensions, so neither of us wanted me to go there. My mother discussed several options with my father. They were still in touch, if only to handle their children's affairs, and they decided it would be best if I moved in with my father and his family in Old Lyme, Connecticut, where I could finish up and graduate from the local high school.

By this point, I rarely saw my father more than once a year, and we weren't at all close. But living with him wasn't as awkward as it might have been because he totally ignored my existence. My mother always had a million questions: Where was I going? Whom was I going with? When was I coming home? But at my father's house there was no curfew, and nobody cared what I did. I was eighteen and dying for some independence, and living there was as close as I had yet come to being on my own.

Academically, Old Lyme High was a pretty weak place—especially when compared to Stoneleigh. Socially, however, it was much warmer and more open. For the first time in my life, I was popular, and what a difference *that* made. I couldn't believe there were only four months left until graduation, and I began to wish that I had been expelled from Stoneleigh three years earlier.

The previous October, before I left Stoneleigh, I was excited to learn I had been accepted to Elmira College in upstate New York, one of the few all-girl schools still in existence, which I preferred, and a good place to get a general education. But after I graduated from high school, my father told me that the fund Granny Sydney had set up for my education had been all used up at Stoneleigh. "I realize a lot of girls go to college these days," he said, "but I don't think it's really necessary. You're a pretty girl. You'll get married, and your husband will take care of you. If you want to go to college that badly, you can earn the money and pay for it yourself."

Now he tells me!

Not go to college? I thought *everybody* went to college, just as everybody lived in a house and ate three square meals a day. And now my father was making an abrupt and seemingly impulsive decision just weeks before the the college year was to start.

I was furious at him because this clearly wasn't a subject to which he had given much thought. Once I got over the shock, I had to come up with a plan: my father might not see the importance of college, but I certainly did. And while I had no particular career in mind, I had always been interested in fashion, and Geoff's stylish mother had given me a sense of how exciting clothes could be. Given my limited resources, I decided that my best bet was the two-year program at the Fashion Institute of Technology in Manhattan. With the help of a student loan from my mother's local bank, I enrolled at FIT for the 1971 fall semester and chose a major in fashion buying and merchandising.

In order to save money toward my tuition, I spent the interim year working as a receptionist for my father's educational services company. The job was insufferably boring, but at least I was paid—a total of $70 a week. When I finally asked my father for a raise, he turned me down because, he said, it would look like favoritism. When I left, however, my successor was paid $100 a week.

During that year between high school and college, my grandparents suggested that I might like to be presented in November at the annual ball of the Mayflower Society. I had never given much thought to being a debutante, but it sounded fun and glamorous and I accepted immediately. One of the highlights of the entire experience was shopping for a dress. My mother and I went to Saks, where formal-occasion and designer dresses were sold in the elegant Adams Room, which featured a sumptuous French atmosphere with an impressive chrystal chandelier, Louis XIV chairs, and enormous dressing rooms. There were no clothes to be seen: everything was kept in the back, and dresses were brought out individually or, in some cases, modeled. After considering several heavenly possibilities, we chose a gorgeous white peau de soie gown with a high neckline and a hand-beaded bodice. Before we left, the saleswoman recorded my name and the name of the event I was attending, a standard precaution to ensure that no two girls—from this store, at least—would show up in the same dress.

The ball was held in the Grand Ballroom of the Plaza Hotel. The chandeliers were lit, the orchestra was playing, the glasses were clinking, and I felt like part of a movie set. The other debutantes and I were presented after dinner. When it was my turn, a voice called out: "Sydney Biddle Barrows, descended from William Brewster." My grandfather escorted me in on his arm, and I made a deep curtsy to the governor of the society. The whole night was like a dream, and I kept hoping it would never end.

* * *

The following September, I moved to New York and started classes at FIT. I lived in the dorm and took courses in textile science, marketing, draping, retail math, advertising, and art history. Although the courses weren't very challenging, FIT provided an excellent practical education because everything we learned in class was actually going on in showrooms and office buildings all around us.

FIT was filled with all sorts of people I had never met before. Many of them were New Yorkers with thick accents from Brooklyn and Long Island, and some of the students were actually gay—which was a real shock to my suburban sensibilities. The first time I saw two men with their arms around each other, I couldn't stop staring.

To help pay for my tuition and living expenses, I took a variety of part-time jobs in the garment district. At one point, I was a fitting model at a junior sportswear firm. Bell-bottom pants had just become fashionable, along with platform shoes. I worked for a place called Happy Legs, which was walking away with the junior pants business because they were the only ones who made pants long enough to wear with platform shoes.

During the Christmas season I landed a job at Macy's, where I worked evenings and Saturdays. I had hoped to be on the first floor, where all the action was, selling perfume, cosmetics, or gifts, but to my great disappointment I was relegated to girdles and bras. I moaned at the prospect of selling underwear to fat ladies at Christmas.

To my surprise, I found I really enjoyed the work. This was my first experience helping women look and feel better about themselves, and I seemed to have a real knack for it. And I liked knowing that something I had done or suggested had made a real difference to a customer's self-image.

I was soon transferred to lingerie, which was fun because of all the men who came in before Christmas, embarrassed to be there at all, looking for a nightie or some other unmentionable for their wives.

"How tall is she?" I would ask. Almost invariably, the man would think for a moment before replying, "Actually, she's just about your height."

"Is she very busty?"

Pause. "About like you."

No matter what question I asked, the answer was always, "Just like you." Either a lot of women looked just like me, or a lot of men were remarkably unobservant about their wives.

When a customer came in, I would ask him a few questions and then show him a couple of items I thought he might like. I would point out the various features as tastefully as possible, noting a low-cut neckline or the effect of the little slits up the side of a nightie. Often, when I suggested he might want to choose between two items, the customer ended up buying them both. I did extremely well selling lingerie, and my only regret was that I wasn't on commission.

These men would walk into our department blushing and bewildered. Twenty minutes later they were happy and confident that they were walking out with a gift their wives or girlfriends (in some cases their wives *and* girlfriends) were really going to love. This was the first time in my life I had ever done business with men— almost no women came to the lingerie department in December—and I enjoyed it tremendously.

At the time, of course, I had no idea selling lingerie to men was only one step away from my ultimate calling, which also involved marketing lingerie to men. The only difference was that in the latter case, the lingerie arrived with a pretty young lady inside.

I graduated first among the fashion buying and merchandising majors at FIT and won the Bergdorf Goodman Award, which was given to the student with the highest grades. I was also accepted in the training program of Abraham & Straus, the large and well-known New York department store. The program would begin the following September.

The Bergdorf Goodman Award included a cash prize of one thousand dollars, which the recipient was to use to fly to Paris in July for the haute couture fashion shows. Not wanting to go alone, I invited the young man I had been dating to come along with me.

Steve Rozansky, who studied photography at FIT, was so different from me I can only conclude that our relationship was a case of opposites attracting. Steve was Jewish and had grown up in a Bronx housing project; his father had spent his life behind a deli counter. Several years before lofts became popular, he was living in one on lower Fifth Avenue. His friends were photographers and artists whose background and style were very different from the conservative and tailored bluebloods in the prep school set.

As long as we were going to be in Paris, Steve and I decided to spend the entire summer in Europe. I couldn't wait to go: I had graduated at the top of my class, had won a prestigious award, and had a good job waiting for me in the fall. I was definitely ready to celebrate.

This was in 1973, when the spirit of the sixties was still alive, and we were part of a contingent of thousands of young Americans who would congregate in front of the American Express office in each city to pick up mail, arrange for rides, and swap information. We started out in Copenhagen and made our way to Amsterdam on the Blue Goose, a private bus operated by a young American who made a living by taking people from Copenhagen to Amsterdam to Paris and then back again. He had taken all the seats out, covered the floor with mattresses, and installed a stereo tape deck. The ride to Amsterdam was one rollicking party on wheels.

Amsterdam was spectacular. I especially enjoyed walking through the red-light district, where the local prostitutes displayed their charms in storefront windows, discreetly closing the curtains whenever they had a customer. It was amazing to see these women, who were part of a genuine and legitimate business—complete with window displays!

Shortly after we arrived in Amsterdam, Steve and I were sitting waiting for some laundry to dry when we ran into an American who owned a houseboat on a canal. When he invited us aboard to sample some hashish, which was virtually legal in Amsterdam, we were delighted. I was a neophyte with drugs, but in the giddy atmosphere of that carefree summer, I was more than willing to experiment.

We went to the houseboat and sampled our new friend's excellent hashish. After a while, he tactfully disappeared, leaving us together in the shimmering afternoon sun. "This light is perfect for pictures," Steve said, and I was delighted to have him snap some shots of me in my skimpy summer clothes. Pretty soon, he started flattering me: I looked so terrific, the light was just right, so why didn't I take off my clothes and let him shoot some nude photographs?

No, I said, I wasn't interested. But Steve could be very persuasive, and I was high and on vacation, and the sun was bright on the water, and this was Amsterdam, after all, where the boundaries were a lot looser than they had been back home in New Jersey. What harm could it possibly do?

Steve shot some pictures that were very tasteful and not at all revealing. But as soon as we were done, I started feeling uncomfortable. I had never done anything like this before (and I never would again), and I guess my newly acquired bohemianism didn't run very deep. I wished I could push back the clock, and I even remember thinking at the time: Sydney, someday you'll be sorry you did this.

Our next stop was Paris, where I went to all the haute couture shows and got to sigh over some of the world's most elegant and expensive fashions. My chaperone was a former vendeuse from Dior, and I was thrilled to see that we had better seats than the fashion reporter from the *New York Times*. As the recipient of the Bergdorf Goodman Award, I was on the guest list for most of the shows, and by acting as if I belonged, I was able to see almost all the others as well. For the first time I realized how far you can get if you conduct yourself with confidence and poise and pretend that you know what you're doing.

Shortly after our return, as memories of Europe began to fade, Steve and I started drifting apart. Ours had been a summer romance, but it was clear to both of us that the summer was over. Before we parted, I asked Steve for the negatives from that day of shooting in Amsterdam, but he said he couldn't find them. I had my doubts about that, but there wasn't much I could do. Besides, I had other things on my mind, like my new job at Abraham & Straus. As far as I was concerned, my formal education was finally over. And now, at last, my real life was about to begin.

Chapter Three

B_{ack} at FIT, we had been told repeatedly that the best on-the-job training for our future careers was to work in a department store, where we could learn a wide variety of skills including buying, merchandising, fashion, display, advertising, consumer relations, and design. The Abraham & Straus executive training program was said to be the best in the business, and I couldn't wait to begin.

A&S had no Manhattan store, so the training program took place at their flagship store in Brooklyn. My first day on the job, I showed up in a foulard print Ellen Tracy shirtwaist dress and flat brown Papagallo shoes. With my straight hair and virtually no makeup, I looked like an immigrant from Preppyville, off the train from Greenwich, Connecticut. It took me about two minutes to see that I stood out badly in an ocean of trendy New York women, most of whom were wearing bell-bottoms, platform shoes, and the latest hairstyles. The next day, with the help of my A&S charge card and the 20% employee discount, I began to assemble a more fashionable wardrobe.

I loved retailing, and I was excited by buying and selling. But I was even more drawn to all the backstage machinery—the receiving rooms, the marking rooms, the stock areas, and the various behind-the-scenes operations that made everything else function smoothly.

I also had a new boyfriend, a wonderful guy named Steve Winer with whom I ended up living for four years. Steve was also Jewish, and at first I was terrified of meeting his parents. I had heard stories about how if somebody who's Jewish marries outside the faith, the parents go into mourning, just as if their child has actually died. (I learned later that although this extreme reaction is not unheard-of, it's pretty rare.)

Fortunately, Steve's parents were nothing like that; they couldn't have been nicer, and in family gatherings they treated me more like a participant than an observer. We used to visit them on the major Jewish holidays, when there would always be a festive dinner with relatives and friends. There was a genuine warmth in that household, and it made a powerful impression on me. I decided that if I ever had to pick a religion all over again, I would seriously consider Judaism, not only because the Jews I knew were so family-oriented, but also because they had a deep sense of caring and responsibility toward their own community.

The first time I heard "Hava Nagila" played at a Jewish wedding, I shocked Steve and his parents by singing along with the band. I had learned the words years earlier from an old Harry Belafonte record.

"Sydney," said Steve's mother. "How on earth do *you* know that song?"

"Mrs. Winer," I replied, "I *love* Calypso music!"

At Abraham & Straus I started out as a trainee in junior lingerie and then became an assistant buyer for the bath shop. My boss, Mary, was a fabulous teacher who took the time to show me how everything worked and explained why things were done in a particular way. And Mary was one of the few buyers at A&S who

25

allowed her assistants to do some of the buying, which gave me some real hands-on experience.

By including me in the decision-making process, Mary always made me feel that even in my lowly position I had an investment in the store. And because she treated me so well, I worked extra hard to please her. Unconsciously, I filed away a lesson for the future: a boss should always work to create an atmosphere where her employees feel more like colleagues and less like underlings.

A&S was a well-rounded store with an extensive selection of merchandise, mostly at middle-range price points, with a smattering of higher-end goods as well. It was well matched to the clientele, who were an urban mix with an eye for the latest fashions and a real concern for value.

By keeping my eyes open, I was able to learn some valuable lessons about business and marketing. For example, no matter what business you're in, you've got to know your customer and offer the kind of merchandise that he or she will like—even if you hate it yourself. When Mary and I selected shower curtains for the bath department, I would shudder at the colors and designs she chose, which I never would have bought for myself. But Mary knew what her customers wanted, and she was usually right.

Not long after I joined the program, I had an opportunity to be part of a real-life case study of what happens when a business fails to follow this lesson and begins to ignore the needs and preferences of its customers. A few months after I arrived, Federated Department Stores, which owns A&S, decided to upgrade the store to make it more like another of their divisions—Bloomingdale's.

As part of the transformation, we had to get rid of the popular O tables ("O" stood for omnibus), where we sold heavily discounted goods. These tables had been immensely popular, and all of us who had actual customer contact could see that it was a serious mistake to do away with them, especially as few of our customers were showing much interest in our newer, high-fashion, higher-priced goods. If that's what they'd been looking for, they would have gone to Bloomingdale's in the first place.

But the executives who ran the company were out of touch with the customers and failed to understand a key principle of good business: stay close to your public and pay attention to what they tell you. In the early 1980s, entire books would be written—and sell in huge numbers—that would outline business principles as simple and as obvious as that.

The decision-makers at A&S made another critical error when, in an effort to pare expenses, they encouraged the older salespeople to take early retirement. These were honest, hardworking, dedicated men and women who formed the backbone of the store. Although many of them lived more than an hour away by subway, they always arrived on time and rarely missed a day of work.

But when A&S upgraded its image, the retiring old-timers were replaced with young people who were hired to do the same work for less money. Instead of being cost-effective, however, this move was terribly short-sighted. The veterans sold a lot of merchandise. They put the stock away properly, kept buyers informed about what the customers were asking for, and, most important of all, they really cared about the place.

The kids who replaced them at the minimum wage didn't give a damn about Abraham & Straus and what it stood for. They arrived late and took long lunch hours. They weren't familiar with the stock and didn't know how to sell. Here was another lesson that I learned close up: when it comes to hiring staff, don't cut corners. Find good people and pay them what they're worth.

But to be fair to Abraham & Straus, I learned some positive business lessons there, too. One memory that has always stayed with me was how Sandy Zimmerman, the head of the store, used to drop by our department every now and then to walk around the floor with me. And it wasn't just me, either; Sandy knew the name of every employee, down to the stock clerks. From my perspective, it felt great to know that the top guy was taking a personal interest in what I was doing, and I worked harder in order to please him. Another business lesson was being filed away for the future: let your employees know that you recognize and value their hard work. The more they feel appreciated, the harder they will work to earn your approval.

I spent two years as an assistant buyer and was then promoted to department manager of fine jewelry and watches at the Paramus, New Jersey, store. After a year in New Jersey, I took a job with the accessories division of the corporate buying office of the May Company, which, like Federated, owns several department store divisions.

In 1978 I joined The Cutting Edge, a small Manhattan company that served as a resident buying office for independent boutiques all over the country. I was in charge of accessories, which included such items as handbags, belts, scarves, jewelry, and legwear. I loved my job and regularly worked ten-hour days. And because of my A&S training, I was miles ahead of the other buyers, most of whom had no retail experience.

I also worked hard at developing a good reputation with the manufacturers. As a group, buyers were famous for "sampling" items—especially expensive items—which they borrowed to show potential customers and then "forgot" to return. But I made a point of returning everything, even a pair of twelve-dollar-a-dozen socks. When I came across an item I just couldn't resist, I bought it at the standard wholesale price. As people in the business came to know me, they would lend me virtually anything—even if it were their only piece and the Associated Merchandising Corporation buyer was coming in the next day. As a result, I always had excellent samples to show my visiting clients.

The store owners trusted me, too. "Sydney," they'd say, "you know how many handbags I need for spring. Buy whatever you think is best." But what was best for one store wasn't always right for another, so I had to become familiar with the profile of each individual business. This one needed handbags with shoulder straps; that one wanted them all with zippers. This store sold long scarves; that one could sell only twenty-four-inch squares.

The lesson? A store is nothing more than an aggregate of customers, and here, too, the trick was to pay close attention to what *they* wanted, rather than what I thought they should buy because it was the latest rage in New York. As volume grew at The Cutting Edge, the three partners who owned the business decided to bring in a general manager to supervise all the buyers. Carmela was a tall, thin redhead whom I barely saw until, a couple of weeks after she had arrived, she called me into her office. "Here," she said, handing me copies of some orders. "Distribute these to your stores."

I gave her a blank look. Looking through the orders, I saw that she had made commitments for a large number of handbags. But why was she writing these orders without consulting me? When I went to the factory showroom to look over the merchandise, I was appalled. The garment industry had a word for this kind of stuff: *dreck*. Garbage. How could I get my stores to take this junk?

Without insulting Carmela, I had to let her know that her selection was all wrong. "I went around to look at the handbags, but I'm afraid we're already bought up in those categories," I said diplomatically. "Let's see if we can get them to make something different for us instead of this particular item."

She gave me a strange look. "Don't give me that," she said. "I know you can move these handbags if you want to. You have the biggest pencil in the whole office." This phrase was industry slang for the fact that I was authorized to make large purchases.

"You don't understand," I replied. "I buy for more upscale stores. You and I haven't had a chance yet to sit down and discuss what these people really want."

She wasn't listening. She stood up and looked me in the eye. "I'm your boss," she said ominously, "and you'll do what I tell you."

Suddenly, light dawned. Of course—Carmela was on the take! She had bought a huge supply of handbags that the manufacturer couldn't get rid of, and they were giving her a kickback. Come to think of it, she was probably expecting me to ask for a piece of the action. Although I had never come face to face with it before, this sort of arrangement was not exactly unknown in the garment business.

I was horrified and scared. It was a real dilemma: if I didn't distribute the handbags, I'd lose my job. But if I did, I'd lose my reputation. It took me about four seconds to decide.

"You're welcome to write the orders and sign your name to them," I said firmly. "But I just can't do it."

"Then you'll have to leave," she replied coldly. "I'm afraid I can't work with someone like you."

"Don't you think you're being a bit precipitous?" I asked. As soon as the word was out of my mouth I wished it back, as I could tell that she was searching her memory bank for a definition of "precipitous"—which only made her angrier.

"I want you out right now!" she said. "And don't ever breathe a word about this. I'll tell the owners that you and I had a personality conflict, and that you decided to quit."

"They're not going to believe *that*," I said.

"Yes, they will," Carmela replied. "And if you ever want to work again in this business, that's what *you'll* tell them, too."

I was twenty-seven years old and still fairly naive in the ways of the business world. Above all, I was afraid to make trouble. In retrospect, of course, I should have gone straight to the owners and let them know what was going on. Instead, I meekly walked out of the building.

The other girls in the office promised to keep an eye out for part-time work until I found another job. But it was just before Thanksgiving, which was the worst time of the year to be looking. During December and January, the only two words on the minds of retailers are Christmas and inventory.

Except for the fact that I wasn't earning any money, I enjoyed being unemployed. I loved the freedom of not having to report to an office every day, and I was particularly happy not to have heavy responsibilities constantly hanging over me. Besides, I was confident that I'd find something else before too long.

Despite my "big pencil" at The Cutting Edge, I had been taking home only $174.25 a week, and I had virtually no savings. To supplement my unemployment checks, I managed to keep busy several days a week, working here and there off the books, answering phones and filing papers for a variety of companies. As I went from one office to another, I kept running into another girl in a similar situation. Gina had worked for a shirt company that had gone out of business, and like me, she was picking up odd jobs until a full-time position came along. Because we both had so much free time while our friends were all working regular hours, we soon became friends. Each week, we'd spend at least part of a day together, talking, walking through Greenwich Village (where Gina lived), or just sitting around her apartment watching "All My Children" and other daytime TV shows.

One afternoon I walked into Gina's apartment and found her unpacking a brand-new stereo. "Where did you get that?" I asked. "Certainly not from your unemployment checks."

No answer.

"So did it fall off the back of a truck, or what?"

She hemmed and hawed. "Oh," she said casually, "I had a few dollars tucked away."

But I knew that Gina didn't have any money "tucked away." And even if she did, she wouldn't have been using it to buy a new stereo.

"Come on, what's up?" I asked.

"Swear you won't tell anyone?"

"I swear."

She lowered her voice. "I make fifty dollars a night answering phones at an escort service."

"No kidding," I said. "What's an escort service?"

"Well, it's kind of hard to explain. I sit in the office and answer a phone. Men call in, and we send girls out to be with them."

"Do the girls just sit around the office with you until they go out?"

"Oh, no," said Gina. "They work out of their apartments. When a call comes in, I have to determine which girl is right for that client. I call her at home, and she goes over to meet the man at his hotel."

"How much do the girls make?"

"The men pay $125 an hour, and the girls get about half of that."

I thought about it for a moment before asking, "And do they have to sleep with these guys?"

"Come on, Sydney, for $125 an hour, what do *you* think? Nobody charges that much just to talk, not even a shrink!"

I was stupefied. "And all you do is answer the phone?"

"That's it."

"And you make fifty bucks a night?"

"Under the table, too."

"That's really amazing," I said. "If they ever need anybody else to help out, let me know."

"Sure," said Gina, and we let the matter drop.

The whole conversation was so remote from my own experience that I didn't take it very seriously. I knew about call girls, of course, but having a friend casually tell me that she answered the phone for an "escort service" seemed miles away from my glittery, sophisticated image of a high-priced lady of the evening.

I suppose I should have been shocked by what Gina was doing, but I wasn't. After all, she was only answering the phone, not going on dates herself. Besides, if the clients were restricted to men who could afford to pay $125 an hour, perhaps it wasn't as sleazy as I thought.

Fifty dollars a night for answering the phone sounded pretty good to me, but I didn't expect the subject would ever come up again. As far as I could see, Gina's offer to let me know if there was ever an opening was like one of those conversations you have with a guest at a party: she promises to send you a print of the photograph she's just taken, but of course you never hear from her again.

I was wrong. A couple of weeks later, Gina called me and said, "Remember that place I told you about? One of the phone girls is leaving, and the owner is looking for a replacement. Are you still interested?"

I thought about it for a long moment. "Are you sure I won't get into trouble?" I asked. "I don't want to get arrested or anything like that."

"Eddie is very careful," she assured me. "Executive

Escorts has been in business for years without any problems.''

I took a deep breath. "I don't know," I said. "I guess it wouldn't hurt to meet him."

I was definitely nervous. The money was good, and at this point I really needed it. But was this really the kind of operation I wanted to get involved in? On the other hand, Gina clearly wasn't the criminal type, and if *she* was working there, how bad could it be? Besides, I was curious: who was this Eddie, and what was this business all about? I decided to look on the interview as an adventure. After all, talking to Eddie didn't mean I had to accept the job—even assuming that one was being offered.

Gina set up an appointment for the next evening, but what do you wear to a job interview for the position of phone girl at an escort service? I wanted to look good, but not *too* good, because I didn't want Eddie to get the idea that I might be available to work as an escort. In an attempt to look casual yet businesslike, I put on a pair of slacks and a bulky sweater and wore my glasses.

Eddie worked out of his apartment in an ubiquitous white brick high rise on the Upper East Side. When I gave the doorman my name, he called upstairs and directed me to the elevator. When I got to the ninth floor and started looking for Eddie's apartment, I expected the door to be bolted with seven different kinds of locks. But I was wrong: to my surprise, the door was ajar. When nobody answered my knock, I stepped inside.

"Hello?" I called.

"Back here," barked a man's voice. "I'm on the phone." I followed the voice through an empty living room to an ornately appointed office with two desks and two telephones. When he saw me, Eddie motioned for me to come in.

He appeared to be in his early fifties. He was short,

with slick black hair, and he wore jeans and a rumpled gray shirt open almost to the navel. At the time, gold chains were very popular, and Eddie was wearing enough of them to outfit an entire singles bar. From what I could hear, he was obviously having an argument with one of the girls, and I noted with a twinge that he seemed like a pretty gruff character.

When he got off the phone, he asked me a few questions: How did I know Gina? How much did I know about his operation? It was clear that he didn't want me to be overly curious, and I took the hint. Or maybe it's just that I didn't know what to ask. In either case, I must have met with his approval because he asked me how soon I could start working.

It all seemed so easy! My biggest concern had been getting arrested, but after seeing Eddie's office, it was hard to imagine that there was any real danger. And I certainly had no moral qualms because the girls who worked for Eddie were clearly doing so of their own free will and were making good money. According to both Gina and Eddie, the clients were perfectly nice, respectable men, mostly foreign diplomats and traveling businessmen, and Gina had told me, laughingly, that she was on a first-name basis—at least over the telephone—with the duke of this and the ambassador of that. I didn't feel there was anything really wrong with it, and I needed the money, so what the hell: I said yes.

Eddie explained that I would be working three nights a week, from seven in the evening until sometime between midnight and two in the morning, depending on his personal schedule. My job was to answer the phones and explain how we operated. I would start by listing the rates and would then describe the girls who were available that night. If the client was interested, I would make all the necessary arrangements, including calling the girl at home to tell her whom she was seeing, at what hotel, and when. On nights when Eddie wasn't around, I would also be responsible for keeping the books and settling accounts with the girls.

Eddie assigned Gina to teach me how the system worked. I spent the first two nights listening to her and taking notes, and on the third night I started taking calls myself, under her supervision. At first I couldn't keep anything straight, and I was so nervous that I kept tripping over my words. Finally, I asked Gina to go over the pitch with me, and I wrote it down and read it to our callers until I knew it by heart.

While I had never given the matter much thought, I had always assumed that New York call girls were elegant, cool, sophisticated, and probably a little abrasive. But the girls who worked for Executive Escorts were very different from this stereotype. Had I met them in any other context, I would never have guessed how they spent their evenings.

While most of these girls were slightly above average in looks, they were all regular people. None of them looked cheap or tarty, or even especially sophisticated. Many were college-educated, and most had daytime jobs: Alva was a free-lance photographer, Maria was a teacher, Nancy was a nurse, and two or three others were graduate students. With a couple of exceptions, Eddie's girls were genuinely nice. What they had in common was a secret way to pick up a few extra dollars—*quite* a few, in some cases.

The girls had something else in common: they all hated Eddie. He made them work seven nights a week, with no time off and virtually no opportunity for a social life. Not surprisingly, the escorts came up with a steady stream of excuses to explain why they wouldn't be available that night. In the three months I was there, some girls' grandmothers must have died two or three times.

At one point, a girl's father really *did* die, and she told

Eddie that she was going back to Texas to be with her mother. This was on a Wednesday, and Eddie said, "So I'll see you on Monday."

"No," she said. "My mother wants me to stay with her for a couple of weeks."

Eddie was annoyed. "Why so long?" he demanded.

She started to cry: "I told you. My *father* died."

"So what do *you* care?" said Eddie. "He probably left you lots of money!"

A real sweetheart, that Eddie.

The girls collected $125 an hour from the clients, cash or personal checks only, out of which they paid $60 to the agency. This, I learned later, was the usual split in the escort business, but Eddie didn't trust anyone, so the girls had to come back with the money *that night*—no matter how late it was. Even if you had been working for Eddie for two years and it was four in the morning in the middle of a snowstorm, he wouldn't let you keep the money overnight.

And if you were seeing a new client, you had to stop at Eddie's place first to pick up one of his brochures. It would have been a lot easier, of course, to give each girl a stack of brochures which she could then give out on her own. But at the time, no other escort agency in town had brochures, and Eddie was always afraid that somebody was going to steal his idea.

He went to great lengths to prevent the girls from meeting each other, and he had us stagger the times when they came back to pay. Presumably, he didn't want them talking together about how rotten he was. The only exception was on a multiple-girl call, when two or more girls went out together to be with two or more men.

And what terrible taste he had in clothes! He would take the girls shopping at Alexander's, which is like going on a dinner date to Burger King. Invariably, they'd come back from these excursions with outfits that made them look cheap. One girl returned from one of Eddie's shopping trips in a red chiffon number that made her look as if she were working Forty-second Street.

As Gina explained it, Eddie's real purpose was to keep the girls in debt, which would give them an ongoing economic incentive to continue working for him. That may explain why he insisted that they all buy full-length evening gowns, despite the fact that there was never any reason to wear one. But if the whole point was to get the girls to spend their money, I still don't know why he didn't just take them across the street to Bloomingdale's.

While I didn't actually meet any of the men, I did speak to them on the phone. Many of the clients were highly placed in their organizations or were entrepreneurs, and quite a number were foreign diplomats. With a handful of exceptions, they came across as well spoken, intelligent, and obviously successful.

A few months before I met Eddie, Gina had suggested to him that he advertise in the *International Herald Tribune*, the English-language daily published in Europe, the Orient, and the Middle East. No other escort service advertised there, and because the *Tribune* was frequently distributed on overseas flights into JFK Airport, it was a great place to be listed. It wasn't that Eddie's ad brought in a huge volume of calls, but the people it did attract were invariably successful and well-heeled gentlemen who liked to have a good time.

I remember one girl who came back to the office glowing after spending six hours with the head of a Swiss chocolate company.

"It sure looks as if *you* had a good time," I said.

"I really did," she replied. "He was absolutely fascinating. We spent most of the night drinking champagne while I listened to this charming man describe how fine chocolate is made. He had all these samples with him, and he'd describe each variety before he'd let me taste it. It was so much fun that I felt guilty taking his money."

On nights when Eddie wasn't around, I would talk to the girls and listen to their stories. Except for having to deal with their boss, most of them genuinely enjoyed the work. From what they told me, I came to understand that while sex was an essential part of the business, it wasn't necessarily the major part. The clients who used Eddie's escort service were on the go from morning until night. Most of them lived out of town, and during their visits to New York they would rush from one appointment to another, including business breakfasts, business lunches, drinks after work, and dinner meetings.

For some of these men, an hour or an evening with an escort was their only opportunity all week to drop their guard, be themselves, and relax. As a result, the girls were far more than sex partners. They also functioned as friends, confidantes, companions, even therapists.

Working for Eddie, I was struck by the fact that his operation was successful even though he consistently violated every rule of good business—not to mention common sense. By forcing the girls to work every night, he invited their resentment and encouraged them to make up excuses. By never setting limits on the behavior (or lack of sobriety) of his clients, he made the girls feel powerless and occasionally degraded. By not trusting the girls to keep the money overnight, he created an atmosphere of suspicion which kept them on their guard.

I remember a client who one evening arranged for five girls to drive up to his mansion in Westchester for a party with a few of his friends. When one of the men didn't show up, the fifth girl spent most of the evening alone, reading a book in the living room. The men gave her $100 as a consolation, and instead of insisting to the client that she be paid in full, Eddie demanded that she turn over half of the money!

Eddie had a policy that every tip over $100 had to be shared with him, so the girls responded by not telling him about the big tippers. When a client gave one of our girls a case of wine, Eddie made her give six of the bottles to him, even though he himself didn't drink wine. And when a girl came back with a box of fine candy, Eddie had the nerve to tell the client, the next time he called, that in the future he ought to give the girl two boxes because the boss had a sweet tooth.

It was clear that Eddie's behavior was undermining his business, and I started to channel my annoyance into a kind of competitive game: What would I do in this situation? How would I handle tips? How would I treat the girls? The answers to these questions did not strike me as especially difficult, and I knew I could do a lot worse than running a business by deliberately doing the opposite of everything Eddie did. Before long, the idea of running an escort service—and doing it *right*—had become enormously appealing.

The more time I spent working for Eddie, the easier it became for me to separate the business from the way Eddie ran it. When you stripped away the moralism and hypocrisy of conventional society, it became clear that this was a service business, just like any other, and the mere fact that Eddie ran it poorly did not mean it couldn't be run well. Courtesans and call girls had an old and honorable history, and done right, the management side of the business might be an interesting way to make a living. And when I realized how much money Eddie was taking in, the fantasy of running my own escort business became increasingly powerful.

One night when Eddie was out, Janice, one of our most loyal girls, came into the office to make a payment. When the phones were quiet, she asked me to follow up on a check she had brought in three weeks ago because she hadn't yet received her share. But Eddie hadn't left an envelope for her, so I told Janice I'd check with him and get back to her tomorrow.

The next night, I asked Eddie if it was all right to pay Janice the $250.

"Tell her the check didn't go through," he said.

The same thing had happened twice before, and both times I had been suspcious. This time I was sure he was lying.

"Come on, Eddie," I said. "She needs the money."

"You heard me," he said angrily. "Tell her it didn't go through."

Carrying out Eddie's policies was one thing, but cheating the girls was something I just couldn't tolerate. That's when I decided to quit.

The next morning I called Gina to tell her about Eddie's dirty dealing.

"Doesn't he just make you sick?" she said.

"I'm never going back. You know," I blurted out, "we could run this business so much better than Eddie. What do you think about really trying it?"

I hadn't meant to share my secret fantasy, but there it was, out on the table.

Gina was silent for a moment. "Don't think I haven't considered it," she said. "In fact, I should probably tell you that Deborah and I have had several conversations about starting our own agency."

Deborah was one of Eddie's girls. I knew that she and Gina were friendly, but I was startled to learn that they had been discussing a joint venture. Deborah had street smarts, but she didn't have any business experience or organizational skills.

"I think you'd be a lot better off with me," I told Gina, and on the spot, I started selling myself to her. I told her about my classes at FIT and about winning the Bergdorf Goodman Award. I stressed my business training at Abraham & Straus and my short-lived success at The Cutting Edge. I also told her exactly what I thought of Eddie, not as a person—that was obvious—but how he consistently made bad business decisions.

"Besides," I said. "I'm ready to do it. I'm prepared to start talking this afternoon."

I must have made a good case because Gina said she was coming right over to continue the conversation. I hung up the phone and looked in the mirror. "Sydney," I said, "I know you like a good adventure, but are you sure you want to go ahead with something like this?"

A moment later, my reflection answered back: "Absolutely."

Gina and I agreed that she would spend a few more weeks working for Eddie while I embarked on a crash course about the escort service business in Manhattan. I got in touch with a couple of girls who had once worked for Eddie, and when they saw how eagerly I listened to their stories, they passed me on to some of their friends, who in turn introduced me to some of *their* friends.

It soon became clear that Eddie's operation was actually one of the better ones! After all, he never sent girls to any of the other boroughs or to sleazy hotels, and if a girl complained about a client, she wouldn't have to see him a second time. Most of the other services in town failed to show even this much respect for the girls—not to mention the clients. When a new client called and asked to meet a girl who was, say, tall, blond, and busty, he would be told to expect her in an hour. Two hours later, who would show up at his hotel? More often than not, a short, chubby brunette.

In most cases, the client wouldn't bother to complain. After all, he'd been waiting two hours, she was reasonably attractive, and he didn't want to wait another two hours. Besides, if he had dealt with escort agencies before, he didn't expect any better. So he paid the hourly fee and made a mental note not to call this particular service again.

I found that many agencies sent girls not only to the outlying boroughs, but even to the client's office. Apparently, there were no limits to where an escort could be sent, and one girl told me in detail about a client who insisted that she meet him at two in the afternoon in Bryant Park. He had the whole thing planned: she was to arrive in a limousine, dressed in a black plastic raincoat with nothing on underneath. She was then to proceed directly to a park bench, where the client would meet her ten minutes later. At that point, with neither of them uttering a word, and somehow without attracting undue attention, she was supposed to provide an act of oral gratification.

For this unusual favor, the client was to pay her a thousand dollars in cash. He gave her an envelope, and everything went smoothly. But after he walked away, she found the envelope filled with ten one-dollar bills, instead of the ten hundreds she had been promised. When she went back in tears and complained to the owner, she was told, "Sorry, honey, but that's the chance we all take."

Because Eddie had always done his own hiring, Lucy and I had no idea how to interview potential escorts. We decided that I should read over some ads and show up at a couple of job interviews to see what the process was like.

Joan, the first person I interviewed with, met me in the living room of her apartment. To my surprise, she didn't even ask to see any identification before she told me all about her operation. And while she took the basic precaution of using a false name, when I went into her bathroom, I saw a prescription bottle on the sink with her real name on the label.

The interview was just as casual. As far as "Joan" was concerned, half an hour of small talk was more than enough time for her to hire me and tell me what she thought I needed to know. There was no preparation at all, and no discussion of how she wanted the escorts to represent her agency, both of which I thought were critical before a new escort could start working. And in sharp contrast to Eddie, Joan gave all her girls deposit slips so they could put the clients' checks into the agency's bank account themselves.

"Okay," she said, "can you start tonight?"

"W-well," I stammered, "that's a little soon for me, but I'll get back to you later in the week."

As I was leaving Joan's apartment, I remember thinking that her business probably wouldn't last more than six months. I was wrong: six years later, as I write these words, she's still in operation.

I went to another place, where the owner, claiming to be a therapist, actually kept a casting couch in his office. In the most gentle and polite manner you could imagine, he explained to me that I would have to "audition" for the role.

"No, thanks," I said with a smile. "I don't give samples."

A couple of days later, I walked into the office of a large, well-advertised escort service. The man who greeted me didn't even introduce himself. He just handed me a condom, pulled down his pants, and said, "Okay, let's see if you know how to put this thing on."

I was so shocked that I couldn't even speak. I whirled around and ran out of there so fast that I don't think I took another breath until I hit the street.

*   *   *

One afternoon, as I was leafing through *Show Business* magazine, I came upon an intriguing ad: "Escorts, earn $1,000 a week and more, for part-time work."

I immediately showed it to Gina. "A thousand a week?" she said. "There's no way they can do it." At the time, Eddie's girls were taking home only $65 an hour, and even his top girls weren't making $1,000 a week. Something fishy was going on here, and although I had already seen a few places too many, I decided to make one more trip.

I called the number, asked for an interview, and was told to show up at a brownstone in Greenwich Village at eleven the next morning. I was greeted at the door by a uniformed maid who showed me to a dark living room filled with bizarre African masks and statues. As I sat there, half trying to read a magazine, two other uniformed maids were cleaning up around me. Upon closer inspection, both of the "maids" turned out to be men in drag, but this was the Village after all, so I tried to act blasé.

After half an hour or so, the maid showed in a girl in black spandex pants and matching halter top who introduced herself as Linda. She had wild orange hair, lots of eyeliner, and plenty of green eye shadow, all of which gave me the distinct feeling that one of us was out of place and that it wasn't Linda. Like me, she had seen the ad in *Show Business* and had come to learn more about the job.

After a long wait, we were greeted by a pudgy woman in a jogging suit who had clearly just rolled out of bed. Olga, as she called herself, had pasty skin, puffy little eyes, and no spark of energy. Between yawns, she proceeded to tell us about the job, but she was so vague about the details and so incoherent and scattered that neither Linda nor I could understand exactly what she was talking about. There were scattered references to fantasies and role-playing, and to ordering clients around, but it wasn't really clear what, exactly, we would be *doing*—assuming we got the job.

This much was obvious: despite the ad, this was not an escort service but some kind of brothel, which meant that all encounters took place on the premises. Olga, then, was the madam, although it was hard to imagine a more unlikely candidate for that title. But from what she seemed to be saying, the girls who worked for her weren't expected to sleep with the clients.

We were interrupted by the arrival of a male visitor, and while he waited upstairs, Olga told us that he was one of her regular clients. "I'm glad he's here," she said, "because now you can get a better idea of what this place is all about. Give us ten minutes, and then I want you to creep up the stairs just as quietly as you can. We'll be in the second room on the right, and you can peek in underneath the door. Joseph is a doctor, and he enjoys being humiliated. I'll order him to wriggle across the floor, and I'll let him know what a filthy little worm he is, and that he's not even good enough to lick my boots."

The whole business sounds pretty distasteful, I thought. I don't believe anyone would pay money for *that*. This woman must be off her rocker.

I wanted to leave, but I had already invested two hours of my time, and I had yet to understand what was going on. Ten minutes later, Linda and I tiptoed up the stairs. When we got to the room, Joseph was naked, lying on the floor with Olga's boot pressing down on his head. But because the "crack" under the door was a good four inches high, he spotted us at once and complained to Olga, who yelled at us to go away. I assumed that this show of anger was merely an act for Joseph's benefit, and Linda and I hurried back downstairs.

When Joseph finally left, Olga came down and apologized for her outburst. Then she leveled with us. This was a house devoted exclusively to dominance, which she ran under her working name—Baroness Von Stern. (It was difficult to keep a straight face when I heard that.) As she explained it, most of her clients wanted nothing more than verbal abuse, and some even arrived with a script which the "mistresses," as the girls were known, would be asked to read. Apparently, Olga's clients were very explicit about how they wanted to be humiliated.

Just then another client arrived. By this time I had heard more than enough, but Olga put her arms around Linda and me and herded us back upstairs. "There's someone I want you to meet," she said. There, slumped in a chair, was a fat, bald, naked, pitiful-looking man. "Stand up, Henry," barked the baroness. "This is Mistress Linda, and this is Mistress Sheila. Both of them are experienced mistresses, and they won't put up with any nonsense from you. Now which one would you like to see?"

Omigod, I thought, what if he picks me? I certainly hadn't anticipated *this*, but there I was, face to face with a client, and I started to panic. I sent up a quick prayer: "Make him pick *her*!" Mistress Linda certainly looked right for the part, but who knew what might turn this guy on?

When he picked Linda, I was weak with relief. I looked at my watch and said, "Oh, my, I had no idea it was so late. Baroness, I'll call you tomorrow."

"Wait," she said, "you can't leave *now*."

"Why not?" I asked. I couldn't get out of there soon enough; who knew what other surprises she might have in store?

"Just let me show you around. It will only take five minutes, I promise."

Unable to be downright rude and refuse, I reluctantly

followed the baroness as she gave me a tour of the house. One room featured a rack, where the "victims" were stretched, and a pulley system where they could be strung up. Another was fixed up to look just like a jail cell, complete with iron bars and an uncovered toilet.

It was like a nightmare. "I *really* have to leave," I insisted, promising that I'd call her tomorrow. Outside, the sun was shining and the air was bright and clear. Lucy's apartment was only a few blocks away, and I ran over in record time. "That's the last interview I'm ever going on," I gasped as I flopped on her sofa. "You're not going to *believe* what I've been through!" And I proceeded to tell her the whole story.

By now I was starting to understand just how big the commercial sex business really was. Gina showed me a copy of *Screw* magazine, the New York tabloid, and I couldn't believe how many ads there were for escort services and houses of prostitution. There was an entire *industry* here, and I had never even known it existed. Eddie's operation was only the tip of the iceberg.

I also realized the meaning of a puzzling incident that had happened to me a few months earlier, when I had decided to take a close friend to a fancy restaurant to celebrate her engagement. Because we were both dressed up for the occasion, she suggested that we stop first for drinks at the Plaza Hotel's Oak Room, where neither of us had ever been before. As we tried to walk in, a security guard blocked our way. "I'm sorry, ladies," he said. "The bar is too crowded."

I looked past him and noticed at least a dozen empty chairs. "It's not *that* crowded," I said, but he only shook his head and said, "I suggest you go elsewhere." It wasn't until I interviewed some of the working girls, as call girls refer to themselves, that I understood why the guard had stopped us. Obviously, he had assumed we were independent working girls looking to pick up a client. Ironically, we ended up at an elegant bar across the street, which, I learned later, was reputed at that time to be one of the biggest call-girl spots in town.

A day or two after I returned from the baroness, Lucy came up with a good suggestion: she thought it might be useful for us to visit one or two madams who ran high-class brothels—not as potential employees, but as businesswomen. Gina had a friend who managed one of these places, and because we would not be in direct competition, the woman agreed to let us come over one morning to learn about her operation.

This particular establishment operated out of a town-house on the East Side. The clients would enter through the first floor, which featured a cozy little bar and a small dance floor. The rest of the house was decorated in an Oriental motif, with flower displays, Japanese prints on the walls, and subtle, artistic lighting. The bathrooms were loaded with plush towels and stocked with the finest men's colognes. After being introduced to several girls in the living room, the client would make his selection and go upstairs with the girl of his choice.

The manager—she definitely did *not* want to be called a madam—explained that the place was open from eleven in the morning until two A.M. and that the girls worked in two shifts. There was a heavy lunchtime trade, a few afternoon visitors, and then a number of commuters who stopped by for a quickie before getting on the train to Connecticut or Long Island. The house was open to members only, and you had to be a member for five years before you could bring in a guest. And that wasn't all; there was even an armed guard at the door.

"Why the guard?" I asked. "Do you mean to tell me that if the police show up, there would be a shootout?"

"Oh, no," she said, amused at my naiveté. "If the cops show up, it's all over. We're much more concerned about robberies, which are a big problem for private houses. Think about it: if somebody breaks in and makes off with the day's receipts, what recourse do we have? Who can we *tell*?''

Many of the houses had a common security policy: a new caller had to be recommended by an old client, and even then he wasn't told where the place was. Instead, he would be asked to call again from a pay phone on a specific corner. When he called, one of the girls would go out and look him over while another girl chatted with him on the phone; if he looked safe, he'd be invited in. This little arrangement also prevented new clients from showing up without an appointment. Otherwise, a man might note down the address, put it in his wallet, and then suddenly appear three months later at two in the morning.

I had always assumed that bordellos had gone out of business long ago, that they belonged to San Francisco in the 1890s or New Orleans in the 1920s. But from what I could gather—and I doubt if anyone knows the whole story—there are something like fifty brothels operating in full swing in Manhattan alone. The majority are fairly small, with no more than half a dozen girls, and most of the places are not very plush because their owners are reluctant to invest much money in a business that could easily be shut down tomorrow. A few of the houses are downright seedy and consist of little more than mattresses on the floor and thin partitions dividing the "rooms."

Although the house we visited was certainly impressive, I couldn't help but see it from the girls' perspective. The shifts were long, and unlike escort services, where sex was often only one part of a longer evening, the clients here came for just one purpose. And while the money was good, there was a lot of dead time when the girls were prisoners of the house while they waited for somebody to show up. A house may be a nice place for clients to visit, but for the girls who worked there it was no bargain.

Despite the vast amount of sleaziness and deceit in the escort industry, I believed it didn't have to be that way. I was sure we could provide a dramatic alternative to what was available, and I was motivated by the challenge of doing something better than everyone else. Several years later, when I read Lee Iacocca's autobiography, I was fascinated by how he explained his enormous success in 1964 with the Mustang. As Iacocca describes it, the normal procedure in Detroit was to build the car first and look for the market afterward. But with the Mustang, Iacocca and his team tried the opposite approach: first they identified the market, his potential consumers—in this case, the baby boomers—and then he proceeded to build a car that would appeal to them.

In retrospect, I was motivated by a similar principle. From working at Eddie's and from keeping my eyes open, I knew that there were thousands of decent, respectable businessmen out there who called escort services. They were often dissatisfied by their experiences, but if they were willing to pay for female companionship and didn't happen to know a private madam, they really had no alternative. I was determined to create a business that would appeal to these men, who constituted the high end of the market. With the right approach and a little luck, I didn't see how we could fail.

I was sure that we could turn our agency into one hell of an operation—successful, elegant, honest, and fun. I had seen enough mistakes in both the escort and retail businesses to know what *not* to do. And I had no "moral" problems, because escort services filled a human and age-old need. As I saw it, this was a sector of the economy that was crying out for the application of good management skills—not to mention a little common sense and decency. I had never really thought of going into business for myself, but here was a chance to do something nobody had ever done before. I couldn't wait to begin.

Chapter Four

*I*n April, 1979, a month before we planned to open our new business, Gina and I still hadn't come up with a name. Determined to get it over with once and for all, we spent a long afternoon poring over a dictionary and a thesaurus. I came up with Cachet; she chose Caprice. But while I liked Caprice, I didn't want to give my business the same name as a car.

Cachet, however, had several advantages: an elegant ring, a French flavor, a hint of mystery, and a dictionary definition that read, in part, "distinction, prestige, a mark or sign showing something is genuine, authentic, or of superior quality." *That* was more like it! There was a further advantage to Cachet: you had to be reasonably civilized to know how to pronounce it, which might intimidate some of the less desirable callers.

The following month, Gina and I drew up a formal partnership agreement. We opened a corporate bank account in the name of Cachet and got ourselves a federal ID number and a business certificate. On application forms, whenever we were asked to specify the nature of our business, we wrote "temporary help agency." We didn't want to lie, but when there was no other choice we tried to stay as close to the truth as possible.

Technically, we would have no employees: the girls would work as independent contractors and pay us an agency commission. This way, there would be no payroll, no withholding taxes, and no other administrative headaches. Otherwise, we'd need to hire a staff just to handle the paperwork.

Thanks to Eddie, we had a clear idea of what not to do. We agreed, for example, that in contrast to our old boss, we would ask our girls to work only three nights a week. (They were free to work more often than that, but most chose not to.) Moreover, we would allow them to choose their own days—as long as they let us know a week in advance so that we could coordinate the master schedule.

Next, we decided that our clients would never be asked to pay until the evening was over. In my view, asking for payment in advance implied a certain level of distrust, which meant starting things off badly. Besides, it was awkward for a girl to walk into a client's hotel room or apartment with her hand out. In every service business I could think of, the client was asked to pay only after the service had been rendered. Why should we be any different?

I knew at the time that this policy represented a radical departure from other escort services. I didn't know quite *how* radical until recently, however, when I read *Working Women,* an excellent study of prostitution in New York by Arlene Carmen and Howard Moody. As the authors note, "There is no area of prostitution—the streets, parlors, houses, or call girls—where the fee is not paid up front. It is considered stupid, if not irresponsible, to trust a customer to pay afterward."

Call me irresponsible, but I've never regretted that decision. Our first-time clients were invariably startled by our payment policy, and many men called us again simply because they appreciated being treated like normal people instead of potential criminals.

We also decided to limit our business to Manhattan. We felt more comfortable knowing that we'd be physically close to the girls in case they ran into problems, and because we knew Manhattan well, we had a good sense of the safety of various neighborhoods. Besides, except at the airports, there are few (if any) first-class hotels in the other boroughs, and we had no intention of sending our girls anywhere where they wouldn't feel entirely comfortable. Finally, it wasn't easy to hail a cab outside of Manhattan; you had to depend on a car service, which made transportation much more problematic—not to mention expensive.

We made one more resolution: even if our honesty resulted in a little less business, we wouldn't lie to our clients. If a man called and asked whether the girl we were describing was beautiful—and she wasn't—we would say so: "No, I wouldn't call her beautiful. But she's really quite attractive, and she has gorgeous eyes." If the client asked specifically for a girl who was tall, blond, and busty, and nobody fit the bill, we would say, "I'm terribly sorry, but we don't have a girl with all of these qualities who's available right now. But Carolyn has beautiful blond hair, or if you'd like to see somebody tall, Shawna is a delightful redhead."

However, even honesty had its limits. Proud as we were of our business ethics, we both knew that this wasn't the sort of enterprise we wanted to operate under our own names. So for business purposes, Gina became Gloria O'Malley and I chose the name Sheila Devin. To keep things simple, I had wanted a name that began with an "S" and was easy to pronounce—especially for the foreign travelers, who, I expected, would constitute a significant share of our clientele. As for "Devin," it was inspired by Devon McFadden, a former character on "All My Children," my favorite daytime TV show.

In retrospect, "Sheila Devin" wasn't really such a good choice. On the phone, many people I did business with resisted "Devin" and insisted on changing it to Devlin or Devon. I also learned that half of New York can't spell "Sheila." On the other hand, they can't spell "Sydney," either, so I was already used to that.

Using different names for different parts of my life definitely took some getting used to. At first, when I called somebody on the phone, I'd often forget: was I Sheila or Sydney? These days, people often ask me if Sheila and Sydney were more than simply different names, whether they were in any sense two different people as well. They weren't. It's just that they were in different lines of work: Sheila operated an exclusive escort service, while Sydney supposedly ran a small accessories business.

Initially, Gina and I split all the work down the middle: I would do the books for a month, and then it would be her turn. But I'm so bad with numbers that she had to correct everything I did, so we soon made a more practical arrangement: I wouldn't go near the books. Gina had spent months working for Eddie, so she knew a lot more than I did about the technical details of the business. At Cachet, she took care of the banking, the printing of our brochures, and various other administrative details, which left me free to concentrate on what I really cared about—advertising, marketing, and personnel.

Gina's first notable achievement was convincing the bank to let us accept Visa and Mastercharge. When she explained that as a temporary help agency we often had to process the credit cards at our clients' offices, the bank even provided us with miniature credit card imprinters called Port-A-Prints, which the girls would bring along in their handbags.

We worked out of our apartments. We both had a second line installed and, with the help of call-forwarding, each of us answered the phone three nights a week without leaving home. We were closed on Saturdays because we both wanted a social life. Besides, at Eddie's, Saturday had always been the slowest night of the week. Most traveling businessmen are home for the weekend, and foreign diplomats generally find parties to attend or have other social obligations.

Following up on Gina's inspired suggestion to Eddie, we too started advertising in the *International Herald Tribune*. The ad, which listed our name and number, described us as "New York's most exclusive service," adding, "We're not for everyone," and then, in smaller print, "For those who can afford to be discriminating, Cachet introduces a new standard of elegance and distinction."

Today, of course, escort services advertise freely in the Yellow Pages and—at least until I was busted in 1984—in the back of *New York* magazine. But when Cachet first opened, our options were far more limited, and just about the only New York publication that would accept our ad was *Screw,* the sex tabloid. This was far from the kind of environment we wanted to be associated with, but we had no other choice. As a matter of fact, the readers of *Screw* proved to be generally indistinguishable from the men who later called us from the Yellow Pages.

Still, we made sure that our ad was completely different from all the others. Ours was one of the very few, for example, that actually listed the price. (When we opened, our rate was $125 an hour, the same as Eddie's. At the time, most of our competition charged between $60 and $80 an hour.) It was also tasteful and discreet, in sharp contrast to the others, some of which actually portrayed naked women with their legs spread apart and tag lines such as "Cum into my valley."

To find the caliber of girls we were looking for, we placed an ad in *Show Business*, a trade magazine read by actresses, models, singers, and dancers:

> One of York's finest escort services is seeking a small number of attractive, articulate, well-educated young ladies between 19 and 28 for part-time evening work. Fluency in one or more foreign languages is helpful but not a necessity. For an appointment, please call 555-1310.

Soon afterward, I tried to place this same ad in the *Village Voice*. When it was rejected, I went to their office to meet the head of classified advertising. "I run an honest escort service," I said, "and if you're going to carry ads inviting men to come to 'luxury spas,' which we all know are brothels, you have no right to exclude me for advertising in Help Wanted."

"That's a good point," he said. "I'll see what we can do."

Two weeks later we were in the *Voice*.

One of the young women responding to our ad had a voice I immediately recognized as belonging to Eddie's girlfriend. She described herself as being twenty-two, blond, and beautiful, and although that description was far from accurate, it would certainly appeal to any escort service hiring new girls.

I realized at once that this was Eddie's way of checking up on the new kids on the block, but I played along and pretended to take her seriously. She asked a number of questions, and I answered them all. But when I described our policies, I couldn't resist getting a dig in at our former boss. "At Cachet," I said, "we ask our girls to work only three nights a week. Around here we don't believe in slave labor.'' She said she'd call us back soon to make an appointment, but of course she never did.

That was the end of it—or so I thought. But two days later I walked out of my apartment to find that somebody had spray-painted the front of my building, the downstairs hallway, and the sidewalk. In huge letters, the message read; ''Brothel in 5R,'' with a big arrow pointing up to my apartment, and, ''Cachet Whorehouse—upstairs.'' Although I had congratulated myself for recognizing Eddie's girlfriend over the phone, it had never occurred to me that she might just as easily have recognized me, too.

I was shocked and horrified. I flew back up the stairs and called Gina, who jumped into a cab and came right over to help me clean up the mess. Meanwhile, my landlord was demanding an explanation. Tearfully, I explained that I had been doing some modeling and had recently turned down a man who was dying to go out with me. ''You know how some fellows can get when you hurt their pride,'' I said with all the innocence I could muster. ''I mean, really, do I look like a person who runs a brohel?'' That seemed to be convincing, and the matter was dropped.

Gina and I spent all day with rubber gloves, paper towels, and turpentine, trying to clean up the mess. We did a good job on the walls, but we just couldn't get the paint off the sidewalk. Finally, Gina came up with a solution: she bought some spray paint and covered the previous inscriptions. It worked, but only temporarily. From time to time, the rain would wash away the top layer and the original words would start to show through. Whenever that happened, I'd go out and spray it all over again.

Although both Gina and I had learned a great deal from working at Eddie's, neither of us had been involved in the recruiting process. We realized, however, that finding clients would be the easy part; the hard part would be finding the right girls. We began by hiring two girls who had worked for Eddie and quit, but despite the obvious temptation, we agreed not to steal any of Eddie's current escorts—or any of his clients, either. Not that he didn't deserve it, but we wanted to start off fresh and clean.

Looking back, I'm appalled at how casually Gina and I handled the recruitment interviews during the first few months. When girls called us for interviews, for example, we came right out and told them on the phone that they would be expected to go to bed with the clients. "We want to be sure you understand that sex is usually included," we said, and while our motives were above reproach—we wanted to be straight with the girls and not waste their time—we were hopelessly naive. We were exceedingly careful about what we told the clients, and never discussed or even hinted at anything sexual, but somehow it never occurred to us to take similar precautions with the girls who called us. Any of them, of course, could have been a policewoman from the vice squad, and only later did I realize how lucky we had been.

Although escort services are technically legal, they are at times raided by the police and forced to shut down—if only temporarily. To protect ourselves from being arrested under the prostitution laws, we always made it clear to our clients that we were charging for the girls' *time*. In other words, the client paid the same amount no matter what went on—or didn't—in the privacy of his hotel room or residence.

Looking back, I think we neglected to take appropriate precautions with new girls because we never truly believed we were doing anything wrong. As we saw it, we were making a lot of people happy without hurting anyone: the men enjoyed the company of an attractive and well-educated escort, and the girls enjoyed the opportunity to make a good income in just a few hours a week. And we were so aware and so proud of the differences between our service and Eddie's—not to mention everybody else's—that it was some time before we fully appreciated how easily we could have been busted.

But when word got out that one of our competitors had been raided by the police, we suddenly became far more discreet. We no longer said *anything* on the phone that might be incriminating, even at the risk of misleading potential employees and clients. When a new girl called, I started asking if she had *worked* before and hoped that my use of that word would convey what I had in mind.

"Yes," one girl answered, "I worked in Philadelphia." But when she came in for the interview, it soon became clear that the job had been strictly social. After a few such misunderstandings, I would pursue the issue a little more aggressively on the phone: "When you worked," I asked, "was it strictly social, or did it occasionally get a little more personal?"

Gina and I interviewed new applicants every Thursday. At first we asked the girls to come to one of our apartments, but before long we started using a fancy office on the Upper East Side. With wall-to-wall carpeting, a wall paneled in mirrors, and a French antique desk, it was more in keeping with our upscale, sophisticated image. And because we used the office only for interviewing, we would not be compromised if a new applicant had come to gather information for the police—or for one of our competitors. There was nothing incriminating there; the office belonged to a friend of mine, a decorator who rented it to us one day a week when he visited his clients.

At first we booked individual interviews, but we abandoned that idea after a few weeks because only about one candidate in five would show up as scheduled—even after we called them to confirm. This ratio applied to the girls who had never worked; for those who had, the attendance rate was even lower. A few girls took the trouble to let us know they wouldn't be coming, but only one girl in ten showed us that minimal consideration.

To get around this problem, we began to hold the preliminary interviews in groups. We ran two separate sessions: one for girls who had never worked before, one for girls who had.

Over the phone, I would tell the applicants to come dressed as though they were going to lunch with their grandfather at 21. You should have seen some people's versions of what they considered appropriate attire for that occasion! One girl showed up in a Danskin top, an Indian print wrap skirt, and water buffalo sandals. Many others came in jeans.

We paid close attention to what the girls wore, because if a potential escort didn't dress appropriately for the interview, she probably wouldn't work out well even if she looked like Christie Brinkley. Besides, a girl who showed up properly dressed gave us the opportunity to see how she'd look on the job.

Despite our precautions, a few surprises managed to slip through. One morning, Gina called from her apartment and told me to come right over. When I got there, she explained that she and her boyfriend had bought one of the first videocassette recorders and that they liked to watch dirty movies together. As we moved into the living room, she said, "I've got something to show you."

"Okay," I said, "what's going on?"

"You'll see," said Gina as she turned on the VCR. I almost had a heart attack, for there, on the screen, was Robin, one of our new girls. And she wasn't merely having sex, either. Without being too graphic, let's just say that she was causing an amazing range of inanimate objects to disappear into some highly personal hiding places. And that was just for openers.

I stared in horrified fascination. A moment later I snapped back to the real world. "I've seen enough," I said, and started walking out of the room.

"Wait a minute," said Gina. "The scene with the goat is coming up!"

"Some other time," I told her. "Like maybe after I'm dead."

Robin had mentioned that she had worked briefly before joining Cachet, but obviously she hadn't told us the whole story.

"Listen, I said to Lucy. "What are we going to do if any of our clients find out? How many people has she seen so far?"

"I checked," she said. "Only eight."

"That's good. But what are we going to do?"

"We've got to fire her," said Gina. "You know we can't afford to keep her."

"I know. I just can't believe it."

"Believe it. And believe this, too: she's made a number of these movies. Apparently there's a whole *shelf* of them!"

My biggest worry was losing our reputation. We couldn't risk anyone finding out that we weren't as sterling and as pure as we promised—and as we wanted to be. Here we were telling our clients, and believing ourselves, that our girls were practically virgins, and now we had a porno queen on our hands!

We had been doing everything possible to give our business a certain image, and every detail of the operation—including our advertising, our telephone style, the kind of girls we hired, and the way they dressed—

was part of our marketing effort. Robin violated that image, and I had no choice but to fire her at once.

From then on, we grew even more cautious. When new applicants came in for the preliminary interview, we passed out application forms and asked to see identification. We required two IDs, one of which had to include a picture and date of birth. We were aware that this policy might scare away a few good people who preferred to come to us anonymously, but after the incident with Robin we weren't prepared to take any chances. Besides, we were sending our girls into the homes and hotel rooms of wealthy clients, and while a photo ID was no guarantee that a girl wouldn't turn out to be a thief, it did give us an extra layer of protection.

When we interviewed girls who had worked (or were still working) for other escort services, Gina and I learned far more from the discussions than they did. People love to complain, and with most escort services there was plenty to complain about. Many of the girls were only too eager to tell us exactly how these places operated.

It always angered me to hear stories of how both the girls and the clients were being exploited. I listened to a number of sad tales, and on more than one occasion I was tempted to hire a girl just to show her that working for an escort service didn't have to be a degrading experience. But even two or three months at most of these other agencies was usually enough to ruin a girl's attitude toward men and toward the escort business in general. We rarely hired girls who had worked before, and of the few we did, most didn't work out.

When dealing with girls who had never worked before, I would talk in great detail about how we operated while skipping over any explicit references to sex. Instead, I would mention that the escorts generally took out-of-town clients to museums, nightclubs, and fine restaurants. If an applicant came right out and asked if sex were involved, I said that it wasn't. Among other reasons, I didn't want any girls I had rejected to contact the publications that ran our ads and complain that Cachet was actually a prostitution ring. For our own protection, I decided that only girls who were actually working for us had to know the whole story.

Although some applicants didn't even ask about sex, others raised the question in a variety of ways. Some were blunt: "I don't have to go to bed with these guys, do I?" Others were more discreet: "There isn't anything else involved, is there?"

I promised every girl that I interviewed that I'd call her later in the week to tell her whether we had any openings for someone of her type. Even if I knew that a girl wasn't for us, I would always make a point of calling her back. After all, she had given up a lunch hour to come and see us, so this was the least I could do. If she wasn't our type, I would say that I was sorry, but we had no openings in her category. "But if you like," I would say, "I'll keep your name in our call-back file in case something comes up."

If a girl who hadn't worked before seemed like a good prospect, I'd take a different approach: "I have bad news and good news. The bad news is that I don't have any openings in your category right now, and I'm not sure how soon I will. But if you'd like, I'll put your name in the callback file.

"However, there is something else I should mention, although you probably won't be interested. We do have a small number of clients who occasionally see the girls on a more personal basis. It's done very nicely. The clients are carefully screened, the pay is high, and the men are terrific. You would never have to stay with a man you're not comfortable with. If this is something that might interest you, you might want to come in again and I'll tell you about it in more detail. Otherwise, no problem. I'll still be happy to keep your name in the callback file for the strictly social service. If there's ever an opening, I'll call you."

If the girl said she wasn't interested, I never pushed her. "Fine," I said. "I would never compromise you. I just wanted to let you know what was available."

If she was ambivalent, which was often the case, I would urge her to come in to hear what I had to say at the reinterview, which was, in effect, a mini-training program for the girls I wanted to hire. "There's no obligation," I would tell her. "If at any point during the meeting you don't like how it sounds, feel free to get up and leave. I won't be offended, because I realize that this type of work is not for everybody."

Although some girls who came to the reinterview decided not to work, nobody ever left the meeting before it was over. As one girl told me, the material was just too interesting to walk out on.

For a girl who was wavering, the presence of two or three other girls at the reinterview was often enough to win her over. When she saw there were others who had decided to give it a try, she would feel tremendously relieved. Before the reinterview, she might have seen herself as a "nice girl" who was in danger of being corrupted by a collection of hookers, drug dealers—and who knew what else? But once she met the other escorts, you could just see the change as she slowly began to relax.

Every now and then, I would see a girl in a preliminary interview whom I just didn't trust. Generally, she'd give herself away either by asking too many questions or by playing dumb and then coming up with fairly sophisticated inquiries.

Sometimes, though, all I had was an intuition that something about the girl just didn't add up. In these cases, I would reveal as little as possible and later, on the phone, politely explain to her that at the moment we didn't have an opening for someone in her category. But if I was fairly sure that a girl had come in order to learn details of our operation and report them back to her boss, I would feed her misinformation to make us sound even smaller and more innocent than we actually were.

"You know," I might tell her, "I can see that you're very pretty, and I'm sure that at the XYZ agency you're one of the top girls. You're probably used to making a lot of money. Unfortunately, there's just no way that you could make that kind of money here. We wouldn't permit you to work any more than three nights a week, and you would only be allowed to see one gentleman per evening."

"Then how do *your* girls make any money?" she might ask.

"All of our girls have straight jobs," I would explain, "and they work for me only a couple of nights a week to make a little extra money." Even if the applicant was not a spy, she would spread this information to the other girls at her agency, where it would become part of the gossip. As I saw it, it was in our interest to have *everybody*—the police, the competition, potential thieves, and even organized crime—under the impression that we were small potatoes.

I was very selective about whom we accepted, and one of the girls I interviewed in our second year told me that the standard for attractiveness at Cachet was said to be so high that the word was out: "Unless you're a Ford model, don't even bother to interview with Sheila."

I always paid close attention to types of girls: I knew, for example, that I could use only a certain number of tall brunettes.(Tall, busty blondes were another story, and I could always have used more of them.) There was only so much work available for each type, and if I overhired in a certain category, those girls would work less and would become disgruntled.

One year, right after Thanksgiving, just as our busy season was coming to an end, four gorgeous tall brunettes walked into my office and wanted to work. I was really stuck: if I didn't hire them, they would end up somewhere else and build another agency's reputation. But if I did take them on, I couldn't give them as much work as they might normally expect. I decided to hire them anyway and explained that the busy season was over. I counted on the fact that they would realize they were better off with me, even if they worked a little less. Fortunately, business continued to be strong that season, and there was enough work for everybody.

Good looks were not enough to get a girl hired, and those who were slightly less pretty invariably made up for it in personality. Once, we signed up an escort who was positively plain. But Ginger was so exuberant and dynamic that we were willing to overlook her complete lack of physical attractiveness. Some clients, we found, were intimidated by beauty and weren't comfortable seeing anyone who was gorgeous, so Ginger was always busy. Needless to say, we would never send her to a client who had specifically requested a girl who was pretty. But the overall level of attractiveness at Cachet was so high that most of our regular clients were happy to see anybody we recommended because they knew from experience that we wouldn't let them down.

With our less beautiful girls, we would prepare the client by saying, "I just want you to know that she's not one of the most attractive girls we have. But she's such a fabulous person that we know you'll have a great time." Nobody ever complained, and these girls were often invited back by the same clients, so I can only assume we were right.

I turned down a number of beautiful girls who were

not very articulate or well spoken, or who had strong New York accents. For an out-of-town client, a thick New York accent might represent a bit of a novelty, but to a residential client it would more likely sound offensive. I hired several southern girls, most of whom had worked hard at losing their accents. This was unfortunate, as I would have loved to book them as pretty southern belles. Michelle was our only southern girl who retained her accent, and I made a point of urging her to resist the temptation to talk like the rest of us.

I would reject even the most stunning girl if she couldn't look me in the eye, or if she never smiled, or if she had a hard edge to her personality, or if she just didn't like men. This latter problem is widely thought to be common among working girls, but that wasn't the case at Cachet, although I certainly came across it now and then in girls from other agencies who applied to work for us. These applicants usually had an attitude problem, and no wonder: they had been taught to relate to men as little more than machines from whom they were expected to crank out as much money as possible.

While good looks were generally important, I was more concerned about the *right* look. Men have always responded to the way I dress, and I decided that the elegant, classic look that worked for me would also work for the girls. Although I never put it in these terms, I didn't let the girls wear anything that I wouldn't wear. I took many of them to Saks to help them shop for suits and dresses, and I often steered them to the Richard Warren line, which was ladylike and conservative, but still feminine.

Quite a few of the new girls had no money and nothing appropriate to wear, so I would either lend them something of mine or take them to Saks and charge whatever they needed on my credit card. They would pay me back from their future earnings.

I also suggested that the girls wear gloves and hats, although I did not require them. But girls who wore hats found that men loved them, which was something I had learned several years earlier when I was dating a man who was mad for hats. I found that when I wore a hat, complete strangers would come up to me in restaurants to tell me how attractive I looked. I also found that hats with veils were especially appealing to men, and I urged the girls to try them.

I wanted our girls to look like business executives, and I was always on the lookout for too much eye makeup, seamed stockings, or anything else that might suggest a stereotypical call girl. Underneath their handsome suits and dresses, however, I required all the girls to wear a matching set of lingerie, consisting of bra, panties, and garter belt—which soon became our trademark. When it came to lingerie, colors were important. I advised the girls not to wear white, which was too virginal. Beige was too dull, and black underwear was appropriate only for girls who were more sophisticated or exotic; for somebody we had described as the girl next door, black would have been all wrong. For most girls, I recommended pastel colors such as blue, lilac, pink, or peach, although white with colored ribbons running through it was also acceptable.

Matching sets of lingerie were sometimes difficult to find, and I usually had to send the girls to Enelra, a lingerie boutique all the way down in the East Village. While they were there, several of the girls picked up corselettes (which are also known as bustiers or merry widows). When they reported that the clients loved them, I quickly spread the word.

I think I know why our clients responded so well to lingerie. When these men were young the first naked women most of them had ever seen were usually dressed in frilly undergarments in a magazine like *Playboy*. As a result, seeing a woman dressed only in lingerie would create a powerful, nostalgic yearning that many men found irresistible. This made the experience more pleasant for the girls, because the more excited the man was as the evening became intimate, the easier things would be when it came down to the nitty-gritty.

Except for one or two girls who were very small on top, a bra was part of our dress code. I used to recommend the underwire kind, which make you look a little bigger than you are. Some people think that going without a bra is sexy, and with certain girls in certain outfits, I suppose it is. But however paradoxical the claim may appear, Cachet was a very conservative operation. Once, when Kelly and two other girls went to see three men at the Helmsley Palace, one of the other girls called me later to complain that Kelly hadn't been wearing a bra: "You should have seen her, bouncing up and down," she said. "I was afraid we'd all be stopped by security."

I also insisted that the girls wear stockings, preferably sheer ones, even in the summer. Having grown up in the age of panty hose, most of the girls had never actually worn stockings before. New girls would often ask whether stockings were really necessary, especially in the summer, and I would explain, again and again, that bare legs, even when they were sleek and tanned, were just not the look I wanted. "A *real* lady," I would explain with a hint of reproval, "wears stockings no matter *how* hot it is."

Because the girls often carried large amounts of cash at night, some of them would hide the money in discreet parts of their clothing. Once, after a two-hour call, Elise tucked four hundred dollars into the top of her stocking. As she left the elevator and walked through the hotel lobby, Elise felt the money start to slip down her leg. She was wearing a dress, which meant that at any moment the wad of bills was going to appear below the hem and everyone in the lobby—including the security men—would see her little secret. Elise had us convulsed with laughter as she tried to duplicate her awkward walk, one leg rubbing up against the other so that the money would not be visible. By the time it reached the crease behind her knee, she put her hand over the back of her leg and limped out, pretending she was injured.

Another time, Kate was wearing thigh-highs under her dress. She had just left a hotel on Central Park South and was walking over to Columbus Circle. She had been sick the week before and had apparently lost a few pounds. Suddenly, she felt her stockings beginning to slip. Once the elastic gets past the thigh muscle, you're in big trouble because there's nothing left to hold up the stocking. When Kate looked down, she saw both her stockings collapsed around her ankles. So much for the high-class call girl! There she was on Central Park South, which happens to be classic hooker territory. As Kate was leaning against a building, pulling up her hose, a long black limousine glided up to her and the back window rolled down. "Excuse me, miss," said a man's voice from inside. "Would you like me to give you a hand with that?" Kate talked her way out of that one, but from then on she went back to garters.

But garter belts also took some getting used to. Sharon, an Israeli who had served in her country's army before coming to America, once told me that she had never experienced a problem getting in and out of her sophisticated military gear. "But for the life of me," she said, "I'll never get the hang of how to put on a garter belt!" Before her first call, Sharon actually had to come over to my apartment so I could show her how to put it on.

I strongly suggested that the girls wear half-slips under all unlined skirts. Most women don't realize it, but a slip makes almost any dress or skirt fall more smoothly and look better. In my view, every woman in America ought to wear one.

Although we had a strict dress code, within that range I saw the girls as representing a variety of types, based, of course, on their own natural features. Claudette, for example, embodied a sophisticated, elegant New York look, so she always had a more fashionable hairstyle and very chic accessories. Tricia, by contrast, represented the girl next door, and she tended to wear dresses rather than suits—especially dresses with a Peter Pan collar or puffy sleeves. Both her hair and makeup were less elaborate than that of some of the other girls.

Michelle was a model. She was very tall, and her clothing would be slightly trendy, with more dramatic hair and makeup. Melody's look was that of a young student: tousled hair, simpler clothing, and perhaps a skirt and sweater set when that was appropriate.

Colby represented the healthy, outdoorsy type, with a wind-swept, off-the-farm look. Marguerite, by contrast, was exotic and tended to wear tighter skirts and a little more makeup than the others. Kate was a business-woman who wore conservative suits, lower heels, and less jewelry than most of the other girls.

In many cases, I would work with a girl to help her develop a suitable wardrobe and a flattering hairstyle that corresponded with her "look." Sometimes my ideas were a little different from hers, so I had to be tactful and diplomatic. Tara, a Rubensesque blonde, liked to dress in vintage fashions from the 1940s. One evening, she came by the office in a red suede jacket and a long black skirt. "You look terrific," I told her. "That's a great outfit for you, and you wear it well. But we need a different look for the agency. If it helps, think of it as a uniform."

A few days later, I took her to Saks, where I helped her select a handsome business suit and a silk blouse.

As I told the girls more than once, "If you're walking through the lobby of the Pierre at midnight, you want to look as if you belong there."

Some of the girls who worked for us were preparing for a career in show business, and it took time to feel comfortable in a Wall Street look. I tried to be patient, and I made a point of looking over their clothes at every possible opportunity and, if necessary, giving them advice on how to complete the ensemble. I recalled that Eddie was often critical of his girls' appearance, so I went out of my way to be constructive and supportive.

Because I have never responded well to an arbitrary set of rules, I always made a point of providing the rationale for our dress code. "Remember," I would say, "you're a fantasy for these guys. Think back to what your image of a high-class call girl used to be before you became an escort. That's who this client is expecting *you* to be. You just can't walk in there looking like the women he sees every day at work."

I went on to explain that although the executive women in his office may wear business suits, they were not generally very feminine or fashionable. Our girls chose more stylish suits and glamorized them with a soft blouse, a colorful belt, high heels, and fancier earrings. There was no comparison: the look was totally different.

"Have you ever seen a famous movie star walking along the street?" I continued. "It happens all the time. But if she's not dressed up and not looking her best, don't you feel a little disappointed? Imagine how the client feels when he's paying top dollar for an elegant escort, and she comes to his hotel room looking less than spectacular."

As another feminine touch, I also asked the girls to wear nail polish on their toes. I was less strict about their fingernails, however, because manicures can be expensive and time-consuming. My only rule was that if they were going to do their nails in the first place, they had to be scrupulous about keeping them up.

Perfume was tricky; although some clients loved it, others, who were married, were afraid that their wives would detect the aromatic evidence of their liaison. And I would warn the girls not to spray on perfume just as they were leaving a client, as this was a dead giveaway to hotel security. "It's possible that you might be leaving a business meeting at eleven-thirty at night," I said, "but how many women would apply perfume on the way out?"

New girls, who were often intimidated by all the grooming rules, would sometimes acknowledge that the guidelines made sense when it came to out-of-town clients. But for resident New Yorkers, they would ask, "Shouldn't we be able to show up in a pair of jeans?"

"No," I said, and launching into my favorite analogy, I explained why. "What if a customer walked into The Four Seasons simply because he lived in the neighborhood and wanted to eat there? And what if the maître d' decided that even though this customer was paying the same amount of money, he wasn't entitled to as fine a dinner because he doesn't happen to be a high-powered businessman from Paris or London? Would that be fair?

"It's the same with residentials. All our clients are paying the same amount, whether they're living at home or staying at the Pierre. And it doesn't make any difference if he's a first-time client or if he calls us every week; in either case, he deserves the best we have to offer. The reason these gentlemen call us in the first place is that our girls look great every time they go out. I'm counting on you to help us maintain that image."

Chapter Five

After the preliminary interview, those girls who were interested in taking the job or in learning more about how we worked would come in for a reinterview. This mini-training program, as we often referred to it, contained all the information the girls needed to know before they could start working. Like the preliminary interview, it was held in the office of my friend, the East Side decorator.

Shortly after we opened, Gina and I had spent a couple of long evenings with two girls who had previously worked for Eddie, and they agreed to give us a moment-by-moment description of a call. I took careful notes on everything they told us and adapted their information to fit our own style. When Cachet first opened, the reinterview lasted only an hour, but as I paid attention to what our girls were learning, I started to expand these sessions with additional information. Within a year, the reinterview was running between four and five hours.

Unlike the initial interview, for which they had to dress up, the girls could come to the reinterview in more comfortable clothing. I asked them to bring along a pen and a notebook because they couldn't possibly remember all the information I was going to throw at them.

Based on the feedback we got as the business grew, the reinterview material was continually refined and updated.

Usually, reinterviews were held on Thursdays, starting at two P.M. But in order to accommodate girls with tight schedules, we sometimes had to hold them in the evenings or over the weekend. If only one girl was involved, we would usually be finished around six; with more than one girl, the sessions often lasted a little longer. In general, I could count on fifteen extra minutes for each additional girl.

What follows is a greatly condensed version of what I told the girls at the reinterview:

Now, before we start, I know that you, Lisa, are here just to listen, and that you haven't made up your mind yet as to whether this kind of work is right for you. If you decide to join us, we'd be delighted to have you. But if at any time during the afternoon you decide that this job just isn't for you, feel free to leave. We're going to be here a long time today, so don't feel that you have to stay to the end just to be polite.

Let me begin by saying how glad I am that you all were able to make it today. I'm going to be giving you a lot of information this afternoon, and if anything's not clear, feel free to interrupt me. Or you might want to jot down your question, because I'm going to be as thorough as possible, and you may find that I'll be answering your question anyway as I go along.

First of all, we're open from four P.M. until one A.M. every day except Saturday, when our hours are from six P.M. to one A.M. I ask the girls who work for me to give me three days a week of their choosing. Just give us a call every Friday before six P.M., and let us know which days you'll be working during the upcoming week. If you don't call, we'll simply assign three days to you. If you don't really care which days you work, please make that clear when you call, and we'll fit you in when we need you.

If you know your time of month is coming up, please be sure to calculate that in your schedule. It's funny, but it often seems as if all the girls are on the same cycle, and suddenly nobody is available. So please keep an eye on that.

If you want to work more than three nights, that's fine. You can let us know when you call on Friday afternoon, or you can always call that night and say you're available. For the extra nights, you can sign on and off whenever you want; otherwise, we expect you to be available no later than seven.

We also ask everybody who does not have a full-time office job to give us one day a week starting at four P.M., which is when we open. You'd be surprised at the number of people who want to see somebody before they go to dinner, or before they leave for the airport. There's not a lot of business in the afternoon, but there's enough, and of course you'll be one step ahead of the people who sign on later.

Many of our calls come in between six and eight. Then there's usually a lull between eight and ten-thirty, when the phones start ringing again. You may feel discouraged if we haven't called you by eleven-thirty, but don't give up. For some reason, twelve-fifteen is usually a very busy time: everything will be quiet, and then suddenly, just after midnight, three or four phones will start ringing all at once.

On the nights you're scheduled to work, you must call us any time before three-thirty that day on a special phone number that I'll give you. The machine will answer, and all you need to do is say what time you'll be ready to go out that evening. "Ready to go" means that your hair is done, your makeup is on, your bag is packed—I'll get to that in a moment—and your clothes are laid out. If you tell us that your ready-to-go time is six-thirty, you should be able to be out of your house by six forty-five if we need you that early. In other words, you have fifteen minutes to be out the door from the time we call.

While you're waiting to hear from us, please don't leave your house for any reason unless you tell us, because the moment you go to put your laundry in or take out the trash, you just know that's going to be when we call. And if you're not there, we don't know if you're gone for two minutes or two hours. We will keep trying you for five or ten minutes, but if we can't reach you, we'll have to call somebody else and give her that booking.

So even if you're just running out to buy cat food at the corner store, please call us at the office to let us know. Don't feel that you're bothering us; we'd rather know where you are than call you and get no answer. By the same token, please don't get involved in any projects that you can't drop at a moment's notice, such as doing your nails. If you're going to do your nails, or clean your oven—because that happened to us once—let us know that you won't be available until you're finished. If you do get involved in anything like that, the best time to do it is during the slow period between eight and ten, when most of the hotel clients are having dinner. But you'd be surprised how many residential clients get home around eight-thirty and want to see somebody right away.

Naturally, you'll want to keep your phone free. Most of the girls have call-waiting, and I strongly recommend it. If your line is busy for more than five minutes, we'll arrange for an emergency interruption. These are awkward and difficult to explain, and they cost money, too, so please do get call-waiting: it's not expensive, and it's a good investment.

Some girls find it more convenient to use a beeper, which leaves them free to go shopping or out to a movie while they're waiting for us to call. So if you get stir crazy sitting around the house, this is something you might want to consider. But remember, if you do use a beeper, you have to be all dressed and ready to go from wherever you are.

Please be sure to keep a notepad and pen in your pocketbook, or by the phone if you're at home. When the phones at the office really get going at night, especially if there's only one assistant working, things get very hectic. So in case we're in a big hurry, you've got everything you need right there.

Now, before we go any further, I should tell you that we don't permit any of our girls to work for anybody else while they're working for us. We also tell our clients that you're not a professional escort, but that you do this to earn a little extra money on the side. On a night when we're totally booked, we don't want him calling another agency and ending up with you, because it would make both of us look bad.

As honest as we are, we do tell our clients one big lie; that you only see one gentleman per evening. If he believes you've already seen somebody else, he won't respect you as much. But if he thinks you work only one or two nights a week, and that you see only one gentleman per evening, then it's really more like a blind date and he'll feel better about you. If the subject comes up, explain that this is one of our strictest rules, and that it's one of the main reasons you work for me.

You may already have noticed that I'm a fanatic about punctuality. I've had so many compliments over the years from clients who say, "You know, not only does she look great, but she's always there when you say she'll be there." If you're chronically late, you'll be fined on the order of $50 for every five minutes. So please don't get yourself into this situation.

It's also important to keep in shape. These guys are not paying $200 an hour to see somebody who's overweight or flabby. Those of you who need to shape up know who you are. Staying in shape can be especially difficult during the winter, and I've had to suspend people for letting themselves go. I don't like to do that, but I also don't like getting a call from a client who says, "You said she was slender, but I have to tell you, Sheila, she seemed pretty hefty to me." You wouldn't want to go in a restaurant and order veal and then be served chicken. So I expect all of you to be in great shape and to stay that way.

As you already know, we go for a very straight, classic look. I'm afraid that pants, or culottes, or anything that resembles pants, are not allowed. You must always wear a skirt or a dress. Please don't wear anything very short or very trendy. Our clients are rather conservative businessmen, and they don't always understand the latest fashions. They feel much more comfortable with somebody who is dressed in a simple but elegant manner.

Now, I realize that this kind of outfit may not represent your personal style, so if it helps, think of it as a uniform. Basically, you'll need at least one suit—a nice, feminine suit rather than something severe in navy blue or gray. You'll also need a dress, which should be ladylike and tailored, with no frills or ruffles. If you're at a restaurant and one of the client's colleagues walks in, it's important that you look like a business associate and not like a girlfriend he keeps on the side.

The only concession we make to overt sexiness is the highest heels you can manage to walk in without falling over. In our experience, men just adore high heels, so please try to find some. If you like, I can give you the names of a couple of shoe stores which have a good selection.

Always keep in mind that what these men expect is a fantasy. If someone asked you to sit down and spell out your description of what a high-class New York call girl would be like, you'd probably say, "Well, she'd have a beautiful hairdo, gorgeous makeup, she'd be very pretty and elegantly dressed, and sophisticated." That's exactly who our clients expect *you* to be.

I know you're sitting there thinking, Well, I'm just plain old Peggy. But these guys are expecting a fancy, high-class New York call girl, and it's very important that you live up to that expectation, and that you don't look like the secretary who works in his office, or the wife he goes home to, or the girls he passes by on the street. That's not why he called us. If he wanted that kind of girl, believe me, he'd call another agency and spend a lot less money.

When you look great, and you *know* you look great, you'll have a better time because you'll feel more confident and more in control. You'll also find that when you're all dressed up and looking fabulous, you'll be treated better and given bigger tips.

It's really true. Which brings me to the basic rule that you should always keep in mind: The more you act like a lady, the more he'll act like a gentleman.

Now let's talk about the items you should carry in your bag. First, a little Ziploc bag with an extra pair of nylons and a few panty shields, because you don't want to ruin your undies. You should also carry little miniature makeups for on-the-spot repairs. You'll find that the less elaborate your makeup, the easier it will be to fix.

Other items for your bag: a shower cap, bubble bath, mints, especially if you smoke, and a few quarters for phone calls. Often, you'll be going somewhere else after your first call, and you'll need to give us a ring to get all the information, because you obviously can't write it down while you're still with the first client.

What else? A pen and a notebook. A Port-A-Print for credit cards, which we'll talk about later. For cabs, you should always carry a few five-dollar bills, because you'd be surprised how many cabdrivers can't change a ten or a twenty, and you don't want to go circling around late at night, looking for a store that's open so he can get some change.

We don't use prophylactics in this agency unless the client prefers them, so it's always at his request, not ours. For some reason, though, these clients don't always provide their own, so be sure to keep a couple of condoms in your bag. Do yourself a favor and buy the expensive kind. The cheaper ones will save you some money, but they're so much thicker that believe me, it will take five times as long to get anything accomplished that's going to get accomplished. It will be much more comfortable for both of you if you buy the very best.

Okay. So there you are, sitting at home. Your makeup is on, your hair is done, your bag is packed, and you're ready to go. Suddenly the phone rings. We'll be giving you the following information: who he is, where he is, how old he is, and some other details about him, such as his profession and perhaps a little about his personality. The only thing you'll need to write down is his name and address.

If you're organized, it should take only ten to fifteen minutes to finish dressing and another fifteen or twenty to get to the client. Just to be safe, we'll tell him to expect you in about forty-five minutes.

If you carry a beeper, be sure to turn it off before you get out of the taxi. Somebody could always dial a wrong number, and it would be embarrassing to have your beeper go off when you're with a client.

When you're going to a hotel, be sure to memorize the client's name and room number before you get out of the cab. The last thing you need is for somebody from hotel security to come up to you and ask if they can help, and you have to pull out a piece of paper and say, "Um, I'm here to see Mr. Smith, room 1240." That looks very suspicious.

We use only the better hotels, and all of them have security teams. Some of these people will be in uniforms, and some won't. But many of them like to harass working girls because they've got nothing better to do, and they're jealous of the kind of money you make. Obviously, you'll want to avoid these people. The way you're dressed will be helpful in this regard, but so will your mental attitude. Always think of your visit in terms of going to see an old friend, or your uncle, and always act as if you have a right to be there—which you do. Never act furtive or guilty, because the security guards are trained to spot people who look or act that way. So it's very important to get yourself into the right frame of mind.

Some hotel lobbies are so enormous and complicated that you can't always tell where the elevators are. Instead of skulking around and trying to find them, just walk right up to any clerk or security guard and say, "Excuse me, could you tell me where to find the elevator to the twelfth floor?" They're not expecting someone in our line of work to do that.

So you get in the elevator and you go on up. Before you knock on the client's door, be sure to look at your watch, because it's important to know what time you arrived—and nobody likes a clock watcher. Incidentally, it's helpful to wear a watch that's especially easy to read in a dim light with just a glance. And never take off your watch: we had one client who actually turned back a girl's watch while she was in the bathroom so she would stay longer without realizing it.

After you knock on the door, stand back a couple of steps. A face is such a subjective thing: how many times have you looked at a guy across a room and thought, Boy, is he cute! And then five minutes later you see him close and you say to yourself, On second thought, I could probably live without him.

It's the same thing here. It's important that the client gets the full image of you when he first opens the door—the total you, rather than just your face. If you stand too close to the door, your face is all that he sees. And you might not be exactly what his fantasy was, because, let's face it, there's almost no way you could be. But if you're standing back a couple of feet, he's going to get a more complete picture of you, and it's more likely to be positive.

Now, before you go in, please ascertain that he is dressed. If for any reason he isn't, say; "Oh, my goodness, I'm so sorry, I must be a little bit early. You haven't had time to finish dressing. Why don't I wait here until you're ready."

Of course, the last thing he wants is to have you standing out in the hall, so let him coax you inside. But stand right by the door until he gets dressed. If he refuses to cooperate, tell him that you don't feel comfortable going in. Leave the hotel, and give us a call to let us know what happened.

When you walk in, take a look around the room and at him. Make sure that he's someone you don't mind spending some time with. Five other girls may have thought he was terrific, but maybe there's something about him that you personally don't like. For all we know, he may have girlie magazines lying all over the room, and he never did that before. Or perhaps he did—and it didn't bother the other girls, but it does bother you.

Once you're in the room, ask if you could please use the phone. At first you'll be seeing only old clients, so he'll be expecting you to call us. In fact, he may even remind you, because these gentlemen soon become familiar with our little ways. Call the office at the special number I'll be giving you—remembering to dial 9 for an outside line—and say, "Hi, this is so-and-so. I'm here." Please don't say, "Hi, this is me," because we've got a lot of "me's" out there. Obviously, this is not the time for a conversation, because you're there on business.

Whoever picks up your call will say, "Is everything all right? If you say no, we'll start to guess what the problem could be, so that all you'll have to say is "yes" or "no." If we can't guess, then we'll ask if you feel comfortable staying, or if you'd prefer to leave. There may be something going on that you don't particularly like—perhaps you think somebody followed you up on the elevator—and you might want us to know that, even though it's not serious enough to make you want to leave.

If you do want to leave—and this won't happen very often, and it may never happen—you could either ask us to handle it, or you could take care of it on your own. Obviously, it's nicer if you do it yourself, but if you're not comfortable, then we'll take care of it for you. If something's wrong, act as if it's your very first call and you just can't go through with it: "I'm terribly sorry," you say, "and I made them promise not to tell you, but this is my first night. You are certainly very nice and attractive, but to tell you the truth, I just can't go through with it." That way, nobody can take offense.

We have a girl named Lindsay who once went to see an Arab client. When he opened the door, she saw this dark little man in a baggy white robe and a kaffiyeh on his head, and she just couldn't deal with it. She called me, and by her answers to my questions she let me know that something wasn't right.

I asked her if I should send somebody else, and she said yes, so I told her to call me as soon as she got out of there. When she explained what had happened, I called the client and apologized, and asked him if he'd like to see Elise, who was more than happy to go. And you know what happened? Elise went over there and they really hit it off. The next night, the client called back and took Elise out to dinner. The third night, he took her to a fancy nightclub. She had a wonderful time, and she made a lot of money, too. So remember, even if you don't like a client, somebody else might.

Most of the time, after he has taken your coat, the client will ask if you'd care for anything to drink. Very few clients will ever ask if you'd like anything to eat, and even if they do ask, they're usually just being polite. However, if it's early in the evening and there's a good chance that he may not have eaten yet, this may be your opportunity to have a nice dinner. But unless he's going to order something for himself, tell him that you had a little something before you came over. If it's clear that the client would be much happier if you ordered something, I recommend a plate of fruit.

We do not drink hard liquor in this agency, which means no gin and tonics, no margaritas, no Scotch. We drink Perrier, soda, wine, and champagne. A lot of these guys will be happy to order a bottle of wine or champagne, but it would be inappropriate for you to volunteer that you'd love a bottle, because that's hustling and we don't go in for that. On the other hand, if you specifically ask for a glass of wine, that may be all you get. So your best response is, "I'd love some wine, thank you." In other words, keep it vague.

If you're not a wine drinker and you'd prefer champagne, you can say that you'd like a kir royale, which is a glass of champagne with cassis in it. Now that he knows you like champagne, he may just go ahead and order a whole bottle.

Now, when somebody does take the trouble to order a bottle of wine or champagne, don't sit back and act like this happens to you all the time. Especially if he orders Dom Pérignon or Cristal, act a little excited, as if he's doing something that you consider a treat. Remember that these men want to please you as much as you want to please them, so let him know that you think he's a fabulous guy to be doing this and that you're tickled pink.

You should be aware that in some hotels, the room service staff works with the security people. So please be sure that whenever room service does come into the room, you are fully dressed and not sitting on the gentleman's lap. If for any reason you're not fully dressed when room service knocks on the door, you'll want to disappear quietly without letting the client know that you're afraid of anything. You might say, "Why don't I just go and wash up while you take care of this."

Incidentally, some men get a kick out of having the room service person come in and see him with a beautiful, half-dressed girl so they'll know what a ladies' man he is. But just excuse yourself politely without making it seem that you're nervous or guilty.

If you smoke, it's very important for you to realize that most of our clients are such gentlemen that if you ask them if you can light up, they'll say sure—when in reality they would rather you didn't. So until you see him lighting up a cigarette, please do not smoke. And while we're on the subject, don't smoke in the cab on the way over, either. When you've been smoking in an enclosed car, people can really tell, believe me. You're being paid a lot of money, so please don't smoke unless he does.

Now, when you're talking with the client, please don't refer to us as the office or the agency. Let's face it: none of these guys wants to admit, even to himself, that he found us through the Yellow Pages. Every man has the fantasy that he's calling a private madam—or that he would, if he only knew one—and we try to foster that image. Instead of saying, "I have to call the office," say, "I have to call Sheila," or "I have to call Lucy," depending on who's answering the phone that night. Always use our names, and make it sound like we're all good friends.

Talk us up as much as you can, because everybody likes to feel that they're with the best. Every client wants to be associated with the agency that "all the politicians and diplomats use," and there's no reason we can't persuade our clients to think that we're that agency. You might mention that two of our girls just came back from the Caribbean, or that you had a chance to go to Washington the other day with a prominent diplomat, but that you had to say no because you had an important class you couldn't miss.

Now, the only way to extend a call is to keep the conversation going, because once things become intimate, the evening is probably near an end. And since both you and we are getting paid by the hour, you'll want to be a very stimulating conversationalist.

With some men, that simply means you've got to be a good listener. But whether or not you do a lot of talking, you ought to keep up with what's going on in the world. Our clients are busy, active people, and many of them are themselves newsmakers. At the very least, you should be reading *Time* or *Newsweek* and watching "60 Minutes" on a regular basis. Nobody is going to give you a test to see how much you know about the World Bank, but it would be nice if you knew that there *was* a World Bank.

Incidentally, a lot of our clients are foreigners for whom English is a second language. With these gentlemen, you've got to remember to speak a little more slowly and to enunciate your words more carefully. One of our girls knew she was in trouble when the client asked her to speak "slowlier."

You should always have an upbeat, positive mood and demeanor. We've had girls who have mistakenly believed that if they went in there and acted like they were a sad case, the client would feel sorry for them and offer to help them out. Not true. These gentlemen are looking forward to a pleasant evening. They may have had a rough, difficult day, and the last thing they want to hear is a hard-luck story from a girl who is there to listen to them. If you ever have such a tough day that you can't sustain a positive, upbeat mood, please do us all a favor and tell us you can't work that night.

Some clients consider it a real challenge to get your real name and phone number. Naturally, this is something we don't allow. If he persists, let us know and we will speak to him about it the next time he calls.

If he is especially persistent, you might say; "Sheila and I have a deal. She promised me that she would only send me to the nicest people, and that if it didn't work out, she'd take care of everything. And I promised her that I wouldn't give out my personal phone number." If he argues that Sheila will never find out, you can tell him that you can't do something you feel is dishonorable. When you put it that way, very few people are going to argue with you.

Now we come to the most difficult part of all: trying to figure out if he wants you to stay for more than one hour. If the client you're seeing generally books a girl for only one hour, we'll let you know that in advance. But if he's a new client, or if he has a history of keeping girls for varying lengths of time, then before too long you've got to determine how long you'll be staying.

While it's obviously in your interest—and ours, too—to stay longer, we don't want you to manipulate him or hustle him in any way. You can't very well turn to him with only five or ten minutes left in the hour and say, "I'm sorry, but if you want me to stay any longer, it will cost you more money."

After you've been together half an hour or so and things are still in the talking stage, you're going to need to know one way or the other. At this point, you have two choices. The chicken's way is for you to excuse yourself and go to the bathroom. While you're in there, you can be sure that he will look at his watch. If he feels that time is getting short and that he'd like to get the show on the road, he'll probably get up from where he's been sitting. Or he may simply loosen his tie or give some other small indication that he's ready for a shift in the mood.

But what if you come out and he's still sitting there exactly where you left him? In that case, you'll have to take the more confrontational approach, as in, "I took a look at my watch when I was in the bathroom, and I couldn't believe what time it was. I've been having such a good time, and you're so interesting, that the time has really flown by. I really don't want to rush you, but I do have to call Sheila in a little while and tell her if I'll be staying or leaving."

At this point, you should get a little flustered. You don't want to come right out and ask if he wants you to stay a little longer, but you do want to know the answer. The more embarrassed you act, the less calculating you will appear. He'll probably realize what's going on, and he'll either say, "Well, why don't we get comfortable now," or else he'll suggest that you call Sheila and let her know that he'd like you to stay for another hour.

The other option is to skip the trip to the bathroom and go right into the confrontation. The tricky part here, though, is somehow to work the theme of time passing into the conversation in a fairly casual way without making it look like you've been watching the clock.

Now let's assume that he's asked you to stay for another hour. If he's an old client who has used us a number of times before, he knows that he's got to pay for the second hour. But you'd be surprised how many of these guys really think that you like them so much that for the second hour you'll be staying on your own time! Believe me, this happens a lot more than you'd think.

This is why you must call in and say, "Hi, this is Amy. Mr. Jones has told me he'd like me to stay for another hour." We'll ask you if you two have discussed compensation. Sometimes it's more comfortable for the client to discuss this with you. He'll say, "Gee, if I have you stay for another hour, how much will it cost?" And you say, "It's the same as for the first hour." But don't quote a price, because if you name a specific figure, it makes the whole transaction seem too commercial.

After you've spoken to us, put the client on the line, and we'll say: "We're so glad that you like Amy. She just told us that you'd like her to stay for another hour, and we were wondering how you'd like to take care of it."

We also allow a client to extend your visit for an additional half hour at slightly more than half of the hourly fee, and if that's what he asks for, please don't try to stretch it to a full hour. That's not fair, and it's not what we're about. Be considerate of his wallet: not everybody can write this off on a company credit card. Some men will be making $175,000 a year, and they may not care about an extra $175. But if he's making, say, $70,000, and his wife isn't working and he's got two kids, that extra $90 is a lot of money.

Some of our clients are made of gold, and you'll meet your share of them. But that's not true for everybody. In some cases, the evening he spends with you will be his biggest treat of the year.

Now usually, when the client wants to get down to the nitty-gritty, he'll say, "Let's make ourselves comfortable," or words to that effect. I once had a foreign girl who didn't know what this phrase meant, and who replied, "Thank you, but I *am* comfortable."

At first, the only gentlemen we will be sending you to will be old clients whom we know really well and who have used us many times before. A lot of these guys really love to see new girls. Your first three or four calls will all be your "first" call, so you'll have a good excuse to be nervous. These clients will all be nice and very considerate of the fact that you're new at this.

Now, most of our gentlemen like to watch you get undressed, so please don't go into the bathroom and come out with nothing on as if you've just popped out of a cake. The reason you're wearing pretty underwear is that clients like to see it. I'm not asking you to do some kind of strip-tease show, especially if that sort of thing makes you uncomfortable, although the girls who have tried this approach have had great feedback. But I think you all know there is a way to get undressed that is enticing and maybe a little seductive.

Please don't make a big issue of hanging up all your clothes neatly. Certainly I don't want you to take an expensive outfit and just fling it over a chair. But it looks a little too neurotic to make sure that your clothes are hung up the way you would hang them if they were going into your closet for the night, okay?

After you get undressed, some of the men may ask you to walk around the room or to strike a few poses as if you were a model. Those of you who have never done modeling may feel a little silly doing this. But keep in mind that professional models are probably making $100 an hour, which is how much you're making. And nobody is taking your picture, and nobody is seeing you except this one gentleman. Maybe you'll feel more comfortable practicing this sort of thing at home in front of a mirror so that you know what looks sexy and pretty. Most men are too embarrassed to ask their wives or girlfriends to do something like that, and most of the wives or girlfriends would be too embarrassed to try it even if they *were* asked. So don't forget—this is one of the things you are being paid for.

By the way, let me give you a little tip about the garter belt and nylons. At home, when you're getting dressed, be sure to put on the garter belt and the nylons first, before your panties. As you'll discover, there are a number of gentlemen who like you to keep your garter belt and nylons on the whole time. But not being able to get your panties off would obviously hamper things a bit.

Now, these men know that you're there for the money, but that's not something they want to be reminded of. So it's very important that they not feel you think they're repulsive or distasteful in any way. These guys really want to be loved. They want to be hugged and kissed and caressed. They want to feel that you like them, that you're interested in them, that you enjoy being with them.

But before you really get down to business, you've got to go down there and check everything out just to be sure that they don't have anything you don't want to catch. We all know they like you to go down there anyway, so let me give you an idea of some of the things you should be looking for on your travels.

[At this point, I would give the girls a brief lesson in identifying venereal warts, herpes sores, and other unwelcome sights.]

What if he wants the lights off? Believe it or not, I've only heard of one man who ever wanted the lights turned off completely. But if it happens, tell him that you think he has a great body and you just want to see it. If that doesn't work—or if it would be ludicrous to say it—just tell him you hope he understands that you're very cautious and mindful about your health. He's not going to like it, but he's certainly going to get the message.

What if you find something? First of all, you don't want to scare him. Believe me, he's going to be freaked out enough if he suspects that you think there's something wrong with him. So try to be delicate. Say something like "You probably don't check down here very often, and there probably isn't anything to worry about. But you do have a little bump here, and if I were you, I'd have a doctor look at it."

At this point, most men will deny it—not because they're trying to con you into believing it's not true, but because they need to deny it for themselves. You may also hear some creative excuses such as "My zipper got stuck." Some men may be angry because you're the bearer of bad news. But stand your ground. Explain that you're not a doctor and you could be wrong, but that you're very cautious about your health.

Now, I don't want to alarm you. You should know that this sort of thing has happened to us only two or three times. But it is a possibility, and I do want you to be prepared for it. Don't worry about the money; I'll take care of that. Just get out of there as gracefully as you can and call the office after you leave.

You should know that there are certain gentlemen, especially of English and French extraction, who don't bathe as often as they might. We have a number of Arab clients, and they happen to be exceptionally clean; some of them will wash before, during, and after. But if you have the feeling that the gentleman you're with could really use a bath before things progress much further, here's where your bubble bath packet comes in. Tell him you happen to have some bubble bath powder with you, and wouldn't it be fun if we took a bath together? Incidentally, a bubble bath goes especially well with champagne, in case he's ordered some.

If that doesn't work, you might want to talk about taking a nice shower, and how you'd like to lather him all over. If *that* doesn't work, just look him straight in the eye and say, "Well, then, I'll wait here while you take one." Don't let him get away without it; if he needs one, he needs one. And if he won't take a shower, you can say, "I hope you understand that I'm very fastidious. I certainly took a shower before I walked out my door, and I hope you can appreciate that I think you should do the same. If you'd rather not, I would be more than happy to leave."

This sort of thing hasn't happened yet with any of our clients, and I hope it never will. But here, too, I do want you to be prepared. Again, if you have to leave, I will pay you. I just want you to know that you don't have to get near anyone who smells.

Now, a lot of girls come to me after a few calls and say, "Sheila, I must be doing something wrong, because all they do is lie there." Well, a lot of men *do* just lie there. These days, with all this women's lib around, some men are intimidated because they feel pressured to please a woman in bed—which is one of the reasons some of them call us. As they see it, they don't have to prove anything to us. Another reason men just lie there is that they may feel intimidated because they think you're so experienced that you'll judge them as incompetent. Other men just lie there because they simply prefer it. They feel that as long as they're paying for it, why not? So just do your best.

If they request certain things that you don't mind

doing, please do them. Some men may want you to talk dirty, and if that's something you can do comfortably, then by all means go ahead. If it isn't, you can say, "This might sound silly to you, but I wouldn't feel comfortable doing that. I'm sorry, and I hope you understand."

Some people might want you to touch yourself while they watch, and here, too, the rule of thumb is that you shouldn't do anything that makes you uncomfortable. Sometimes he might want to touch you back there. Technically it's known as Greek, and we don't allow it at all. We do not touch them there, and they do not touch us there, for any reason whatsoever. I don't care how much money he offers you. For health reasons, it's not permitted under any circumstances.

By the same token, we do not permit clients to use any battery- or electrically powered devices. To avoid getting into an argument with a client, the best policy here is simply to tell the truth: "Sheila won't let me do it." That makes it harder for them to argue. You can say, "I made a deal with her, and she made a deal with me." If he becomes insistent, you can say, "It's obvious that I'm just not making you happy. I think I should leave now. I'll tell the agency that you really do prefer to do different things, and perhaps they can refer you to somebody else." That will put the fear of God into them because the last thing they want is to get kicked out of the service.

Moving on to another delicate subject, many girls ask me how much they should appear to enjoy themselves. You've probably heard that a call girl never actually enjoys her work, but many of our girls find that isn't true. Obviously, your enjoyment will depend on who you're with, but many of these gentlemen are handsome and kind, and from what I'm told, a few of them are very good lovers. So you may be surprised by your reactions.

But should you pretend it was "good for you" if it really wasn't? In most cases, no, especially if the man hasn't spent much time or effort on making you feel good. These men aren't dumb, and if you fake it, you'll be insulting their intelligence. On the other hand, if he's gone out of his way to make things pleasant for you, or if it's clear that he just won't stop until you've done your thing, then you might consider a little dramatization. But please be subtle about it; don't go and splatter yourself all over the ceiling.

Now let's get into another delicate area. This is not something I especially like talking about, but we need to go over it because there have been some misunderstandings in the past, and I want to make it clear what my policy is.

There are those gentlemen who would prefer not to finish things up in the regular way. Some men happen to like it orally. I just want to make one thing clear: you do not have to swallow it. But I've also had a client call up to complain about how the girl ran to the bathroom to spit it out. Naturally, at two hundred dollars an hour these guys get a little upset by that, and you can't blame them.

[At this point, I would give the girls a few pointers on how to avoid swallowing it in a way that was not obvious to the client. Because it's a very visual lesson, I am unable to put it into words.]

What happens when you're all finished? Let's say you've got fifteen or twenty minutes left. Now, these gentlemen are technically entitled to "get happy," as we like to phrase it, twice in one hour. But of course we don't volunteer this information. If it comes up, so to speak, it comes up. Otherwise, don't worry about it. You'll probably see more clients who don't do it at all than those who do it more than once, so it's not really much of a problem.

In the event that you only have a few minutes left, but he's interested again, you might say, "I'd really love to, but I hate to rush things. I just don't think that would be fair to you. Why don't I call Sheila and tell her I'm going to be staying an extra half hour."

That way, nobody will feel rushed. In general, *whatever you do or suggest, always make it sound like you're doing it for his pleasure and convenience.*

But what if you'd really rather not go at it again? Tell him what a great back rub you give. Ask him to roll over on his tummy and give him a nice back rub. In ten or fifteen minutes, believe me, the only thing on his mind will be sleep.

Now, the one thing you definitely do *not* want to do when everything is finished is jump up and run into the bathroom and scrub yourself down as if you're trying to rub off the germs. These men would be hurt by that. They took pains to be clean for you, and they don't want you to feel that they're dirty. So please be careful about that.

When you're all done, stay with him and stroke him, and try to maintain that loving mood. Then, five or ten minutes before it's time to leave, say, "Oh, gee, I'm afraid that I just have to get up and start getting ready." Make it sound like you're sad to do it. Then say, "Now don't move; I'll be right back." Go into the bathroom, get a hot washcloth and a towel, and run back and do your little geisha girl routine. After all, it's not fair for you to hog the bathroom and leave this poor guy out there without a chance to wash up.

Most of the gentlemen prefer to get dressed to say good-bye to you. I know that sounds odd, but they really do. So you might ask if he'd like to use the bathroom before you go in there. Most of them won't. At that point, gather up all your gear and go in.

This may sound silly, but once you're in the bathroom, jump up and down a little bit and let gravity do its work so that you don't mess up your underwear. Otherwise, you'll be going down in the elevator, and all of a sudden—whoosh! But please do your jumping quietly.

Then take a look in the mirror and assess the damage. Sometimes one side of your face will be totally gone. Sometimes you'll be pristinely clean and gorgeous, and on other nights you'll be a total wreck. Please keep your makeup simple so this doesn't take half an hour. You really have only about five minutes to put yourself back together again.

Still, you want to look as attractive going out as you did coming in. For one thing, you want to leave him with a good memory of you. For another, you don't want the doorman or the security people to notice that you look different from when you came in earlier in the evening. Also, we might be sending you on another call, and you'll have to look as good for the second guy as you did for the first. Don't think you can fix yourself up in the cab. I want you to get dressed in the bathroom where there are bright lights and a mirror.

Many clients seem to have a thing about girls taking a shower while they're there. You can stay in the bathroom for ten minutes and you'll never hear a peep. But if you're in there for five minutes, and you take a shower, I'll start getting phone calls about how you spent an hour in the bathroom. I don't know what it is about showers that drives these guys crazy. So unless you really need one, and most of the time you won't, see if a sponge bath will do the trick. If you really need a shower, you have your shower cap with you, so hop in. But please make it quick.

Now it's time for him to pay you, and a lot of men get

embarrassed at this point. Some of them will hand you the money in an envelope. Some will try to put it in your bag or your coat pocket, or will leave it for you on the table. Others will give it to you directly. However they give you the money, if it's cash, it's your responsibility to count it before you leave. I realize this can be embarrassing, and if it helps, you can say something like "I really hate to be counting it all in front of you, but I hope you understand that I'm responsible for this."

Sometimes they'll give you the money before you call the office to say you're leaving, and sometimes afterward. You'll say, "Hi, this is Amy, I'm leaving," and we'll say, "Okay, you should have $195 in cash"—or whatever.

If he hasn't paid you yet, you can get off the phone and say, "Sheila says I should have $195." If you'd rather not discuss money directly with the client, we'll be happy to do it for you. After all, that's one of the things you pay us for. You can simply give him the phone, and we'll take care of it with him.

If he owes you $195, which is one of our hourly rates [this was the price in 1984], and he's cheap enough to ask for change, you can give him $5 if you have enough small bills left for the cab. But you don't want to be in the situation of taking a cab home with two hundred-dollar bills in your wallet and nothing else; it's almost as bad as having no money at all.

If he owes you $175 and he wants $25 back, that's a little more legitimate, and if you have the money, you should give it to him. If you don't have it, and the money seems important to him, suggest that he call the office and we'll put a credit on his file card that will be applied against the next time he calls.

Now, every once in a great while there will be a discrepancy, and he won't give you as much as you are supposed to have. You must always act as if this must be a terrible mistake. You've counted it twice, and you're supposed to have $750, and you only have $650. Just say, "I'm sure Sheila told me I'm supposed to have $750, and I only seem to be able to count $650. Would you count it again for me?"

If it doesn't come out right, he will usually make up the difference. Now and then there's somebody who just wants to see if he can get away with it. If he gives you a hard time and insists that he was supposed to pay only $650, say, "Let me just make sure and give Sheila a call." When we answer, say, "Hi, this is Amy. I just want to make sure how much that was again. I have $650 here." We'll ask if you're having trouble. You'll say yes, and we'll ask to speak to him.

As long as you give us the opportunity to try to get the money, you'll be paid in full even if we don't succeed. But don't come bopping back to the office saying, "Sorry, that's all he gave me," because by then it's too late.

When you call us to say you're leaving, we'll say one of several things: "Okay, fine, we'll see you soon," means you should come over to the office. "Okay, give me a call from home," means just that. Occasionally we might tell you that we have a second booking for you, and you should give us a call from an outside phone. We'll try to tell you what hotel he's in so you'll know what direction to start walking. But of course you'll have to call us back for more information after you leave the client's room.

Before you leave, be sure to thank him for calling us, and tell him you had a lovely time. At this point, he may give you a tip, and if he does, be sure to thank him. If the tip is more than $20, and especially if it's $50 or more, let him know that you're thrilled. The clients like to give you a tip not only to thank you, but also because they want to make you feel good. So don't accept it as a matter of course, and don't act as if it's not important.

The tip belongs to you—all of it. But please do let us know about it back at the office, because the next time this gentleman calls, unless he specifically asks for you, we'll try to send over a girl who hasn't had a tip in a long time. Some other night, of course, we'll be doing the same for you.

On your way out of the hotel, I'd rather you didn't use the public telephones in the hotel lobby. A lot of girls who work for the cheaper agencies sign up with half a dozen different places. After they finish with one call, they check in with their answering service, see who's called them, and go out again. They even try to arrange their schedules so they can see two or three clients in the same hotel. The hotel security people are wise to this, and they often stand around the phone bank. You should always try to minimize the time you spend in the lobby, and that goes for using the house phones, too. Unless we tell you that the hotel requires you to call the room before you go up, don't bother. Just sail through the lobby as if you belonged there.

Now, before we finish up this afternoon, I'll be asking each of you to go into the dressing room over there to take off your clothes. I'm going to have a quick look at you, not directly, but by seeing your reflection in the full-length mirror. Believe me, I hate to do this, and if it makes you uncomfortable, I can certainly understand why. It's not something I would look forward to, either.

The reason we do it is that a couple of months after we opened, a client called me to complain that the girl we had sent had a gigantic tattoo of a dragon on her back. Another girl had horrible scars from a breast implant operation, which I also heard about from a client. So I hope you understand that I just have to take a look.

While you're undressing, I'll be standing behind the

door asking you questions for my notes, such as whether you have a roommate, how we can describe your background to our clients, whether there are any types of men or any ethnic group that you'd rather not see, and whether you're willing to see clients who use drugs. After you get dressed again, we'll take a few moments to choose a working name for you, and then you'll be free to leave.

Tonight, or whenever you start, it would be a good idea to come by the office and introduce yourself to the assistant who's working. You'll see what the office is like, and the assistant will get a sense of who you are and what you look like, which will make it easier for her to match you with the right client. And remember to call the office tonight and let us know what your schedule will be for the rest of the week.

I think that's about it for now. Any questions?

Chapter Six

I still remember the name of our first client, a businessman from London who was staying at the Plaza and had seen our ad in the *International Herald Tribune*. He was entertaining a business associate, and we sent over two girls for an entire evening of dinner, dancing, and whatever. (We had a strict rule, however, that whenever a call involved more than one girl, the "whatever" part of the evening took place in separate bedrooms, with no swapping allowed.) As most calls at escort services were for an hour or two, Gina and I were beside ourselves with excitement. Like a couple of anxious parents with two daughters at the junior prom, we waited up until 2:30 A.M., when the girls finally called in to say they were back home—safe, happy, and a couple of hundred dollars richer.

A few days later, we were contacted by a man who wanted to hire two escorts for a bachelor party. As soon as I heard that phrase, I told him we weren't interested. From my research, I already knew that a girl who was hired for one of these events was often expected to have sex with everybody at the party, although in some cases it was only with the groom while the other guests cheered him on. Either way, this was definitely not the sort of event to which we would send our girls, and I suggested to the caller that he contact another agency.

"Oh, no," he said. "I know what you're thinking, but that's not at all what I had in mind." He had called our service because he admired our ad, and the event he was planning for his best friend, the groom, was to be a genteel, black-tie affair for a group of recent Princeton graduates. He wanted two of our girls to attend as the personal dates of the groom and the best man, posing as their old girlfriends. The girls' interaction with the other guests, he assured me, would be strictly social.

He sounded trustworthy, and two of our girls were more than willing to go. The party turned out to be a formal dinner on a boat that circled Manhattan, and our girls were met by the best man at the bar of the Carlyle Hotel, where a limousine was standing by to take them all to the pier.

"You should have seen the groom," Clarissa told me later. "Not only was he in a tux, but he was actually wearing patent-leather shoes with *bows* on them. It was a very fancy crowd, and four of the guests had actually flown over from London on the Concorde just for this party. They were very sweet and refined. I only wish I could meet men like that in my personal life!"

For Clarissa, that party had been a real eye-opener. She was a blond, red-cheeked farm girl from Ohio who had moved east to study veterinary medicine, and she worked for us five nights a week for two years until she had saved up enough money to put herself through school. This was her first call, and I was happy and relieved that she had such a good time.

Whenever a girl returned from seeing a new client, her description of him was entered in our client log, a loose-leaf record book with a page for each man. Even if he had called us only once, we kept a fair amount of information on file: his name, his address and phone number (if he lived in town), how he heard about us, his credit card number (if that's how he paid), or the number of his driver's license if he paid us by check. We also listed some personal details including his age, place of residence, hobbies, his business or profession, a line or two about his personality and conversational style, and what type of girl he preferred.

Contrary to some of the press reports after we were busted, there was no mention on these records of the client's sexual preferences, although if a man was *very* well endowed, we would note this fact with the code LP. (The original designation was BD, but we changed it when I realized that if we were ever raided by the police, those letters might be interpreted as a reference to bondage and discipline, which was definitely not a service we provided.) The only sexual indicator that might appear on a client's card was the word "easy" which meant that the intimate part of the evening moved along fairly quickly.

On the other side of the page, we would list the name of each girl this client had seen, the date she saw him, the length of the call, and the size of the tip—if any.

Although we had no serious problems during our first year, we did have our share of anxious moments. Arlene, a dark-eyed beauty who in her daytime life was a Wall Street lawyer, once ended up in the wrong room at the Waldorf Towers, where the elaborate lettering on the doors made it difficult to distinguish between 18T, where the client was waiting for her, and 18J, which was down the hall. Without realizing it, Arlene knocked on the wrong door. When a distinguished-looking fellow greeted her warmly, she called us to say she had arrived, then proceeded to enjoy a bottle of wine with her gracious host.

About half an hour later, Mr. Wexler in 18T called to say that Arlene had still not arrived.

"Are you sure?" I asked him. "Because she called us half an hour ago to say she was there."

"You said she was petite," said the client, "but you didn't say she was invisible!"

We were really puzzled. Fortunately, one of the girls who had come by to settle up had recently been to the Waldorf Towers, where she, too, had had trouble making out the letters, and she surmised that Arlene might have ended up in 18J. Nervously, I called 18J to see if Arlene might be there. The phone was picked up by an English gentleman whose voice reminded me of Alistair Cooke introducing "Masterpiece Theatre," and who informed me, most graciously, that yes, a young lady by that name was indeed there, and would I care to speak to her?

"I don't suppose you would be Mr. Wexler, then," I said.

"No," he replied, "my name is Miller."

"Well, Mr. Miller, I don't know quite how to say this, but I'm calling from Cachet. We're an escort service, and earlier this evening we sent Arlene to visit another gentleman in your building. I'm afraid she must have knocked on your door by mistake."

"You don't say?" said Mr. Miller, trying gallantly to mask his disappointment. "I'm awfully sorry to hear that. I only wish it had taken you a little longer to discover the error."

Five minutes later, Arlene was in the right room. The intended client took it all in good spirits, and as for our British friend, I called him back and asked if he might care to see another girl—on the house, of course.

"Well," he replied, chuckling, "that's awfully kind of you. I did rather enjoy the young lady's visit, and she did put me in something of a romantic mood." Within twenty minutes, Diane was on her way. Mr. Miller had a pleasant evening after all, and I wasn't at all surprised when he called Cachet a few weeks later—and at regular intervals thereafter.

Although most of the girls ended up in bed with the clients, some of the calls were purely social. Occasionally a client would simply want to entertain a girl for dinner or drinks in his hotel room. Other men were interested in a companion for the theater or an important social event. Lonnie had a fabulous time at the premier of *Return of the Jedi* with a film producer from California who had wanted an attractive and intelligent date and didn't know any eligible women in New York.

One evening we received a frantic call from one of our regular clients: he had just had a fight with his girlfriend, and he needed a date for a formal dinner at the Pierre that was being hosted by Henry Kissinger. Ninety minutes later, one of our girls met him in the lobby in a gorgeous evening gown. "Next time you call me for a formal dinner," she kidded him as they entered the ballroom, "I'd appreciate knowing about it at least two hours in advance."

Several clients, including one man who was gay, would call us because they needed a suitable "girlfriend" to bring to family weddings and bar mitzvahs—not only for their own companionship, but to ward off the inevitable intrusive queries of overanxious mothers and aunts who wanted to know when Michael or Mark was finally going to settle down and get married. Fortunately, we had a girl named Natalie who just loved these events and always knew exactly what to wear.

When Natalie left us to open her own interior design business, Michael and Mark were crushed. They had come to depend on her and were suddenly forced to concoct sad and elaborate tales of an irrevocable breakup. Mark's mother actually asked him for Natalie's number to see if *she* could talk some sense into that lovely but misguided girl.

While I was dealing with the girls, Gina was a ball of fire behind the scenes. One morning she was out shopping, and when she paid for her purchase with a check, she was so impressed by Telecredit, the national check-guaranteeing service, that she signed us up with them the very next day. She also used her connections to arrange to have our books done by a prestigious accounting firm, which also helped us set up a comprehensive health plan for the girls—a benefit that was simply unheard-of in the escort business.

Gina also designed our brochure, and we could hardly wait for the first carton to arrive from the printer. She had picked out the type herself, and it gave the brochure, which was designed to look like an invitation, a cool and elegant appearance. She had persuaded a friend of hers who worked in advertising to write the copy, and he was a master of euphemism: "For an evening of dining, dancing, or theater, Cachet provides a companion who will also join you in your hotel room or apartment afterward." Elsewhere in the brochure, there was a reference to the possibility that a client might "require an escort until morning."

In retrospect, of course, this kind of language was far too risky, and within a few months we put out a revised version. But Gina's friend was justifiably proud of his work and included our brochure in his portfolio. He told us later that it led to two or three new accounts, who told him, in one form or another, "If you can make that kind of business sound this good, we want you to be working for us."

Within four months we were operating in the black. With fewer than a dozen employees, we weren't exactly a threat to General Motors, but on good weeks Gina and I were each taking home as much as $500, which was far more than we had ever earned before. Our policies were beginning to pay off, and the two girls on our staff who had worked before were amazed at the number of our regular clients (or "repeats," as they were called at other agencies). We even had a handful of men who would call us a week in advance to be sure that their favorite girl would be available when they came to New York.

Before long, we started getting calls from overseas, and Gina and I were thrilled to hear from men in London, Zurich, Paris, Kuwait, and Saudi Arabia who had seen our ad in the *International Herald Tribune* or had heard about us from a friend and wanted more information. Another thrill was our first overnight call—overnights were $1,000, of which the girl got $550—which was all the more exciting because the client had originally booked Stacey for only an hour. But he was lonely, and he simply wanted to hold her all night long. And while Stacey didn't get a good night's rest, she consoled herself with the thought that this was very good money for sleeping.

Gradually, the girls got to know each other, and after a particularly fascinating evening, one of the escorts might come back and mesmerize a small group of us with a description of a client's gorgeous apartment, or his magnificent art collection, or an exciting new business deal that would be written about in the *Wall Street Journal* six weeks later.

We were continually refining our operation, but as the following story makes clear, not every administrative problem could be anticipated. Debbie, one of the first girls we hired, once saw a new client named Robert, who owned a sportswear company. She had a wonderful time and reported back that he was young, handsome, and a great lover, and she couldn't wait to see him again. As always, I noted this information in the client book.

When Robert called again the following month, I told him about Christine, whom I thought he would like because she was in the fashion design business. (We never recommended a girl the client had already seen, on the assumption that if he wanted to see her again, he would have said so.) I called Christine to tell her about the booking, and, following our procedure, I read her the information on Robert's card, which included Debbie's glowing report.

"Sounds like you'll have a great time with this guy," I told her.

"I'm counting on it," she replied.

When Christine arrived at Robert's apartment, she called to check in.

"Is everything okay?" I asked, following the script.

"No."

"Do you think he's a cop?" I asked.

"No."

"Is anyone else there?"

"No."

"Should I send somebody else?"

"I don't think so."

"Then you'd better come right back."

Five minutes later I called Robert. "I'm terribly sorry," I told him, "but nothing like this has ever happened before. Normally, I'd be happy to send you somebody else, but I'm afraid we're completely booked tonight."

When Christine came back she was furious. "How could you do this to me?" she asked.

"What do you mean?" I said. "He was supposed to be so fabulous."

"Tell me about it! When I got to his building, it was so decrepit that I was sure there had been some mistake. But once before I had been to a shabby-looking building where the client turned out to have a terrific apartment, so I thought that might be the case here. The elevator wasn't working, so I had to walk up six flights of urine-smelling stairs, half of them without lights. I expected to be attacked by a junkie at any moment. It was the pits. I'm lucky I made it all the way to the top.''

"And then?"

"When I walked into his place, guess what I saw? A bare light bulb hanging from the ceiling. A mattress on the floor with sheets that looked like they hadn't been changed since Lincoln freed the slaves. Beer cans all around. A rickety old kitchen table and one chair. Sheila, I was afraid to even touch the *phone!*''

I was horrified. "So what did you do?" I asked.

"Just what you said. I told him that it was my first night on the job, and that I just couldn't go through with it. I said I was terribly sorry, and I hoped he would understand. Actually, he was very nice about it.''

"I can't believe this," I said. "Debbie raved about this man. She said he was terrific."

"What's her number?" said Christine. "I'll give that girl a piece of my mind.''

"Don't worry," I said. "I'll take care of it."

Now I started to be concerned: Debbie was a real showpiece, and we had been sending her to a lot of new clients. Oh, Lord, I thought, what else has crept in here that I don't know about?

As soon as Christine left, I called Debbie. "Do you remember a client named Robert about a month ago?" I asked.

"The sportswear guy?" she said. "I'll be right over."

"Keep your shirt on," I told her. "You're not even working tonight. I'm calling because Christine just walked out of there in disgust. She said he lives in a pigsty.''

"I wouldn't go *that* far," said Debbie. "It's not *House Beautiful,* I'll grant you that. But who cares about the apartment? Didn't she just think he was fabulous?"

This was the first time that I realized how subjective

our information really was. Unless somebody took the trouble to correct or update the first girl's impressions, whatever she had reported about a new client was accepted as the truth. From then on, Gina and I would debrief the girls when they came back, to make sure that their observations corresponded with our data. If necessary, the client cards would be changed or at least expanded to reflect the reactions of different girls.

On another occasion, a new girl complained to me about a client who had been calling us for months. She had gone over to his apartment and had been shocked to find that there was virtually no furniture in the place—just an old fold-out couch and a small TV perched on a chair. The client was dynamic and successful, and very interesting to be with, but the way his place was furnished had made her feel cheap—and I couldn't blame her.

When I checked with two of the other girls who had been to see him, they said more or less the same thing: "He's an old client, so I assumed you knew." But of course I didn't know. I didn't go on calls myself, so my information was always limited to what the girls reported.

So I wrote the girls a memo: "Just because a client has been around for a while, don't assume that he's perfect. If anything about him or his residence disturbs you, tell us and we'll make a note of it."

If two or more girls had a similar complaint, I would always take action. We had one client, a resident at the Columbia Presbyterian Medical Center, who would work straight through, as residents do, for two or three days without sleeping. When he finally came home, he would call us. But because he hadn't shaved in a couple of days, several of the girls complained to us that it was physically uncomfortable to be with him.

It was an awkward situation, but it had to be dealt with. The next time he called, I brought up the problem.

"Dr. Burton," I began, "this is a little difficult for me to talk about, but our girls take a lot of care of their appearance, and they spend a lot of time getting all showered and dressed up before they go to see you. I realize that after you get home from the hospital you probably just want to collapse. But I hope you understand how much the girls would appreciate it if you could take ten minutes to shower and shave before they arrive."

I knew that my comment could have antagonized him into calling another service. But I had no choice because it was absolutely essential to me that the girls feel good about the clients I sent them to. This, after all, was what made our agency different. Fortunately, our doctor was very understanding, and there were no further complaints about him. But not every client took our criticisms so well, and several men never called us again after I confronted them.

Still, I encouraged the girls to be assertive when the situation called for it. "When you're in somebody's apartment," I said, "sometimes you've got to come right out and say, 'Which towel is mine?' or even, 'Can you let me have a clean towel?' As you probably know from your own dating experience, there are some perfectly nice men out there who live like animals because they've never learned to survive without a woman in the house. So if his towels or his sheets aren't clean, tell him nicely that you'd prefer fresh ones. If you can't bring yourself to say something, be sure to tell me and I'll take care of it for you."

One hot night in August, Shawna came back from a call looking as if she had spent the day trekking through the Sahara Desert. "Never again," she said. "He didn't have air conditioning, so I took three showers in two hours. And when I asked him for something to drink, the fridge was empty and all he could offer me was tap water in a paper cup.''

I wanted to call him on the spot, but I realized that nothing would be gained from my outburst, so I waited until the next day. "I'm not asking you to buy a case of Dom Pérignon," I said, trying to be diplomatic, "but would you mind keeping a few cans of diet soda in the refrigerator? I know the girls would really appreciate it.''

No problem, he said, and it never was again. I'm constantly surprised at how many problems can be resolved if you're willing to confront them politely and directly. And I'm even more surprised by how many people are afraid to do just that.

All hotels have security teams for the protection of their guests, so it was important that our girls look as much as possible like executives who were there for a business meeting—or even as guests at the hotel. Some girls would carry a large manila envelope as if to announce that they were not there for social reasons. I encouraged all the girls to carry briefcases, and except for the height of their heels and a touch more makeup than one would wear to the office, they looked as if they were en route to the boardroom rather than the bedroom.

While many hotels in New York are not all that particular about who walks in and out, we sent our girls only to the better ones. We soon knew which places would not allow an unescorted woman in the lobby after nine o'clock, although in some of the very fanciest hotels in town nobody would even blink if three girls marched through the lobby at two in the morning wearing tophats— and nothing else.

Security wasn't our only concern, however, as the girls spent the bulk of their time in the client's room, not the lobby. Most of our girls felt much more comfortable in suites with a separate living room or, at the very least, in large rooms that included a sitting area. They reported that the rooms they went to in some otherwise respectable hotels, such as the Barbizon Plaza, the Gramercy Park, the Lexington, the Summit, and the Roosevelt simply did not meet these standards, and so we did not accommodate the men who called from those places, no matter how nice they were on the phone. If a call couldn't take place under ideal circumstances, in a hotel room that was well appointed, spacious, and comfortable, we preferred not to accept it at all.

With constant feedback from the girls, Gina and I soon knew as much about Manhattan hotels as any travel agent in America. The girls were excited when a spectacular new hotel opened up in the heart of midtown, near Grand Central Station, but they soon discovered that above that dazzling lobby the rooms were cramped. The rooms at the Park Lane had all king-size beds. The Pierre really *was* as glamorous as it looked. And one internationally famous luxury hotel was a special favorite because room service was so slow that if a guest picked up the phone to place an order, the call would usually last an extra hour.

When a regular client called us from what we considered to be a borderline hotel, we would let the girl decide: "Mr. Jones is a good client, and he's staying in the Lexington. Would you like to see him?" But if we didn't know the man, it was always a little awkward. After all, we didn't want to say, "We're sorry, but we only send our young ladies to the better hotels." We had to use some version of that, but I hated to do it because of how it must have sounded to the caller.

After all, it certainly wasn't *his* fault. He had come to New York on business, and a travel agent had booked him into a hotel that we didn't think was first class. I imagined these lonely men sitting in their rooms, already depressed because they could see that the hotel wasn't what they had hoped, and now being told that at least one escort service wouldn't even send a girl there!

But even the best hotels could pose unexpected problems. One winter evening, we sent Mary to see a foreign client at the Waldorf. She arrived at eight o'clock, called in as usual, and at midnight, she called again to say she was leaving and on her way back to the office.

Half an hour passed, and there was no sign of Mary. After an hour I began to worry. At one A.M. I called the client, who was very tense and clearly not interested in talking. "There's nobody here," he snapped, and hung up.

Gina was sure that Mary had been stopped by hotel security, and although that had never happened to one of our girls, it was certainly a possibility. At one-thirty, with all of the girls back, I took a cab down to the Waldorf to look for her. I asked for the head of security and told him that my roommate had been visiting somebody in the hotel, that she had called an hour and a half ago to say she was leaving, and that she still hadn't returned.

The security officers were skeptical, but I prevailed on them to check around. There was no sign of Mary. I wandered around the lobby, close to tears, not knowing what to do. Just as I was starting to imagine that she had been kidnapped—or worse, as there had recently been a murder at the Waldorf—I caught a glimpse of her running out the door.

I caught up with her on Park Avenue. She burst into tears, and in the cab home, she told me what had happened. The previous day, her client had picked up a call girl in a bar and brought her to his room. After several glasses of champagne and a roll in the hay, he had fallen asleep. When he awoke, the girl was gone—along with his briefcase full of cash and his expensive watch. He had told his sad tale to the head of hotel security, and just as Mary was about to leave, two men from the hotel's security staff knocked on his door to ask him a few more questions about the robbery.

But now he had another girl in his room, and he was embarrassed. He hurried Mary into the bathroom and told her to lock the door. The security men stayed for nearly an hour, going over the previous evening's events in great detail. When they finally left, Mary couldn't get the bathroom door unlocked, and neither could the client. Despite her pleas, he refused to suffer the indignity of asking the hotel for help.

Eventually, the two of them did manage to open the door, and the client paid Mary and added a hundred-dollar tip. She told me that she had seriously considered not taking it if it would have meant spending another minute in that place.

We laughed about it later, but it had been a traumatic experience for both of us, and at Mary's request we never again sent her to the Waldorf.

A few girls simply refused to go to specific hotels; others, because of their daytime careers, wouldn't see any residential clients and felt safer with men from out of town. But whatever her preferences, we allowed each girl to set her own limits. Christie, who worked in advertising, would not see any men in that profession or in publishing. Arlene, the lawyer, would not see any attorneys. Other girls had more general concerns, refusing, for example, to see any client who was more than a little overweight, or who smoked, or used drugs, or was over fifty-five.

Some girls were reluctant to see Oriental men. "You're making a mistake," I would tell them. "Our Oriental clients are all such gentlemen—very clean, very nice, very easy. Unless you feel strongly about this, why don't you go on this one call and see if I'm right?" No girl who saw an Oriental man ever said a negative word about him.

Several girls actually preferred Japanese clients because they were less demanding sexually. For one thing, they normally took less time in bed. For another, they tended to be . . . well, let me put it this way: For his monthly column in *Esquire,* Bob Greene once paid a visit to a New Jersey factory where Trojan contraceptives are manufactured.

At one point, Greene tells the plant manager that when he was a teenager, he and his friends used to believe that condoms came in different sizes. As a matter of fact, the manager replies, there really *are* two sizes—one for American men and one for Japanese.

"What's the difference?" asks Greene.

"The Japanese size is smaller," the manager replies. "When you lay one of these goods flat and measure its width, it is fifty-two millimeters wide and seven point one inches long. The Japanese standard is forty-nine millimeters wide and six point three inches long."

From that time on, some of the girls used "six point three" as their private code word for Japanese men.

Not all of our problems occurred in hotels. We had one client who used our service every Sunday night, when his wife went out to play cards with her friends. One evening, I sent over Tess, a cute, bubbly girl with an optimistic attitude and a great sense of humor. An hour into the call, at a most inopportune moment, the intercom in the client's apartment started buzzing repeatedly.

"Your wife is here," said the doorman. "I've done everything I can to stall her, but she's on her way up. And she's loaded for bear."

Tess started to giggle, but to the client this was no joke. He raced around the room, picked up all her clothes, shoved some money at her, and pushed her, naked, out into the hall. Tess ducked into the stairwell just as the woman was getting off the elevator, and as she hurriedly pulled on her clothes, she heard the angry wife storming around the apartment, opening doors and then slamming them shut. "Okay, Richard," she shouted. "I've caught you this time! Now where the hell is she?" Tess was shaking, but she walked safely down the stairs and out of the building.

On another occasion, Tess had been to see her gynecologist to be treated for a yeast infection. He treated the problem with gentian violet, a bright purple liquid that he applied liberally to the infected area. When Tess asked if she could continue working that week, the doctor, who knew the whole story, assured her that there would be no problem.

But little did he know. That same night, Tess went to see a new client. Suddenly, near the end of her visit, he started screaming.

"What's wrong?" she asked.

"Look!"

Which Tess did. To her vast amusement, his prized possession had turned a bright shade of purple. But here, too, Tess's sense of humor was not shared by the gentleman she was seeing. "My God," he cried, "what if this stuff never comes off?"

Tess calmed him down, but not surprisingly, the poor fellow never called us again.

I had forewarned the girls in the reinterview that there was always the possibility that a man might get out of line or suggest something that made them uncomfortable. Most of the girls were quite young and not very assertive, and it wasn't hard for them to be intimidated by the rich and powerful men they were seeing—who were, after all, paying them handsomely for their time.

This situation could create a feeling of obligation—that whatever the man wanted, he deserved.

"It's natural to feel that way," I explained, "but it's the wrong attitude. Instead, always keep in mind that you're doing the client a favor by going to see him. If he ever gets belligerent or obnoxious, just smile at him and say, 'I'm sorry, but I'll have to leave now,' And don't worry about the money; I'll take care of it."

I was proud of this policy, and I wish I could say that it was operative from the very beginning. But in fact, it came out of a situation midway through the first year, when Elizabeth returned from a call in tears. She had been to see a client who was drinking, and he had become rude and abusive to her.

"Why didn't you simply get up and leave?" I asked.

"Because I had already been there for two hours," she replied, "and the rent is due tomorrow."

Click! It had never occurred to me before, but the very next day, I sent out a memo with a new rule: "If any client acts in a rude or obnoxious manner, just get out of there and I'll pay you anyway."

"This doesn't mean you can act like a princess," I warned the girls. "And I'm sure you understand that not all of our clients are Robert Redford. But if there's something you really don't like about him, leave. Because if you stay, you're not going to have a good time with him, which means that he won't have a good time with you. So what do we end up with? Two unhappy people. And in that situation, who wins? Far better to leave and avoid a bad experience."

"But what do we *say*?" the girls wanted to know.

"Make something up. Tell him that something you ate for lunch disagreed with you, that you've been trying to ignore it, but that you feel really terrible. Apologize profusely. Let him know there's nothing personal about it, but you have to go home. Or you can always say that this is your first time, and that you just can't go through with it."

This new policy was enormously important for the girls, even though most of them never had to use it. But the knowledge that they *could* leave—that they always had the option of walking out if the situation became tense or unpleasant and that I would applaud them for doing it—was a tremendous boost to their morale. And it was one more example of the first rule of the market-place: Treating people well is always good business.

Because most of our girls had never worked before, they didn't always appreciate the little touches that made us different from the competition. But we had one girl, Claudette, who'd had extensive experience with escort services and as an independent working girl in both New York and Europe.

In Geneva, she had operated out of a bar where the waiters served as middlemen. In London, she had worked in a house. Eventually, she made her way back to New York, where she had lived years earlier as a social worker. To supplement her meager income, she had taken a part-time job at an escort service, and like so many girls in that situation, she found that she enjoyed the work far more than she had expected. After a year or two, she developed a roster of private clients who would call her directly. Some of these men would pay through bartering—especially plane tickets, which they would charge to their business credit cards. "A lot of working girls talk about 'around the world,' " Claudette liked to say, "but how many really get to go?"

Although Claudette could have made more money on her own, she signed on with two other escort services, and later with me, because she had grown tired of work-ing every night. An independent working girl soon be-comes a prisoner of her phone, and if she's not available when the clients call, they soon disappear. Besides,

Claudette was happy to give up part of her income in return for having somebody else arrange the bookings and handle the administrative and financial details.

Because she was more experienced than the other girls, we would send Claudette to our more adventuresome clients, and she was free to negotiate her own arrangements with those who wanted special favors. (I didn't even want to know the details, and she never discussed them with me.) But Claudette was keenly aware that most of our girls were novices, and she was always sensitive to the fact that they might not feel comfortable performing all the little tricks in her repertoire. She made sure that every client understood that she operated by her own rules and that he shouldn't necessarily expect the other escorts to share her various interests and inclinations.

I couldn't send Claudette to every client, however, as some of them just couldn't deal with a girl who was slightly older and more experienced. Since most of our clients were conservative businessmen who weren't looking for any unusual activities between the sheets, Claudette could have made more money at other escort services, as she well knew. But she appreciated the sense of security Cachet provided, and she enjoyed the camaraderie with the other girls. But most of all, she said, she liked the way I treated the escorts and went out of my way to make them feel comfortable. Because Claudette had been around the block, her confidence in me meant a great deal.

Most of the girls kept a certain distance from the boss, but Claudette and I became friends right away. And because she had several friends who worked for other escort services, she was a terrific source of information. If there was an easy way to sneak out of a hotel by going through the nightclub rather than the lobby, Claudette would know about it. If the Plaza had a new head of security with a reputation for toughness, Claudette would be the first to hear it. And it was Claudette who had told me how she checked for venereal warts; it was a malady I had never even heard of, but I dutifully passed on the information during the reinterview.

"I always prefer to work for a woman," she told me. "The first couple of years in the business were fun, but this kind of work can be very taxing, both physically and emotionally. And I've never met a man who could really understand what it takes out of you. Sometimes I wish that being a call girl were legal, so I could take a tax deduction for the depreciation of my body."

Because most of our girls worked for no more than a year, I was amazed that Claudette had remained in the business for so long. One day I asked her how she did it.

"Sheila," she replied, "the first thing I learned was that a good call girl always thinks about the money. If you stop thinking about the money, one of two things will happen: either you'll get emotionally involved with the client, which is never a good idea, or you'll become bored, which is just as bad. But as long as you keep the idea of money firmly implanted in your mind, the job takes care of itself."

Claudette had an unusual perspective on her work, and despite what she said about money, it was clear that she enjoyed the excitement and adventure of the job. "There's nothing like working in New York," she told me over dinner one night. "At first, I found it a little overwhelming to be going out at night. But you quickly get used to it. Now, every night is like a drama, and it's always different—different characters, different backdrops, and different scripts.

"Sitting in my living room, waiting for the phone to ring, I feel like a star in her dressing room. Except that I never know exactly when the curtain is going to rise. There I am, bathed, groomed, and made up. When the call comes, I throw on my clothes, check myself in the mirror, and say, 'Showtime!'

"But it's a long way from the dressing room to the stage. Will I be able to find a cab? Will there be traffic? Do we have to go through the theater district, which always slows things down? There's always a little tension, and the adrenaline never stops.

"When I finally get to the hotel, there's the challenge of getting past security. A moment later I'm knocking on the client's door, and the music from *Dragnet* is playing—dum-de-dum-dum. I've gone through a lot to get here: who's going to open the door?

"And then suddenly, there I am, with just one other person in an enclosed little space in the middle of this crazy city. There's me and there's him, and a couple of props, like a couch and a bottle of wine. The curtain goes up, and the play begins. And it's different every night, of course, depending on what we improvise. If we play well together, it's great, and when it's not so great, the money is still good.

"But don't get me wrong. I would never want to see new clients only. They're exciting, but my life is stressful enough as it is. An old client is easier, more comfortable. We already have a relationship. He will notice a new pair of earrings or a terrific new dress that I've put on just for him.

"Some of my male friends have fantasies about doing what I do. They love the idea of getting dressed up, going over to somebody's house or hotel, being wined and dined, and then being well paid to bring pleasure to a member of the opposite sex. If you ever want to sign up a few male escorts, I can give you a long list of volunteers."

Because of her broad experience, Claudette was a kind of mentor to the other girls. Once, a few of them prevailed upon her to conduct an impromptu little seminar on the techniques of oral sex. "The first thing you have to understand," Claudette began, "is that men's penises are like snowflakes. No two are exactly alike." Then, using a carrot, she gave an hysterical lesson on the finer points of fellatio. As an encore, she dazzled the girls by demonstrating a special little trick she had learned in Europe, which consisted of putting a condom on a man without his even knowing that it was there. I won't even try to explain how she managed that one except to say that she used her mouth in ways we didn't think were possible.

Claudette used to carry a "goody bag" in her briefcase, and one cold night, when business was slow, she gave a group of us in the office a guided tour of her toys. I don't remember them all, but among the items in Claudette's collection were harnesses, body paint, paddles, rubber belts, spiked shoes (for both women and men), and something known as a cock ring—which preserves a man's erection until, in Claudette's deathless prose, "he's ready to explode in a blissful burst of pent-up energy."

She also carried a small Polaroid camera, French ticklers, satin gloves, pleasure mittens, massage oil, an elaborate dual-control vibrator known as a "busy beaver," and edible underwear. The girls had a wonderful time, but although the demonstration was fascinating, I was more embarrassed than amused.

The item that most aroused their interest was Claudette's set of ben wa balls, nestled in a little velvet box. Most of us had heard of ben wa balls, but few of the girls had ever actually seen them. As Claudette explained it, ben wa balls were first used in the early Ming period in China—a fact my ninth-grade history text had somehow failed to mention. They're generally made of brass or bronze, and women insert them into the appropriate area, where they knock lightly against each other for added pleasure, especially during intercourse.

Claudette then showed us the deluxe version, a kind of silver egg filled with mercury. Traditionally, she told us, the egg was used in conjunction with a rocking chair, which would cause the mercury to flow back and forth from one end of the egg to the other, with very pleasant results. "But as you can see," said Claudette, "this modern version comes with a small, battery-operated attachment."

Once, when Claudette was having trouble with her bathroom sink, she asked the maintenance man in her building to help her retrieve what she believed was the top of a toothpaste tube that had slipped down the drain. But when he opened up the drain, he found a silver ben wa ball.

"What's this?" he asked.

"Beats me," said Claudette. "Must be a ball bearing."

"No way, lady," he said.

"I copped out," Claudette told me later. "I should have told him what it was."

"Don't be ridiculous," I said. "To the *maintenance* man?"

But Claudette was committed to teaching people about sex, and she insisted that she could have told him the simple truth in an appropriate, neutral way. To her, the incident represented a missed opportunity in her ongoing campaign of sex education for adults. To me, it represented the essential Claudette, and although her outspokenness sometimes made me wince, I couldn't help but admire her healthy, straightforward attitude toward sex.

By the end of the first year, Gina had decided that running an escort service was no longer what she wanted to be doing. Like me, she had found that managing the business was enormously time-consuming, but unlike me, she wasn't especially enjoying the work or our steady growth. She wisely concluded that she would probably be happier pursuing a career in the art world.

For Lucy, the last straw came when the FBI called and asked her to come to their downtown offices. As part of their search for Bernadine Dohrn, a member of Weather Underground and a suspected urban terrorist, the bureau had decided to interview the owner of every escort service in New York. They had been told that Dohrn was now working as an escort, but when two agents showed Gina her photograph, she was astonished. "Are you kidding?" she said. "We would never hire a girl who looked like that!"

Nonetheless, the meeting with the FBI was extremely unpleasant. According to Gina, the detectives harassed her and repeatedly threatened to shut us down. When she returned to the office she was still shaking, and it was just a matter of time before she decided to get out.

I had mixed feelings about her leaving. On the one hand, I could never have started the business without her tremendous energy and administrative skills. On the other, I felt that she was holding me back, that she was ambivalent toward, and even afraid of, our growing success. We were also different types: I was close to the girls, whereas Gina preferred to remain aloof.

Still, when she actually left, I was scared to death. From the start, we had talked together every day, and although I now knew as much about the business as she did, I couldn't imagine running Cachet without her. It took me a couple of weeks to realize that Gina's departure was really more of an opportunity than a crisis, as it would allow me to run the business exactly as I wished.

I had some new ideas I was eager to try out, and now

I was free to experiment without a partner looking over my shoulder. First, however, I would have to compensate for Gina's absence. As I saw it, my immediate priorities were to find an office and to hire some help.

Chapter Seven

*F*inding an office came first. Not only was I getting tired of working out of my little apartment, but I had also interviewed several excellent girls who had boyfriends or roommates and could work for me only if they had somewhere to wait on the nights they were on.

When I told the real estate agent that I was looking for an inexpensive one-bedroom apartment on the Upper West Side, she smiled sweetly and pointed to a pile of applications that must have been six inches high. I didn't expect to hear from her again, but four days later she called back to show me a nice-size place not far from where I lived for seven hundred dollars a month. I took it on the spot.

I set up the tiny bedroom as a back office and brought in a long desk, supported at each end by a two-drawer file cabinet. In the living room I put a straw rug, a floral chintz sofa, two lime-green armchairs, a terra-cotta elephant table with a glass top, a five-section white wall unit, and a television. I stocked the bathroom with plenty of clean towels, as well as shampoo, electric rollers, and a hair dryer. I also had a beautiful vanity built with lights that went all the way around the mirror.

I wanted to make the office a cheerful and comfortable place for the girls, for in addition to those who found it more convenient to work out of the office, other girls were always coming by to settle up their accounts, and they'd often hang around to socialize with whoever happened to be there.

Periodically I would bring over a pile of magazines, including *Glamour, Vogue, Cosmopolitan,* and *New York.* Whenever I came across an article that I thought the girls should see, I would make copies. Each girl had her own mailbox where I could leave her notes, memos, or clippings.

On any given evening, somebody would usually be ordering a takeout meal from Bennie's, a natural-food and salad place, or from one of the many Chinese restaurants in our neighborhood. While they waited in the office, the girls would read, study for courses, watch TV, exercise, or do yoga. Our most overworked appliance was a popcorn machine, and I think we went through more popcorn than the movie house around the corner. We had a blackboard, where the girls would leave me notes when we were running low on soda, coffee, hairspray, or other supplies. Once, when somebody wrote, "Sheila, please buy butter for popcorn," I wrote back, "Forget it, you're all on diets!"

With so many girls coming in and out of the office, we had to be careful about not calling attention to ourselves. All of the girls had a key to the outer door of the building, because the alternative was to be buzzed in, and a tenant on the first floor used to complain that he heard the buzzing all night. But as I instructed the girls in a memo, "If anyone who lives, or appears to live, in our building is around when you arrive, please don't use your key. You'd be a little uncomfortable if you knew that ten or twenty people who didn't live in *your* building all had keys to the front door, wouldn't you?"

To make the traffic less conspicuous, I told the girls to have their taxis stop at the building next to ours. And because the lobby in our building was like an echo chamber, I asked them to remove their shoes as soon as they came in the front door. The last thing I wanted to do was alarm the natives.

With the office in place, I soon developed a regular routine for myself. I would come in every morning to take care of the banking and other paperwork. When that was done, I would leave to do errands—making sure to return to the office no later than three-thirty, half an hour before we officially opened. On my way back, I would usually start to think about which girls were on that night. Some were easier to book than others, and on nights when I had several outstanding girls to work with, I was especially excited. There was no feeling more wonderful than the confidence that came from having a new client call, sending him a fabulous girl, and just *knowing* that he would be surprised and impressed by how lovely and warm she was.

I would always begin the afternoon routine by checking the prebooking board, where previously booked calls were posted. There were often two or three calls already scheduled for that night, which made me feel that we were going into the evening from a position of strength. It was also flattering to know that some men thought we were so terrific they had called us a week in advance to make a reservation.

As I quickly counted down to four o'clock, I felt a small rush of exhilaration. Who would phone us tonight? Would there be anybody glamorous, like a prince or a duke or a well-known deal maker? How would things go for Michelle on her first call? Would there be any dinner calls? Any overnights? Would any terrific girls call us for an interview?

Next, I would go to our hiding place behind a baseboard in the fireplace and pull out a five-section accordion file, which I called the "Inev" (for "incriminating evidence'') file. This included the file cards with my description of each girl, the girls' schedules, our annotated hotel list, credit card information, the "dailies"—a detailed record of the previous night's calls—and the "bank," which was an envelope of cash from which I would reimburse the girls for their credit card slips and checks.

After that, I'd check the master schedule, which I had made up the previous Friday, based on what days the girls had chosen for the upcoming week. I would take special note of who was scheduled to start at four o'clock today, and I might call her to be sure she would indeed be ready that early. On Wednesday afternoons, I would also call the girls who were scheduled to come in the next day for interviews and reinterviews, to reconfirm.

Then I would play back the answering machines and listen to the messages. First came the girls, who had called in to say exactly when they'd be ready to go out that evening; I'd note down the times on my master list. Next, I listened to the clients' messages. First-time callers generally hung up when they called us before four P.M. and were greeted by a recording, but our regular clients would often leave a message and a phone number. By now it was three-fifty or so, and I'd have to hurry because the phones would start to ring the moment we were officially open. At three fifty-eight I'd make a trip to the bathroom, because on busy nights I wouldn't have another opportunity for hours.

On the stroke of four, I'd turn off the answering machine and start taking the calls myself. There would be old clients calling for later in the evening, new callers asking for information, out-of-towners wanting to prebook for the following week, and, invariably, one or two girls who had to start a little later than they had expected or had to cancel altogether. I might have had eight girls scheduled, but between Rebecca's cold and Patty's "migraine"—(the code word for her period), I'd suddenly be down to six. When that happened, I'd quickly call around and try to convince somebody else to work that night.

Now that we were open, girls would be coming in to settle up from the previous night. If the client had paid in cash, the girl would pay me the agency's share. If he had paid with a check or credit card, I would reimburse her with cash on the spot because I had received an authorization for the credit card or the check before the girl had even heard about the call.

At other agencies, the girls routinely wait from four to eight weeks to be reimbursed for credit card payments, although in reality the agency's bank account is credited within a matter of days. In some cases, the owners will lie to a girl, telling her that a particular check or credit card didn't go through—this, of course, was why I had stopped working for Eddie—and a few places actually had the gall to charge the girl for this "problem" by deducting the *full* amount of the check or credit card from the amount they owed her for other calls. In other words, she not only failed to receive her own share, but she also had to come up with the agency fee, which meant that she actually *lost* money on the call.

This was a horrible situation for a girl to be in, for by the time she caught on to this practice and started to complain, the agency might owe her several thousand dollars. And if she quit, she would never see a dime of it.

I was always surprised to see how many of our clients made out their checks to us from a joint account, with their wives' names prominently imprinted underneath their own. And although a check made out to "Cachet" did not indicate that we were an escort service, it always seemed to me that these men were taking a needless risk

—unless their wives never looked through their canceled checks.

Men who ran cash businesses generally paid us in cash, and we had one client, a hairdresser, who invariably paid in crumpled one-dollar bills that he had received as tips. The girls liked him well enough, but it took so long to count up all the money that they would generally wrap up the evening a few minutes early.

Back in the office, there was usually a lull between six and eight. Our out-of-town clients would be having drinks or an early dinner with business associates, and as for the residentials, no man who could afford to call us ever left the office much before seven o'clock. During the dinner hour, I would usually order a takeout meal from one of the many restaurants in the neighborhood, and if the phones were quiet, I would eat in the living room with any girls who happened to be around.

Most nights, the phones would pick up again around eight, with residential clients arriving home, out-of-towners returning to their hotels, and another group beginning to arrive from the airport for meetings the next morning. We would also start to hear from girls who had seen our Help Wanted ads, especially on Wednesday and Thursday nights when the new issues of the *Village Voice* and *Show Business* hit the stands.

The period between eleven and twelve-thirty was usually our busiest, and some nights it would be a real zoo, with three or four callers on hold while I tried to make each one feel special. With a regular, I could explain that we were momentarily swamped and that I'd call back in fifteen or twenty minutes. Meanwhile, I'd make a mental note of which girl I would hold in reserve for him.

While all this was going on, I was also placing calls of my own. Every time I booked another client, I had to clear his check or credit card before calling the hotel to confirm that he was really there. Only then would I phone the girl to tell her who the client was and what time he expected her.

New girls were always asking me which nights of the week were the busiest. I would have loved to be able to answer that question, but the truth was that except for the fact that Friday and Saturday were usually slow, there were no predictable patterns. Still, most of the girls were convinced that they had at least one "lucky night," so Stacey, for example, always made a point of working on Thursdays. We used to close on holiday weekends but would open on the last night, when many of our residential clients would call—either because they had just come back from out of town and wanted to continue the celebration or because they hadn't gone anywhere and didn't want to feel the weekend was a total loss.

With half of our management team in retirement, and no letup in the amount of work that the job required, it soon became clear that I needed one or two girls to help me answer the phones in our office, just as I had done for Eddie. But I couldn't very well put an ad in the paper: "Phone Girls Wanted for Escort Service." Such an announcement would have constituted an open invitation to be infiltrated by the police—or by our competition. Instead, I asked the girls if they knew anyone who would be interested in helping out in the office.

From the start, I decided not to refer to the office staff as phone girls or bookers. Our regular clients had become accustomed to doing business only with the owners, and I knew they would resist talking with anybody else unless they believed she had some stature in the organization. So I called these girls "assistants," because when I wasn't around they had the authority to make decisions and even to discipline the escorts for lateness or other infractions on the rare occasions this became necessary.

The telephone assistants were our public face to the outside world. They were the ones who set the tone, who always referred to the girls as "young ladies," not only because "women" made then sound too old and too liberated, but also because, as I had already explained to the girls, if the client was trained to think of his escort as a lady, then he was more likely to behave like a gentleman.

The assistants also constituted our first line of defense against inappropriate, overly curious, or potentially dangerous callers. And they freed me up to attend to the hundreds of little details that made the business run smoothly.

With an endless stream of applicants coming in for interviews, not to mention the banking and other administrative duties (including continual problems with the phone company), my days were full enough without also having to be in the office every night. When I had other plans, the assistants took over, and in addition to running the business, they served as an extra set of eyes and ears. Was Heather carrying a little extra weight? I needed to know about it. Did yet another client complain about Elizabeth because she seemed "too professional"? Write it down. Was Kelly dressed too provocatively? Be sure to tell me. Was that new client from Texas as nice as he sounded on the phone? Find out and leave me a message.

The first assistant I hired was Liza, whom I had met a few months earlier when she had applied for a job as an escort. Liza had everything I was looking for—good looks, intelligence, and a warm personality. She was studying to be an actress, and I made a note on her application form that she had a fabulous voice. Her only drawback as a potential escort was that she needed to lose a few pounds.

But when I started looking for an assistant, I remembered Liza and realized that she might be a good choice. Not only did she have office experience, but because she had been to the reinterview, she already knew the score. And then there was that fabulous voice. To my delight, she was both interested and available.

A good telephone style was essential for the job, and girls who studied acting usually had a trained voice and were generally articulate and well spoken. I especially didn't want our phone to be answered by someone with a New York accent, like most of our competitors. Whoever answered our phone would set the tone for everything that followed, so it was essential that she speak in a refined, cultivated manner.

I also liked to hire actresses because they were accustomed to repeating the same lines over and over, making them sound fresh each time. A good assistant could make it seem as if she were merely enjoying a friendly, casual conversation with a client, even if, in reality, virtually every word out of her mouth was part of a script. She might be trying to balance three phone calls at once, but with her acting background, she could make it seem as if the client she was speaking to at that moment were the most important man in the world.

An assistant also had to be discreet, not only with potential clients, who occasionally asked more questions than we were prepared to answer, but also with the escorts. The assistants had access to the girls' file cards, and it was critical that the information on those cards remained confidential. Morgan's card, for example, included the phrase "Not attractive enough to send to a new client." I was always terrified that Morgan would somehow read her card and feel betrayed. At some level, she undoubtedly knew that we had hired her in large measure for her enormous breasts, as there were always a few clients for whom a big bust was paramount. Still, there was nothing to be gained from rubbing it in.

Liza turned out to be an inspired choice, and she was as happy about it as I was. For somebody who was bright, sensitive, responsible, organized, and intuitive, it was a rare treat to find a position with flexible hours and good pay where all of these attributes were needed.

Liza was warm and friendly on the phone, and she could get even the most stressed person to relax. She was especially good with difficult clients. One of our regulars, a prominent attorney, called one night when he was drunk, and Liza handled him brilliantly. "You know, Charles," she told him, "you already seem to be having such a good time tonight all by yourself! Why don't you give us a call tomorrow?"

When I complimented her, she just laughed. "Don't think it was easy," she said. "I was dying to say, 'You're soused, Chuck, and you couldn't get it up tonight if your life depended on it.' " That's why it was so good to have an actress answering the phones.

In fact, Liza's telephone manner was so winning that it changed her life. A good assistant would get to know the clients individually, and Liza especially enjoyed talking with a sales manager named Alex who called us every week. Because he was so jolly and generous, Alex was a particular favorite of the girls. He also had a great attitude: once, when I asked him what kind of girl he wanted to see, he answered, "Bright, honest, and happy." Because he was unusually kind and sensitive, he was always a good choice for a girl who was just starting out.

Alex traveled widely, and he'd often call us from San Francisco or Chicago just to say hello. Like many of our clients, he tried to get one of the assistants to go out with him. Liza was seriously tempted, but she always refused. But they continued to talk, and Liza continued to select girls she thought Alex would like.

This wasn't a difficult assignment, because Alex was so warm and outgoing that he could have had a good time with almost anybody. The next day, he'd always want to speak to that girl on the telephone, but because we didn't allow that, he would do the next best thing: he'd call Liza and talk to her instead.

One evening, Alex told Liza that he was planning a Caribbean vacation and really wished he had somebody to go with. He spoke so sensitively about his forthcoming trip, and about being single, that the next time he called, Liza said, "I'm not going away with you, but your description of the beach really touched me. Maybe we should meet after all."

"How about dinner tomorrow?" he said.

"On one condition," she replied. "That our date has nothing to do with the business, and that you'll continue calling us even if it makes you feel awkward."

Alex never did call Cachet again, but not because the dinner was awkward. He and Liza fell in love, and they've been living together ever since. "We got to know each other under very trying circumstances," Alex likes to say. "Before we even met, she had put me on hold more than a hundred times."

An assistant had to be skilled at selling—but in a restrained manner. Ours was strictly a soft-sell operation, and I didn't want anybody to be too pushy. While a hard-sell approach might have worked in the short run, over time it wouldn't pay off. Besides, that kind of salesmanship went against our whole image, not to mention our marketing strategy. Our goal was to attract repeat customers, and their first impressions of us were extremely important.

Although a client who used our services might see a different girl every time he called, he had an ongoing relationship with the assistant. She was his pal and his adviser, and if for any reason he was disappointed with the girl we had sent him, she was there to listen to his complaints.

Except for Alex, no client ever succeeded in meeting an assistant. But it certainly wasn't for lack of trying. Because the assistants were good talkers, and especially because they were invisible to the clients, they often became prime fantasy objects. Men were always asking the escorts about them: "What does Jaime look like?" Or: "Tell me about Ashley."

In addition to her human and social skills, an assistant had to have a good memory and be well organized. Although most of the information she required was written down, on a busy night there wasn't always time to check the records. Which girls are on tonight? During which hours are they available? Whom would they rather not see? What kind of girl does Mr. Harris like? Whom has he already seen, and what were they like? Which clients do I have to call back later to confirm a prebooked appointment, and when?

Administratively, Ashley was superb. She had an amazing memory and not only knew the phone number of every hotel in New York, but also the phone numbers and addresses of our regular residential clients. But what really counted was that just like the corporate executives with whom she did business, she—and all the assistants—had to be able to operate clearly under pressure while thinking five steps ahead.

An assistant also had to be impartial and nonjudgmental. As a matchmaker for one-night stands, she couldn't afford to let her personal feelings about a girl influence the business decisions she had to make. Even if she didn't happen to like a particular escort, she still had to book her if that girl was right for the client.

On evenings when I wasn't in the office, the assistants

would close up at the end of the night. If the last girl out was at a private residence, the assistant could go home—as long as she had given her home number to the girl who was still out. But if the last girl was at a hotel, the assistant had to stay on the job until the escort got home. I wanted somebody in the office in case there were problems with hotel security.

One o'clock in the morning was an unusually early closing hour for an escort service, and although we missed out on a lot of business, I wasn't especially interested in hearing from men who were looking for female companionship at three A.M. (More often than not, these would be drug calls.) And as I always explained to the new girls, we specialized in the more straitlaced businessman who had to be at a breakfast meeting at eight in the morning. Besides, many of the girls had to be at work or in class by nine.

But if a girl had gone out at midnight, or was on an unusually long call, she might not return until three, four, or even six o'clock in the morning, and the assistant would end up sleeping on the couch until the last girl called in on the special escorts' line to say she was safely home. But as long as a girl was out, the meter was running, so even if she were taking a nap, the assistant was still earning $7.50 per hour in commissions for every girl who was still out. All things considered, it wasn't bad money for sleeping.

When a girl returned home from a hotel call, she was supposed to call the office so that the assistant would know for sure that she had returned home safely and had not been stopped by hotel security. But every now and then a girl would come home late, collapse into bed, and forget to call in. Usually her answering machine would be on, so there was no way the assistant could determine whether she had actually returned. As a result, the assistant might be forced to wait in the office until as late as ten or eleven in the morning. Believe me, this was a mistake no escort would make more than once!

If an applicant for the job of assistant seemed to have the range of qualities I was looking for, I would put her through a six-week training program. During this period, she would receive a token fee of $25 a night, which was increased to $75 once she started working. This was the base pay; as an extra incentive, the assistants kept 10 percent of the agency's share of all the business they booked.

As a result, the assistants usually made between $100 and $200 a night, and although the money was good, the job was difficult and the hours were long. An assistant who worked a full shift would arrive at the office at three-thirty in the afternoon to set up the office, just as I did. And on some nights she wouldn't be able to leave until dawn.

The training program for the assistants began with several sessions of discussion, note taking, questions, and role-playing at my place. When I felt that a new trainee had a basic command of the job, I would bring her to the office, where she would listen in, on a speaker phone, to conversations between the assistants and the men who called us.

I wouldn't allow a new girl to go near a phone until we had gone over a long list of details, including such topics as how to describe an escort, how to read the client books, how to put people on hold without making them angry, how to set up the weekly girls' schedule, how to answer questions properly—but without revealing too much information, how to interview a girl who has just returned from seeing a new client, how to keep financial records, and much more.

By the third week, she would be permitted to answer

calls, but only during slow times and under close supervision. When one of our regular clients called, we would ask if Lorraine, our new assistant, could help him out tonight. Invariably, Lorraine would make a mess of it, but that's how she learned. I'd have an internal fit watching a new girl botch up a call with a client, but when she improved, as she invariably did, it was always worth the wait.

When a new client called, the assistant would go into what we called the "spiel," which went as follows:

"Let me tell you a little something about us. Sheila started the agency back in 1979, and one of her most important principles is to hire only girls who work or go to school during the day. In other words, none of our girls are professional escorts. (The word "professional" was to be said with a touch of derision.) A few of our young ladies are aspiring dancers, actresses, or models, but the majority of them are either in college or are employed full time. They work for us two or three nights a week, and we permit them to see only one gentleman per evening on a first-come, first-served basis.

"If you would like to take one of the young ladies to dinner, that would be four hours for $500. Dinner and dancing or the theater would be six hours for $750. But if you would prefer to see someone on an hourly basis, that would be $175 an hour. There is no additional tipping involved unless you would like to specially thank her.

(This was a reference to some of the other agencies, which charged a low initial fee, but whose girls then negotiated an extra price for everything—from kissing all the way up—or down.)

"These are our cash prices. We would be more than happy to take your personal check with proper ID, or your credit card, but the price would be a little different." (Actually, the price would be a little higher, but it was against the law to say this, so, like many businesses, we offered a modest "discount" for cash.)

At this point, the assistant would pause to let the client thank her—assuming he had called for information or to ask a question. If he remained silent, she would continue: "What type of young lady were you interested in seeing this evening?" If she sensed any confusion or hesitancy on his part, she would ask specific questions:

"What age range did you have in mind?"

"Would you prefer a girl who was tall, or more petite?"

"Would you like to see somebody slender, or do you prefer a young lady with a little more to her?"

But it was always a mistake to ask a caller what color hair he preferred, because most men would say "blond," and there were never enough blondes to go around.

"A lot of men will ask for the world," I would tell the new assistants. "So if you sense that this guy is looking for a 'ten,' you must defuse his overblown expectation in a way that he doesn't lose face, and so it won't sound like any other girl you tell him about would constitute a major compromise.

"In this situation, there are several responses you could give. You can laugh and say, 'I wish I had a dozen girls who fit that description!' Or, 'Isn't it a shame that so few girls like that go into this business? Otherwise, I could start looking at co-ops on Park Avenue.' Or, 'That's some fantasy girl you're looking for'—sigh—'I wish I had her here for you.' "

I continued, "At this point, you have to ascertain which qualities are most important to him. Tall? Busty? Beautiful? Check them against the list of available girls, and choose two or three candidates. You may find that one girl in particular will embody nearly all his requests. If so, tell him that you have a young lady (or two young ladies, if that's the case) named X who is close to what he's looking for.

"But don't overdo it. Don't tell him that she's 'perfect' or that you just know he'll love her, or anything of the sort. He'll never believe you, and you'll be sowing the seeds of distrust.

"While you're looking through the list, you might want to make some 'mmmm' sounds to reassure him that you're giving his preferences close consideration. It looks very insincere to brightly assert that you have 'just the right girl' for him the moment he's finished talking. Give him the impression that you've got the lights on and the wood burning, so that he believes you're taking the time and energy to make an appropriate selection just for him.

"Pull out the cards of the girls you are considering, and describe them in a conversational, storylike manner. You don't have to give him the information in the order that it appears on the card. Highlight those qualities that match his requests. Downplay the differences, but don't ignore them, because we're trying to sell to these guys—not con them. Here's an example of what I mean: 'Victoria has long brown hair. It's not blond, but it is long and beautiful.' Or, 'I'm afraid she's not as tall as you had preferred, but she does have outstanding legs.'

"If he asks for somebody very slender, don't waste his time with a girl who's zaftig. He'll know you're trying to hustle him, and he'll be right. So always remember: if you don't have what he wants, say so!

"On the other hand, if you can fulfill the most important parts of his request, tell him, but be sure to mention the disparity. Your ace in the hole is our refusal policy: 'When she gets there, if, for any reason, you do not feel that she is the type of young lady you were expecting, please feel free to give her twenty dollars and send her home. There will be no hard feelings.'

"If he's skeptical about the accuracy of your description, you'll want to counter that skepticism. Here's one argument you might use: 'Sure, I could lie to you and send you just anybody, and we could take your money. But then you'd never call us back, would you? But if I'm honest with you and I send the type of girl who is just as I described her, you'll know that you can trust us and you'll call us back again. That's my goal—for you to call us back and tell your friends about us. And you'd never do that if I ripped you off, would you?' Remember, most of these guys are in business, and they understand that we're in this for the long term.

"Now, after you've described one or two girls, he may ask if there's anybody else. If that happens, you should diplomatically assure him that of course we have other girls, but that based on his stated preferences, the girl or girls you described are the best choices. If he'd like to hear about one more, you can say, 'Let's see now . . . hmmm, Denise might be a good possibility.' Then highlight the matching positive points about Denise. Be sure to mention the differences, and remind him again about the refusal policy.

"But that's as far as you should go. If he still can't make a decision at this point, throwing a fourth choice at him is not going to make the process any easier. Instead, assure him once again that we have his best interests at heart, and that if he'd prefer to call us back later, or on another evening, perhaps we would have someone then who might be more to his liking.

"If he decides not to book, thank him graciously for calling, tell him that we hope we can help him another evening, and get him off the line.

"If he does want to book, you already know how to discuss methods of payment and the other technical details. But if he's a new client, you must also get a little information about him, as follows: 'I'm sure you'll understand that the girls are always interested in knowing a little about the gentleman they're going to see. Would you mind if I asked how old you are? And what type of business are you in? Where are you from? Thank you for being so helpful.'

"You can close the call with some remark appropriate to the situation, which may include a simple thanks for calling, wishes for an enjoyable evening, assurances that he's going to like her, and so forth.

"Do not notify the girl until you have taken care of the necessary check or credit card authorization (if he won't be paying in cash) and have verified his hotel or residence. You must also look him up in the client book to make sure he isn't a DNS."

"DNS" stood for "do not send," and most of the men on that list were former clients whom we had found rude or otherwise obnoxious, or whose apartments were unpleasant to be in. There were also a few DNS men who had never called us, but who had a reputation for being difficult with girls at other agencies. And whenever I read about a businessman who had done something I didn't approve of—such as building an ugly high rise in a residential neighborhood—I added his name to the list, just in case he ever called us.

"Residential clients should be looked up in the phone book to verify that their name, address, and phone number all check out," I continued. "If you can't find him in the book, or if he has told you his number is unlisted, call Information and say, 'Manhattan, resident, last name, first name, address.' If the directory-assistance operator tells you there's no listing or no such person at that address, then you'll know he probably wasn't playing straight with you. If they tell you the number is unlisted, then you'll know that the address is correct, and you'll have to take it on faith that the apartment number is accurate. So far, we haven't had any problems.

"For hotel clients, call the hotel, ask for the man by name, and say, 'I think he's in room 1319'—or whatever. When he picks up the phone, say, 'Hi, Mr. Jones, this is Lorraine from Cachet. I would just like to confirm that Darlene will be with you at nine o'clock. Thank you.'

"After everything has checked out, including payment authorization, DNS list, and verification of hotel or residence *then* and only then do you call the girl and give her the information.

"Now for old clients, the process will be much smoother. A client who calls us at least twice a month is usually not that strict about sticking to his originally stated preferences. There will be some things on which he may not compromise (like bust size, brightness, slenderness), but with most regulars you can usually ignore height, hair color, and occasionally age.

"With the real regulars, you can be less formal. As you get to know them, try to introduce a more personal aspect into the relationship. But remember, business is still business, so don't say too much and don't give away any of our secrets.

"An easy mistake to make with an old client is to recommend a girl he's already seen. You're looking at his card, and you see that he's seen Darlene, say, and there's no indication that he had any complaints, so you assume she'd be a good choice.

"But you would be wrong. Some things are just not done. Unless the client tells you specifically that he'd like to see somebody again, always proceed on the assumption that he'd rather meet a new girl. That way, we never put the client in the awkward position of having to turn somebody down."

All of this training was leading up to the first night when a new assistant would be working by herself. No matter how well she had been taught, this was always a terrifying experience. Not only were there hundreds of details to keep in mind, but there was also the pressure of making the right judgments, as the safety of the escorts was riding on her shoulders.

The first night a new assistant was on by herself, I always made a point of being on call throughout the evening, in case she had any questions or problems. On one occasion, a new assistant walked into the office and froze. She had suddenly forgotten everything she had learned, and I had to rush over to the office to be at her side until she regained both her confidence and her memory.

I always arranged for a new assistant to begin on a Saturday night, which was the quietest evening of the week. For the first three years, Cachet was closed on Saturdays, but during our fourth year, Liza, Ashley, and Jaime came to me and asked if we could be open on Saturdays as well. "If you want to work then," I said, "I have no objection. But I'm never going to work on Saturday nights, and you'll have to swear to me that one of you will always be available." They agreed, and from then on we were open seven nights a week.

As I've already mentioned, we told the clients two big lies—that the girls were allowed to work a maximum of three nights a week and that they saw only one gentleman per evening. More often than not, these "lies" turned out to be true, but this was a result of circumstance rather than policy.

But as often happens with lies, one can quickly lead to another, and an assistant might have to do some quick explaining when a girl who was booked for midnight was unexpectedly asked to stay longer by the client she had gone to see at nine-thirty. At that point, the assistant might call the client to tell him that Barbara's business meeting ran late, or that Melody was tied up because they had to reshoot the entire scene, or that Kate had missed her flight from Texas.

The assistants enjoyed this part of the job because it allowed them to improvise. But I had to remind them not to get carried away. "Your excuse always has to fit the particular girl you're talking about," I said. "And it has to be believable. I don't want to hear any equivalents of 'the dog ate my homework.' "

At times, the assistants found it necessary to take a few other liberties as well—especially when it came to describing a girl's measurements. While many men have an unusual respect, bordering on reverence, for these numbers, they don't always understand what the numbers actually *mean*. Some men, for example, don't realize that it's the cup size and not the bra size that tells them what they really want to know. On the other hand, I'll never forget overhearing Jaime as she patiently explained to a caller, "But sir, you don't understand, forty-four double-D is *very* large."

Every now and then, a man would ask for a girl with specific measurements, such as 36-22-36. But honestly, how often do you see a twenty-two-inch waist? Even among our girls, who had excellent figures, a waistline that small was unheard-of. Our clients never knew the difference between twenty-two and twenty-four, so if necessary, we would tell them what they wanted to hear.

The same was true when it came to a girl's height, and here was an opportunity for our own kind of creative accounting. Gabriella was petite, and when we described her, accurately, as being five feet one, nobody was interested. Perhaps they were afraid, as one man put it, of ending up with "a frail little bird." But when we added three inches over the phone, Gabriella suddenly became rather popular. And when she showed up in four-inch heels, no client who saw her ever complained about false advertising.

Tall girls were always in demand, even with some clients who weren't so tall themselves. But most of the shorter men would not see anyone who was taller, which called for some subtle and diplomatic efforts on our part. Frank, at five six, might feel uncomfortable about seeing Patty, who was five ten and over six feet in heels. But if she happened to be his type, I'd say, "You know, Frank, I just know you're going to like Patty. She's fun, she's interesting, and she shares your interest in sailing. And since you're not going out to dinner with her, or taking her for a stroll in the park, I don't think her height will be a problem. You'll never notice it, and if you don't see her, you'll be missing out on the chance to meet a very pretty, bright, and special young lady."

After listening to my logic, Frank would agree to see Patty, and of course he'd have a very good time. Generally, if a client felt you were really listening to him and looking out for him, he'd be willing to take a chance. After Patty left, I'd call Frank to make sure the evening had gone as smoothly as I had hoped. And Frank would say, "You're right, Sheila, she was terrific. I'm going to listen to you from now on." He would then join the ranks of those clients whose attitude was, "I've liked everybody you've sent me, so next time I'll leave the choice in your hands."

For every man who called us with specific measurements in mind, there were two others who were very nervous or guilty about calling an escort service at all. From their perspective, it must have been a little frightening to call our number with no idea who was on the other end. I can imagine what was going through their minds: "Why are they asking me all these questions? How safe are they with their records? How do I know if I can trust these people? What if they're connected to

the Mafia?" Some of these men, who held very responsible positions in the business world, were so anxious on
the phone that they could barely get the words out. So
another responsibility of the assistant was to calm them
down and make them feel taken care of.

"Do I have to give you my real name?" a man would
ask. "Yes, you do," the assistant would reply. "Of
course we'll hold it in the strictest confidence. But
we're sending you a real person, and we have to think of
her, too. I can appreciate that you'd rather not tell me
your name, but I need it for security reasons."

If she thought it might help, the assistant would elaborate along the following lines: "Would you want to call
the kind of agency that was lax about the clients they
sent their girls to? They would probably be just as lax
about the kind of girls they hired. I'm sure you're looking for a nice girl from a respectable place, not somebody who will come in and rip you off. We're very
careful about the girls we hire, and we're equally careful
about the men we send them to. Besides, you have our
phone number right there in the Yellow Pages. I can
certainly understand that you might be nervous, and I
don't blame you. After all, you don't know who I am,
and we've never met. I guess you'll just have to trust
us." This approach usually worked.

We also had our share of strange callers. Our *clients*
were mostly gentlemen—if they weren't, we wouldn't
do business with them—but you should have seen (or
heard, really) some of the people we turned away. I'm
talking about weirdos, not just the usual gang of idiots
and nut cases who get a cheap thrill out of making
obscene calls to escort services. Jaime once picked up
the phone and was greeted by a sincere-sounding man
who calmly told her that he was interested in spending
the evening with a woman who was lactating. She hung
up on him, not knowing whether to be grossed out or to

feel sorry for him. "I thought I'd heard everything," she told me later, "but I guess it's a big world out there."

Not every oddball identified himself so clearly or so quickly, however, and it would sometimes take a new assistant several months before she mastered the knack of spotting the nuts. There was one man, for example, who called us three or four times a month. His voice was perfectly normal, and there was nothing strange about his requests—except that at the very end of the call, when we'd ask for his room number at the hotel, he'd hang up abruptly.

Another regular pest, who soon became known simply as "the creep," would call up and pretend to be a new client. He'd talk very softly: "Yes, I'd like some information please." The assistant would then go through the whole routine with him, including a description of two or three of the girls who were available that evening. If the assistant mentioned Margot, he'd say briskly, "I've seen Margot before." But because he always gave a different name, we had no record of him.

If the assistant disputed his claim that he'd already seen Margot, he would become haughty and say, "Well, it's not *my* problem that you don't have me in your records." He would then proceed to describe Margot in some detail, using information he had picked up from previous phone calls. It was never clear what his point was, but there he was, night after night, wasting our time—but not, apparently, his own.

The strangest call of all came from an anonymous caller who said, simply, "Marsha has fake tits," and then hung up. It was true that Marsha's upper torso had always seemed a little too good to be true, but who was this man, and why was he telling us this?

Then there was the fellow with the slightest trace of an English accent who wanted to make sure that the escort would not feel uncomfortable if he had the urge to try on her clothes after she undressed. We might have been able to accommodate his predilection, but as soon as he mentioned that clothes would be removed during the evening, we were forced to terminate the call. There was just no point in taking chances with the law.

We were always very circumspect about what we said on the telephone. The moment a client mentioned sex or even alluded to it, we'd say, "We're terribly sorry, but you've called the wrong agency. We don't do that sort of thing." As Gina had pointed out to me before I ever dreamed I'd be running my own escort service, most people understood that they weren't being asked to pay over a hundred dollars an hour merely for conversation. Still, in a business like ours it was always frustrating not to be more explicit.

Or more direct—when that was called for. While our assistants were invariably polite and discreet, a first-time caller might turn out to be fairly crude. Sometimes, after we described one of the girls, the man would ask, "Is she clean?"

"Is she clean?" Jaime would say. "Well, she certainly seems well groomed. She washes her hair regularly, and I've never seen any spots on her clothing."

If the caller persisted and mentioned the word "disease," Jaime would go into her medical-alert routine: "Sir, if a young lady has so much as a cold, I won't permit her to work. If you're that concerned about disease, I would suggest that you use the stairs at the hotel, because if somebody sneezes in the elevator, who knows what you might catch?"

On another occasion, one of the assistants threw the inquiry back in the caller's face: "How do we know if *you're* clean? Are you wearing clean underwear? Did you brush your teeth after dinner? And while we're on the subject, is there, by any chance, a ring around your collar?"

There were men whose choice of language told us more than we wanted to know. For the man who asked, "Whaddya got tonight?" the answer was a dial tone. To the caller who said, "I'd like something five six and blond," I said, "I think I can find you a doll that might fit that description, because I assume you're not referring to one of our young ladies. I suggest you call somebody else."

Most of the men who called us, however, were far more refined, and their preferences and requests were fairly routine and predictable. Almost everybody preferred long hair, and any girl with a short haircut knew full well that she was risking her income. And I had to let a couple of girls go after they got perms, because our clients disliked that frizzy, ill-kempt look.

Blondes were always high on the list, and we never had quite enough to satisfy the incessant demand. On the other hand, there was almost no call for redheads—I don't know why—and over the years I had to turn down some stunning ones. Back at Abraham & Straus I had learned the importance of trusting the customers' tastes rather than my own, which is why I never had more than one redhead on staff at a time.

Busty girls were always popular, and a client who requested a well-endowed young lady would rarely compromise. For this reason, unless a client asked specifically for a busty girl, we would send him somebody smaller because there were never enough busty girls to go around. Many men asked to see a girl who was slender, but almost as many said they preferred "somebody with a little more to her."

Black girls were difficult to book because most of our American clients associated them with street hookers. This was a shame because we had some absolutely wonderful black girls. British clients, however, did not share this prejudice, and I told the assistants to keep that in mind whenever they heard a British accent on the phone.

The best clients were those who asked for a girl who was nice, bright, and a good conversationalist. If a gentleman didn't seem overly concerned about a girl's measurements, or if he specifically said that he wanted to be able to talk to her, I could almost guarantee that both of them would have a good time. By the same token, a man who had a preconceived idea of the physical qualities he was looking for in an escort might be very difficult to please—even if we sent him a girl with the qualifications he asked for.

In the case of a new client, or an old client who had seen a girl we had talked him into, I or one of the assistants would call him a few minutes after she had left to be sure he had enjoyed the evening. If the client was genuinely unhappy, which was rare, we would always make it up to him. "I'm awfully sorry that happened," the assistant would say. "We try very hard to send someone you'll like, but we're not infallible. I'm very sorry you had this experience, and I'm going to make a note here that the next time you call, we'll send you someone for an hour on the house." (The girl would still be paid, of course.)

When Liza first started answering the phones, and I explained this policy to her, she thought I was kidding. "With a policy like that," she asked, "how do we make any profit?"

"Because *your* job is to match them up so well that the clients never need to take advantage of it."

As I constantly tried to impress upon the assistants, the name of the game was service. If an escort was more than ten minutes late, we always called to apologize. It was important to us that he knew that *we* knew she was late and that we were concerned about the problem. Our apology made the waiting easier and also defused his anger.

Once, on her way to a routine call at the Halloran House, Claudette got stuck in the elevator of her building. Claudette was very dependable, so when half an hour went by and I still hadn't heard from her, I called the client a third time and said: "Mr. Dexter, I just can't imagine what the problem is. Claudette is always on time, and if she's this late, I'm sure there's a very good reason. I realize that this doesn't help you very much, so I'm going to send you somebody else—at no charge. You could see her tonight, or you could wait until to-morrow night and call us then." Mr. Dexter chose the second option.

Jaime, who was helping me on the phones that night, thought I was being overly generous. "He's never even called us before," she said, "and you're giving him a freebie?" But treating people well was part of the business. I should add that thereafter, Mr. Dexter phoned us whenever he came to New York and nearly always booked a dinner call. "I was so impressed with the way you handled that problem," he told me the following month, "that I would never even consider calling another agency."

Of the various assistants who worked for me over the years, Jaime was one of the best. Like most of our girls, she was a college graduate from a stable, upper-middle-class home, and like most of the assistants, she had come to Manhattan to pursue an acting career. "You reach a certain age," she told me when we first met, "and you don't want to keep going back to Daddy to ask for more money."

She had grown up in Georgia, and the transition to Manhattan was not easy for her. From time to time she'd go back to visit her family and her old high school friends, and she always returned with mixed emotions.

"Maybe I made the wrong choice," she'd tell me after one of these visits. "My friends are all married and living in fabulous homes. My rent is twice as much as their mortgage, and I'm barely surviving in a converted tenement."

Like most of the assistants, Jaime was referred to me through a girl who was already working for me. She was attracted to the money, but she equivocated for several weeks because she couldn't imagine how her inquisitive boyfriend in Boston would take to her being unreachable on some evenings until two or three A.M. She finally told him she worked the night shift at an answering service, which was at least partly true.

Jaime was definitely attractive enough to have worked as an escort, and once or twice she toyed with the idea. But she could never quite make the leap. "I've rebelled enough," she told me. "Remember, I went to school with nothing but debutantes."

I laughed. "I know where you're coming from," I replied.

At the same time, Jaime was openly envious of the escorts, and she used to fantasize about becoming one. From her perspective, their lives seemed exciting, risqué, and glamorous, while she just sat in the office all night and answered the phones. I was delighted that she never made the switch, because a good assistant was invaluable, and Jaime was as good as they came. She never had to be told what to do, and she always took the initiative whenever there was a problem. And as more than one client remarked, she gave great phone.

Jaime managed to maintain a friendship with many of the girls, although I'm sure this wasn't always easy. Technically, she was their boss: when I wasn't around, she and the other assistants decided who would get which assignment, and the girls followed their directives. At the same time, the assistants were in the strange position of making significantly less money than the escorts they supervised.

Although the escorts and the assistants genuinely respected and liked each other, there was also a subtle tension between them as each side envied the other. From the escorts' point of view, the assistants got to sit around in jeans or sweat suits, order out constantly, and talk on the phone; it looked like a pretty cushy job. But from the assistants' perspective, the escorts were like the popular girls in high school who got to dress up and go out on glamorous dates while *they* just sat around and waited for the phone to ring.

Once, during a job interview, a girl who had worked for another escort service asked me how much money she would keep out of the hourly rate we charged. After I explained the split, which was roughly sixty-forty in the girls' favor, she asked, "And how much of this do I have to give to the phone girl?"

I was horrified. 'If I catch anybody giving one of the assistants one red cent, you're both out immediately. If I ever catch anyone even bringing an assistant a cup of coffee, it's all over. And I'll tell you why: once something like that starts, there's no way to stop it. It escalates, and soon the whole situation gets out of hand. The assistants are paid very well, and they also get a commission from the agency.''

This doesn't mean that personal friendships and subjective impressions played absolutely no part in an assistant's decision-making. But as much as was possible, we managed to keep these things under control.

Although I maintained a strict division of labor between the assistants and the escorts, Jaime did see one of our clients. This was an unusual case, however, as these visits involved no sex, no kissing, no touching, and no intimate contact. As Jaime put it, "For a hundred bucks an hour, I think I can deal with that."

Brad, the client, was in his early forties. Like many of the men who used our service, he worked on Wall Street. Why we had so many men from the financial world was never clear, but they kept calling. As Ginny liked to say, "When the stocks go up, the cocks go up."

When Jaime arrived at Brad's apartment, he would answer the door in a bathrobe, under which he wore a woman's girdle and stockings. As soon as Jaime was seated comfortably on the living room couch, he would casually ask her if she could remember any unusual experiences involving the cutting of hair.

This was Jaime's cue to improvise, and she would invent elaborate tales about haircutting that kept Brad on the edge of his seat. On several occasions, she told him about Harriet, a particularly stunning girl in her college dorm with beautiful golden locks. Harriet was very popular with the boys, while Jaime (supposedly) never had a date. One night, consumed with jealousy, Jaime sneaked into Harriet's room, and as she lay there sleeping, with her long blond locks draped over the pillow, Jaime snipped them all off.

Sometimes Brad would ask Jaime to pretend she was his sister and that they were both going to the hairdresser. Brad would be first, but his haircut supposedly turned out so badly that his "sister" would change her mind, at which point Brad would burst into tears. But usually it was Jaime's job to come up with a story, and to please Brad it usually involved a woman getting a haircut who was very unhappy with the results. Because Brad was her only client, Jaime was able to use a great deal of energy and imagination in her stories. She once joked with me about collecting them all into a book called *Hair Today*.

After story time, Jaime would strip down to a pair of

full-cut cotton underpants and an old-style pointy bra, both of which Brad found extremely sexy. Then, wearing a white sheet—and nothing else—Brad would climb into the "barber's chair" in his living room, where Jaime would pretend to give him a haircut. Brad had all the necessary haircutting paraphernalia, but he was clearly ambivalent about what was to be done, for although he kept saying, "Cut it off," he continually moved his head away from the electric razor in Jaime's hand. While this was going on, Brad would proceed to make himself happy under the sheet. Before Jaime left, Brad always paid with four fifty-dollar bills, telling her to keep the extra twenty-five dollars because "you should always tip your hairdresser."

To the rest of the world, Brad was a highly successful and respected financial analyst. There was nothing in his demeanor to suggest that he often wore women's underwear beneath his pinstripe suit or that he maintained an elaborate collection of women's wigs. He shared his secret life with Jaime alone. And she genuinely liked him, although she used to say with a smile that her one and only client was "quite literally a head trip."

Chapter Eight

Whenever a new girl joined up, the first thing she needed was a working name. Rather than assign one arbitrarily, I would let her choose her own favorite, and if the name she selected was at all suited to her looks and personality, she was welcome to use it. While I tried to be flexible, I had to draw the line when a bouncy, blond, blue-eyed art student insisted she'd like to be known as Natasha.

To me, certain names have always suggested specific images. A girl named Natalie should have long dark hair. Alexandra is tall and stately, and Ginger is a spunky redhead. I gave the name Melody to a girl named Carol whose voice was so mellifluous it made me think of music. When Wilma joined up, tall, sophisticated, and experienced, I knew immediately that she would be Claudette. I encouraged foreign girls to choose familiar names from their country of origin: Sonya from Germany, Kristen from Scandinavia, Gabriella from Brazil.

These new names weren't only for the comfort and convenience of the girls; they were equally important to those of us who had to describe the escorts over the phone. When I or one of the assistants was describing a girl to a client, we would have to conjure up an image of her in just two or three phrases. Her name could be a big help in that process.

One day I had the bright idea of buying one of those *What to Name Your Baby* books as a way to generate more names. ("When are you due?" asked the cashier as I was paying. "Not for years," I replied. "I'm just well organized.") After reading through the book, I wrote down a hundred or so names that I especially liked and started asking the new girls to make their selections from that list.

The girls and I invariably had a good time with the naming process, and before settling on their new aliases some of them would try on and discard different names like dresses in a boutique. Occasionally I would have to veto one of their suggestions, because names like Monique, Noelle, Nicole, and Tiffany made a girl sound like a hooker—which was, of course, just about the last association in the world we wanted to raise in the minds of our clients.

Over the years, several girls preferred to work under their own names. Kate, for example, felt that if she ever ran into anybody she knew, the situation would be complicated enough without also having to explain why she was using a pseudonym. At one point, however, her extreme honesty almost got her into trouble. Before becoming an escort, she had worked for a major steel company and was at home in the world of business. (In fact, one reason she was so popular with our clients was that she was the only girl we had who used to read the *Wall Street Journal* because she *wanted* to.) At one point, she foolishly told a client exactly which company she had worked for.

"Now that's a coincidence," he said. "I've got a golf date on Saturday with your CEO. Would you like me to mention that we're friends?"

Kate didn't miss a beat: "Only if you'd like me to call your wife and tell her the same thing," she replied.

He looked at her in amazement: "Would you really do a thing like that?"

"Not unless it's absolutely necessary," she said. End of discussion.

Three or four other girls agreed with Kate and felt that a working name would only add to the stress they were already feeling. I could never quite understand this rationale, and I would always point out that a pseudonym gave them an extra layer of protection. "When we describe you to a client," I said, "how can you be sure that we won't be talking to your uncle or your former high school principal?" But if an escort insisted on working under her real name, she certainly could.

Many of the other girls, however, found that their working names were an effective way of dealing with their initial anxieties and guilt. "I'm not the one who's doing this," a new girl could tell herself. "It's this other person I'm pretending to be."

For girls who enjoyed acting, the new name was a godsend, for when evening rolled around they could simply go into character. Usually, this persona wasn't much different from the girl's regular self, but occasionally the change was more dramatic. Although most of the girls were deliberately vague about their daytime lives, Tricia, who worked in an office, liked to tell clients that she was a stewardess for Eastern Airlines who signed up with us on her days off. "The men love it," she told us. "They always want to know if I ever make it with the pilots. 'Sure,' I tell them. 'Why do you think they call it the cockpit?'"

One night, when Tricia was spinning her usual tales about being a stewardess, the man she was with expressed a great deal of interest in what she was telling him—and it wasn't the usual prurient interest, either. When he started asking detailed questions about the New York–Miami run, she began to get nervous. Finally, she remembered what she had been told about him but had conveniently "forgotten": he was the president of a major regional airline. From then on, Tricia was a little less casual about her new identity.

While some girls took to their new names immediately, others found the change difficult or confusing. The first time Melody went out on a call, the doorman asked, "Whom shall I say is here?"

"Carol," she blurted out. A moment later she caught herself and quickly made the correction. "On second thought," she added, "my friends call me Melody, and that's probably how he'll know me." The doorman shot her a dubious look as he announced her over the house phone.

Every now and then, a girl would call me in tears because after the third glass of champagne a client had persuaded her to reveal her real name. I would calm her down by telling her that the situation was far less serious than it seemed, because we not only knew *his* real name, but his address, phone number, and several other facts about him. A few men were obsessed with finding out a girl's real name, presumably because their ability to uncover that secret would symbolize a certain intimacy with her that wasn't otherwise available to a client. On some level, almost every client wanted to believe that the girl was spending time with him not for money, but because she found him irresistible.

I always laugh when I hear people speculating about or trying to analyze a girl's "true" motives for working in this business, because to me it's always been clear that, as someone observed long ago, a call girl is simply a woman who hates poverty more than she hates sin. Almost all our girls signed up to make money, although there were two or three who came to me primarily for adventure, and another who actually claimed she was doing it for the sex.

I once overheard Camille telling a few of the girls that she had joined Cachet as part of a secret assignment from *Playboy*. As she described it, the magazine had sent five girls who had never worked before to report on their experiences in Manhattan's most exclusive brothels and escort services.

It made for a good story, especially when Camille claimed that *Playboy* had paid her ten thousand dollars for her one-month investigation and that she had decided to stay on because she was having such a good time. Fine, I thought, if that's what she needs to say, I don't suppose it's harming anyone. Tess used to enjoy teasing Camille by continually asking her when the article was going to appear. For some strange reason, it always seemed to be "tied up in litigation."

Hour for hour, our girls were among the highest-paid professional women in the country. Even though a girl might not go out every night she was on call, by 1984 our escorts were taking home a hundred dollars an hour. But because most calls lasted longer than an hour, and because most clients added a tip, it wasn't unusual for some of our girls to be making up to a thousand dollars a week—with a select few approaching twice that figure. As Ginny liked to say, "I may be good for nothing, but I'm never bad for nothing!"

Naturally, different girls needed the money for different reasons. More often than not, it went for such basics as rent and food. But some girls spent their money on travel and luxuries, and others developed a taste for fine clothes.

Many of our girls worked for Cachet to pay for their education, or their business training, or advanced classes in music, dance, art, or acting. Manhattan is an appallingly expensive place to live, and even a girl making $25,000 a year in an executive training program would have a difficult time paying her bills without a second income.

For most girls, the alternative to working for an escort service was to be a waitress. But the better restaurants in New York don't employ women for the lucrative dinner shifts, and then, of course, there was the money: in one good evening at Cachet you could bring home twice as much money as you could earn in a week of waiting on tables.

Our girls came from a variety of backgrounds. Margot's father was a judge; Suzanne worked for us between Radcliffe and medical school. Barbara, who had a graduate degree in journalism, joined Cachet after working as an intern for her congressman. During the day, Alexia was the manager of the American branch of a German business. Her father was a diplomat, so she refused to see any embassy people or politicians because there was always the possibility that they might know her.

Paige was an heiress whose grandfather was a famous industrialist; she stood to inherit a large sum of money when she turned forty, but until then she had to struggle like the rest of us. Laurie was a real estate agent. Ariana had been a showgirl and a blackjack dealer in Las Vegas. Raviana came from India and lived in Queens with her family, which made it awkward for us to call her at home.

Nancy was a statuesque farm girl from Indiana. In college she had played on the varsity girls basketball team, a fact she happened to mention to one of our clients who worked for a brokerage house. A few weeks later, when his company was scheduled to play a coed basketball game against their major competitor, he paid us the regular hourly rate to have Nancy join his firm's team. Posing as the new secretary, she outscored all but two of the men. Her client's team won, and Nancy returned to the office with four hundred dollars plus a tip, joking that she had just made her debut as a professional athlete.

But despite their very different backgrounds and personalities, the girls had at least one thing in common: they were all nervous before their first assignment. When a new girl came back from seeing her first client, I would always make a point of talking with her about how it went, and if I hadn't been in the office that night, I would call her at home the next day. Except for the few girls who had done this kind of work before, the first call was invariably difficult.

After all, they had been brought up to believe that promiscuity and casual sex were wrong; and that sex in exchange for money was a sin. In the aftermath of her first call, a girl might experience a flood of emotions, including, in some cases, the fear that something was wrong with her because she wasn't feeling the guilt she had anticipated. Whenever a girl came to me with this problem—which was itself, of course, a form of guilt—I would let her know that her reaction was perfectly normal, and I'd help her understand that there was no legitimate reason to feel badly.

"Think about it," I would say. "Are you really doing anything wrong? You're getting money that you really need from a man who can certainly afford to part with it. You're providing a real service without hurting or taking advantage of anybody. You're bringing a little fun and fantasy into the life of a man who was lonely until you showed up. Think about how appreciative he was, and how wonderful you made him feel!"

Although commercial sex was never discussed when I was growing up, I was certainly aware that most people considered it to be wrong. But during the brief period that I worked for Eddie, I developed a more informed position. If some men are willing to pay for sex, and some women are willing to provide it at a price they consider fair, and if nobody is being taken advantage of or coerced, then why is it wrong? Maybe it's my entrepreneurial bias, but when each party has something the other wants, and they're able to make a deal, that constitutes a good and fair exchange.

Some people object, arguing that commercial sex is different because the woman is allegedly selling her body. But a working girl doesn't *really* sell her body; that's just an expression. In reality, she gives the client access to her body for a certain period of time and at a certain price, just as a consultant gives a client access to his mind and his experience on an hourly basis, or as an artist's model provides a different kind of access to her body for a suitable fee.

It may not sound very romantic, but the fact is that sex is a commodity just like anything else. And like every other commodity, it operates on the law of supply and demand. All over the world, some people are in the position to sell, and others are interested in buying. It's ridiculous to make sex the one area of life where people who wish to are not allowed to make a living with their bodies. Our society has no qualms about a masseuse who is paid for touching people, or about laborers, or professional athletes or dancers, all of whom make a living with their bodies. Why should we make an exception for sex?

Although guilt wasn't entirely absent for the new girls, it was never a major problem. One reason may be that the girls who were most likely to feel seriously guilty never took that first step of coming in for the initial interview, however much they might have fantasized about being a part-time call girl. Or if they did come in, they concluded correctly that this job wasn't for them, and they quit before taking any calls.

While no girl ever quit because she felt guilty, there were several who would work for only two or three months at a time, with long stretches in between. And many others had a hard time lying to their families or their friends about why they were busy on certain nights or how it was that they suddenly had a few extra dollars.

But most of the new girls were pleasantly surprised by how much they enjoyed the job and especially by how nice the men were. "Although I had expected to feel guilty," Kate told me, "I never really felt I was doing anything wrong. Maybe it's because the clients didn't make me feel that way." Natalie, on the other hand, was never entirely comfortable in the job, and she once confided to me that she was always afraid she would go on a call someday and the client would turn out to be her father. I discovered that deep down, many of the other girls shared this same fear.

Whether or not they found my reassurances convincing, the new girls soon learned that most of their anxieties were groundless. One girl, who was so nervous on her first call that she actually threw up in the cab, came back to tell me what an ego trip it had been to see a handsome, successful man who thought she was terrific. And many girls came back from their first call saying, "I can't believe I'm getting paid for this!"

On the other side of the street, I'm sure that our first-time clients had fears and anxieties of their own. Those who had never called Cachet before, but who had used other escort services, had reason to fear that the woman who appeared at their door would be a hard-edged piece of work in tight jeans—much like the stereotypical prostitute on television. Although they had seen our ad and spoken to one of the assistants or to me, they were still relieved when they opened the door to an attractive, well-dressed, poised young lady.

To ease the minds of new clients, I initiated a liberal

refusal policy. If the client was nervous—and any man who had used another escort service had a right to be—I would explain it in these terms: "When the young lady arrives, if for any reason she is not the type of young lady you were expecting, feel free to give her twenty dollars and send her home. There will be no hard feelings, and if you'd like to call us back, we'll be glad to send somebody else."

Because we were always honest in describing our girls, very few clients ever took us up on this offer. But just as the girls had the option of leaving at any point, it's clear that the men were gratified to know that such a policy existed for them, too.

Many of the girls found that being an escort increased their self-confidence when it came to dealing with men and helped to demystify these traditional authority figures. Our girls were young, and most of them didn't know many adult men. They had been to college, of course, but the men they had known there were really just boys. And now, suddenly, they were meeting *real* men—who were older and worldly and successful.

To a girl in her early twenties, mature and successful men are still "they," and despite all of the changes in our society, many young women are still intimidated by men—especially when they are rich and powerful, as many of our clients were. But this threatening image gradually faded when the girls realized that these men were regular people who just happened to have powerful jobs. A number of girls told me that the job gave them a new feeling of confidence in dealing with men, whom they now saw as their equals rather than their superiors.

For although we were ostensibly selling sex, what the girls were really providing was companionship and intimacy. Invariably, the bulk of the evening was taken up with conversation, which often consisted of the men talking about their various problems. It wasn't that our clients had more problems than other people; it was just that like most men, they didn't have many opportunities to talk about them.

I'm hardly the first woman to notice that most men just don't have personal conversations with each other the way women do. More often than not, the only time men really talk to each other is when they're engaged in some other activity—like fixing a car or playing racquetball. So the opportunity to unburden themselves and to be really open with a warm, sympathetic stranger who was, not incidentally, a young and attractive woman, was enormously appealing to our clients.

Traditionally, men have told call girls things they don't reveal to their priests, their therapists, or even their spouses. So the girls heard a great many stories and secrets—about money, about politics, about girlfriends— even about wives. In many cases, they functioned as therapists as the men responded to the girls' attentiveness and their own anonymity by talking about their problems, their fears, and their fantasies.

Many men believe that a call girl is inherently worldly and that her sexual experience (real or imagined) somehow endows her with an added measure of wisdom. After all, she is supposed to be an expert at pleasing men. And if she knows how to *please* me, the client reasons, she must therefore *understand* me. At the same time, he thinks, she can't possibly *judge* me, because she's obviously in no position to pass judgment! All of which makes her the ideal short-term companion.

There's another element in this equation: unlike the other women he knows, the call girl is realistic enough to acknowledge the true nature of male sexuality. She realizes that whatever else sex may represent, it also has an important therapeutic and recreational function outside the context of any relationship. Here, then, is a woman who knows how to satisfy certain needs that a man has, and who, at least professionally, accepts the very kind of behavior that other women in his life persist in regarding as immoral or a sign of weakness.

At first, many girls were afraid that clients were going to look down on them. Others assumed that the man would always be in control because he was paying for her company. This was a critical point, and I tried to make sure each girl understood that *she* was the one who was actually in control. "It all depends on your attitude," I explained. "If you act like you're in control, you will be." Some girls had to go on a number of calls before they could really act on this perception, but over time, most of them realized that control was a self-fulfilling prophecy.

In at least one respect, the call girl business is like any other: the people with the best attitude are usually the most successful. Inevitably, there would be difficult clients and awkward situations, and the girl who was mentally prepared to handle these problems was always ahead of the game. Tricia, for example, used to respond to a client she didn't especially like by making it a personal challenge to uncover his good qualities.

In general, the most successful escorts were those who could have a good time with a variety of clients. "A good time is contagious," I would tell them. "If you're obviously enjoying yourself, it's hard for him not to. Your goal should be to come back every night and report that a good time was had by all."

Despite everything I had told them about the job, most of the new girls expected the men to be creeps or worse, and they were always surprised when their imagined stereotypes turned out to be so wrong. "Look at it this way," I used to remind them. "Do you see yourself as having much in common with the stereotypical hooker? Well, they have their clients—and we have ours."

Among our clients were a number of old-fashioned gentlemen who were charming, courtly, and well bred; and most of the girls had rarely spent time with men like that. A well-dressed man in an elegant hotel suite who took your coat and sat down with you to enjoy a bottle of good wine or champagne; who kept his hands to himself and treated you like a lady; who, when the time came, moved graciously and smoothly into the intimate part of the evening—this was so different from what some girls had imagined when they first signed up that it often took a few weeks before they fully believed it.

To ensure that a girl's first few calls would go smoothly, I established some strict ground rules. For her first ten calls or so, a new girl saw only established clients whom we knew well, and whom other girls had liked without qualification. She would not be asked to see anyone who was difficult in any way, or whom other girls preferred not to see, or who sometimes had a little too much to drink.

We would always notify the client whenever we were sending over a new girl, so he could go out of his way to make her feel comfortable. The men were delighted by the idea of being the first one to see somebody new. There were even a couple of times when the girl we sent over was so visibly nervous that the client insisted on keeping the evening on a strictly social basis.

Later, I would always check with the client for his impressions of the new escort. Sometimes on her first call a girl would be so anxious she could barely speak. Or, out of that same anxiety, she might talk, smoke, or drink too much. And a girl might act very differently with a client from the way she had during her interview with me. For all these reasons, the clients' feedback was essential.

At first, many of the girls were reluctant to meet the other escorts because, like the rest of society, they had formed their images of call girls from magazines, movies, and TV shows. As a result, they were usually afraid the other girls would be hard-edged and a little cheap. But when they discovered that the other escorts were very much like themselves, that they, too, were pretty, intelligent, warm, and even wholesome, it came as a tremendous relief.

To help integrate the new girls into the group, and to make the job more fun for all of us, I started to throw a series of monthly parties to honor those girls who would be celebrating their birthdays that month. I would ask each birthday girl to choose her favorite kind of cake, and I'd have a marvelous time picking up each one at a bakery that specialized in that particular item. What a great job this is, I'd think, getting paid to go around to bake shops picking up birthday cakes! We held these parties at the office, on regular working nights, and everybody would come by for cake and champagne.

The parties were a great hit. The birthday girls loved having everyone make a big fuss over them, and for the new girls it was an ideal way to meet some of the other escorts. One or two of our actresses would often perform one of their comic monologues, and somebody would always get up and sing a song. During one summer, the highlight of these parties was a command performance by Ginny, who could easily be coaxed into doing her impression of an evening with "Mr. Tongue," as we called one of our clients whose overriding interest in life was performing oral sex. Ginny would take a cushion from the sofa to represent his head, and she'd place it between her legs. Then she'd lie back and moan, building up slowly to a more powerful writhing and trembling, all of it accompanied by such realistic noises that we'd all be howling with laughter. But Ginny never broke her concentration, and after her "climax" there would be cheers and applause and another round of champagne.

Many of the girls became good friends, not only because they saw each other fairly often and sometimes worked together, but also because if you were friends with another girl who did what you did, then you had the security and comfort of knowing that somebody knew your deepest, darkest secret—and liked you anyway.

One thing I never had to do was sell the new girls on how wonderful our agency was, because the clients always beat me to it. They knew when a girl had just joined us, and they went out of their way to reassure her that she had made the right choice, that she'd love the other girls, and that Sheila was honest and fair. Everybody likes to play on a winning team, and the girls were proud to be associated with the best.

That's why I was delighted the first time one of the girls called me to complain that another girl wasn't dressed properly. Four escorts had gone out together to see a group of four men, and the next day three of them called me individually to complain that the fourth had shown up in an outfit they felt was flashy and inappropriate. They were indignant that her appearance reflected badly both on them and on the agency. To a considerable extent they policed themselves; I would also get calls if a girl drank too much, talked too much (or not enough), or did anything else that the other girls with her felt was improper. And it was not unusual for a client to give us a ring if he thought a girl wore too much makeup, talked too much, or was "too professional."

It happened more than once that a new girl would see a client, they'd have a marvelous evening, and he would promise to call the next night and take her to dinner. The following night, she would be pestering me: "Has Mr. Edwards called yet? He promised he'd take me to dinner tonight." It was hard to see her so excited in anticipation of an evening that I just knew probably wouldn't happen.

"Of *course* he liked you," I would say. "But in one respect, at least, the men you will see through this agency are exactly like the men you date in real life. There's that three-word lie they seem almost compelled to use, especially after they've slept with you: 'I'll call you.'"

When they're paying for female companionship, most men prefer to see a variety of girls. After all, it doesn't cost them any more money, and there's no emotional price to pay, either. So when Mr. Edwards called back the next night or shortly thereafter, and didn't ask specifically for Amy, I would try to protect Amy by telling her that yes, Mr. Edwards did call, but he wasn't going to be able to make it tonight.

Occasionally my protective instincts backfired. While Amy was sitting in the office, another girl would walk in and start raving about her fabulous evening with the man Amy had started to think of as "hers." When this happened, I would talk to Amy and gently tell her that it was nothing personal, but that most men who used our service wanted to meet a range of women.

It wasn't only the girls who occasionally became attached; sometimes the men did, too. To cite an extreme example, we had one client who saw Sunny just about every week for a full year. One night, when she wasn't available, he reluctantly agreed to see somebody else. This made him so nervous, however, that he called us three different times that week to ask that we not tell Sunny about his "betrayal."

Only once did a client and an escort fall in love. One afternoon, Camille called to tell me that she would be taking the rest of the week off. "I'm going to spend a few days with the man I saw last night," she said, "and

I don't want to do it behind your back. But when I walked into his hotel room, we just looked at each other and realized that this was the real thing.'' Real enough, anyway, as their relationship lasted for close to two years. During most of this time, with the man's knowledge, Camille continued working.

One reason we were so successful early on is that, at Gina's instigation, we had made a special marketing effort at the United Nations, with its phalanx of diplomats and continuous stream of visiting dignitaries who came to New York every fall for the opening of the General Assembly. Each year, the UN publishes a mailing list of all the diplomats currently in residence, and it's easy to tell which ones are single by the way they're listed. We sent our brochure to several hundred of these men, with gratifying results.

Another factor that worked in our favor was the huge influx to the United States in the early 1980s of Arab businessmen. At first our girls were excited about meeting Arab clients because they had heard stories about how rich and glamorous they were. But the fact was that most of the Arab men who called us were terrible customers.

In part, this was because they had been brought up to think of women very much as southern whites had once been taught to view blacks. Many Arab clients just couldn't accept the fact that our business was owned and operated by women, and they would often be rude to me or the assistants. When we sent a girl to see an Arab client, he might ignore her completely for the first couple of hours. And if she were much over twenty-one, he might dismiss her altogether.

Suzie was one of the few girls with Cachet (or any other escort service, for that matter) who was tall, blond, busty, and beautiful. She once went on a call with six other girls to visit a group of Arab dignitaries. The men were having a party in an enormous suite, and they ordered fancy dinners and champagne for their visitors. "But they weren't gentlemen," she told me. "They weren't interested in talking. They told lewd jokes. They watched television for hours, and acted like we didn't even exist. Every now and then, one of the men would take one of us into a back room for a few minutes. It was spooky, and I couldn't wait to get out.

"Late in the evening, one of the bodyguards escorted me into a bedroom to see a man who was very short, and who knew all of about five words of English. But from the way the guards were acting, I could tell he was important. We made ourselves comfortable, and he turned out to be wonderful, loving and sweet, not at all like his pals. As I left, he kept saying, 'You come back, you come back.' When I left, the guard gave me a tip of three hundred dollars."

A few months later Suzie was on another multiple-girl call with a group of Arabs when a guard motioned for her to go into one of the bedrooms. And there, reading a newspaper, was the same man she had liked so much last time. When he looked up and saw her, he started shouting her name and smothering her with kisses.

Whenever we did business with a group of Arab men, it was never clear exactly who would be picking up the charges. When we finally uncovered the man who was responsible, he would invariably try to get us to lower the price. There was always some reason why we should give him a big discount, and these people had an inexhaustible supply of excuses. Their friends were coming over next week, and they would certainly be calling us. Or the girls we sent were dancing and drinking champagne much of the evening, so why should he pay for that?

"I'll tell you why," I would explain on the phone. "What if you walked into a clothing store and saw a nice suit for five hundred dollars? And what if you decided you didn't want the vest? Should the store knock off twenty percent because you don't want the vest?"

In groups, Arab men would often order girls like so many pizzas: if there were four men, they might ask for six girls, and then, when the girls arrived, they would look them over and dicker with each other in Arabic as to which girl would go with which man. The extra girls would be given a tip and dismissed.

Typically, these calls would go on for hours. At one in the morning, when we were officially closed, I would take a nap until the girls called to say they were leaving. Two or three hours later the phone would ring, and invariably I would find myself in an argument with an Arab client about money. They would insist that the price was negotiable, but I would stand my ground.

"I can't believe you're doing this," I would say. "I find it difficult to believe that a gentleman would agree to pay a certain amount, and would then go back on his word. I just can't imagine that you're that type of person."

If this appeal didn't work, I would up the ante and make some reference to "honor," which often did the trick. After a few difficult negotiations, I began to make a point of talking about their honor during the initial phone call, and later, when I refreshed their memory, it usually worked.

If all else failed, I would become testy. "Listen," I'd say. "This isn't a camel bazaar in the middle of the desert. The price is the price, and it's not negotiable." I hated to resort to that kind of language, but when I had no alternative, this approach rarely missed.

The most fascinating of all our Arab clients was a nineteen-year-old Saudi prince who used to come to New York with half a dozen bodyguards who never left his side and an official taster to protect him from being poisoned. The royal party would usually occupy an entire floor of one of the top hotels.

The poor boy was never allowed to leave the hotel suite except to play tennis or go swimming—and even then only if the place had been swept for bombs and cleared of other people. He spent most of his time watching television. He was very lonely and had nobody to talk with other than his family, the guards, and two or three cousins. He had everything money could buy—but he was miserable.

According to the girls who saw him, he was a sweet fellow who spoke English very well. Unfortunately, because he was a prince, he had never enjoyed a real childhood. Once, when Jerri was with him, he told her shyly that what he really wanted to do—and he hoped she wouldn't mind—was to jump on the bed and have a pillow fight.

On another occasion, when he was in New York on his birthday, he had six girls come over to the hotel. Earlier in the day, he had sent one of the guards to Tiffany's so he could present each of the girls with a little gift—a gold bracelet. When the girls arrived, the entire group, including the guards, played children's games like pin the tail on the donkey, blindman's bluff, and Twister—where everybody ended up in a tangled heap on the floor. For the finale, there was a long, raucous pillow fight.

The girls who went on that call talked about it for months. They had all enjoyed themselves, but there was something terribly sad about the little prince who was a prisoner of his wealth. When Jerri asked him why he couldn't go out to see the city, he simply said, "I'm not allowed," as though that explained it. Apparently, he had learned to accept his imprisonment.

During our third year, I was finally able to institute two marketing ideas I had been thinking about for some time. One of our competitors had been offering a two-hour call for $300, and they were advertising so heavily that I could only assume they were doing well. At the time, we were charging $150 an hour, but the idea of a two-hour minimum was very appealing. I decided to open a second agency called Finesse, which would offer a two-hour call for $250.

My reasoning was simple: if we attracted a certain amount of business from one ad, we would probably draw almost twice as many calls if we ran a second ad under another name. Nobody had to know that both agencies were run out of the same office.

When it came to staffing the second agency, I thought back to all of the girls I had been turning away. Many of them had been moderately attractive but were not quite pretty enough for us. After seeing hundreds of applicants who worked for other agencies, however, I knew that many of the girls I had rejected were still more attractive than what the competition had to offer. Besides, I hated saying no to these girls. Most of them were determined to work as escorts, and sooner or later they would be interviewed and hired by other agencies. I had liked many of them, and I felt badly, knowing that by turning them down I was in effect casting them out to the Eddies of this world simply because they didn't have the good fortune to have been born a little prettier.

But when I started to interview new applicants with a second agency in mind, I just couldn't decide where to draw the line: if a girl wasn't pretty enough for Cachet, what made her pretty enough for Finesse? The concept had made sense in theory, but in practice I just couldn't make it work.

I decided to retain the idea of Finesse but to staff it with the same girls who worked for Cachet. Because $250 was less than we were charging for a two-hour call from Cachet, I offered the girls a higher cut if they took these calls. But I had to abandon the plan when very few clients showed any interest. Apparently, the initial commitment was too high; to this day, I don't understand how our competition got away with it.

After three months of virtually no business for Finesse, I decided to cut my losses and make the difference between the two agencies one of marketing rather than price. Cachet's image was friendly and warm, and its motto was "New York's most trusted service." Finesse, on the other hand, would be slightly more expensive for the first hour, although there would be a price break if the call went two hours or longer. More to the point, Finesse was targeted at the competitive man who needed to believe he was calling the most exclusive place in town; the tag line here was, "We're not for everyone." In other words, you'll have to prove to us that you're good enough to do business with us.

When a new client called the Finesse number, this is what he was told: "We've been in business here in New York for a number of years, but until fairly recently you could only have gotten in touch with us through a private recommendation. I'll be happy to tell you more about us and to discuss the type of young lady you are looking for. If you'd like to tell me where you are staying, I'll call you back on my private line."

There was no "private line," of course, but it sounded good, and if the man left a number, the assistant would call back to add the following information:

"We are very particular about the young ladies who work for us. They must work or go to school during the day, or be actively pursuing a career in the arts or in modeling. We carefully check all references before hiring anybody. These are girls who just need a little extra money to get by. They may work up to three nights a week and may see only one gentleman per evening."

As I told the assistants, who of course answered the

calls for both agencies, the image of Finesse was supposed to be "desirably elusive." Finesse certainly brought us additional business, although there turned out to be no discernible difference between these clients and the men who called Cachet.

The advertising for Finesse was really quite special. Most escort services who advertised in the phone book left it up to the Yellow Pages to design their ad. But I've always found that if you want to attract professionals, you have to *be* professional. We already had a very tasteful ad for Cachet, but for the Finesse ad I approached a well-regarded employee of Kenyon & Eckhardt, a prominent ad agency (they had the Chrysler account and still do), and had him design it. The Finesse ad appeared the year that Manhattan's Yellow Pages introduced red as a second color, and with its red, hand-lettered logo, it brought in a large number of calls.

My second marketing decision had to do with a new category of escorts. We'd had two or three price hikes over the years, and by 1984 we were charging $175 an hour, of which the girls got to keep $100. To my surprise, I found that these higher prices did not lead to a corresponding decline in business. On the contrary: I kept hearing from men who wanted to know if we had any girls who were *more* expensive, and presumably more beautiful, than the others.

I was fascinated by these requests. Here were men who could enjoy the company of one of our girls for a price that was already high, but who would apparently feel better if they could spend even more. As a responsible businesswoman, I had no choice but to respond to the obvious market demand: if all those men were really so eager to pay us more money, then what the hell, I was going to charge them more.

That's when I hit upon the idea of "C girls," who

were unusually beautiful—and about 25 percent more expensive. A C girl had to fulfill five requirements: she had to be tall, beautiful, blond, under twenty-five, and full-figured. Fortunately I had two or three girls with all of these qualities, so I created a new category just for them.

One of our first C girls was Suzie, who had a mane of blond hair, penetrating green eyes, a firm bust, and a body that wouldn't quit. She was also the proud owner of the greatest rear end in America. I used to think that some of the girls portrayed in *Playboy* couldn't possibly exist in real life and that the magazine made them look that way through trick lighting and other technical wizardry. But when I met Suzie, I changed my mind.

Suzie was the daughter of a former beauty queen, and in fact it was her mother's idea that she join an escort service. She had sent Suzie an article about escort services from *Cosmopolitan,* which included the observation that "hundreds of good-looking men and women are in the business of providing charming company for pay . . . but not 'love and kisses.' They earn between $20,000 and $100,000 a year whiling away expensive evenings in glittery restaurants, at Broadway openings, and at celebrity-packed parties."

Although the article did mention that some escort services provided sexual favors, the general impression was that there were many who didn't. But as *Cosmo* also stated, "Experts generally agree that if a service is listed in the Yellow Pages, accepts credit cards, and the local police have no record of complaints, it's probably not a call girl come-on." It was a reasonable assumption—but wrong.

Suzie was one of dozens of girls who called us for an interview when that article was published. When she learned that we were not as innocent as the magazine had led her to believe, she went home and cried for hours. But she was broke, so she decided to give it a chance. She was very nervous as she went on her first call, but gradually relaxed when she found that the man was young and rather shy. The only strange thing he did was to show her a few photographs of his cat.

Several clients fell in love with Suzie, not only because she was gorgeous, but also because she was so sweet and accommodating. At one point, one of these men came to New York to spend the weekend with her. His wife, apparently, was skeptical about his cover story, and finding our phone number on the family's long-distance bill, she called Cachet one night and asked to speak to her husband. Although this particular problem had never come up before, I had told the assistants that when in doubt, they should say that we were a temporary employment agency, which was fairly close to the truth. For some reason, it did not occur to this woman to ask why an employment agency was answering the phones at eleven o'clock on a Saturday night.

Liza, who took the call, explained that she was just a secretary and that she had never heard of this woman's husband. When the woman finally hung up, Liza didn't know what to do: should she call the poor guy at his hotel to tell him what had happened? It was an interesting dilemma, but my advice was not to call. "Why ruin their evening?" I said. "Let's wait until she's ready to leave. Will it make things any better if he finds out now? At least this way he'll have something nice to look back on when he goes home to face the music."

Maybe it's nature's way of distributing favors, but the C girls were as irresponsible as they were beautiful. You constantly had to make sure that their hair was clean and their clothes were pressed. They were always late for appointments, and they were terrible with money. If they didn't come back to the office right after a call, it could be weeks before they would pay up. We always had a few girls who were never allowed to go home without reporting first to the office—which had been Eddie's policy for *every* girl—and the C girls were invariably among them.

Most of the C girls didn't appear to be very bright, either. I had heard it said that beauty and brains didn't go together, but I never believed it until I noticed that with these girls, at least, the old adage appeared to be true. It was certainly true for Tina, who admittedly was playing with less than a full deck. She refused to worry about contraceptives or a diaphragm because, she assured me, she practiced brth control—are you ready?—through astral projection.

Amazingly enough, she soon found herself pregnant—the only time, incidentally, that one of our girls got into this situation. When Tina told me she intended to keep the baby, I decided it was time for us to have a little chat. A few weeks earlier, Tina had seen a couple of our black clients, and I was concerned how her boyfriend might respond if the baby was born with dark skin.

"Oh, no," she assured me. "The baby definitely belongs to my boyfriend."

"That's a relief," I said. "But what makes you so sure?"

"It's very simple," she replied. "I've never had an orgasm with a client!"

Chapter Nine

*O*ur *clients worked* in almost every business and profession you could imagine, from fish to flowers, from toys to nightclubs, from office supplies and computers to surgical instruments and war materiel. We had doctors and lawyers, bankers and brokers, deal makers and consultants. We had corporate board members who came to New York every month. We even had a judge, as well as two or three law-enforcement officials.

After we were busted, *Newsweek* reported that our client list included "well-known names from virtually every important field of enterprise except the church." It was a good guess, but not an accurate one. We indeed had a few clergymen, including a Catholic priest who liked to smoke marijuana while he burned incense and an Orthodox rabbi who insisted on wearing his fringed prayer garment to bed.

We also had a good number of foreign diplomats, especially during the fall, when the United Nations General Assembly was in session. Many of these men were fairly high up in their respective governments, although they were far too discreet to describe their official positions over the phone. But when an articulate, gracious, and well-spoken gentleman with a foreign accent called from the UN Plaza or the Waldorf Towers, you didn't have to be with the CIA to know why he was in town. Besides, even a man who was secretive on the phone was inclined to loosen up with a bottle of champagne and a pretty young woman whom he wanted to impress.

We could always count on the fact that business would double when October rolled around. In addition to the delegates themselves, the annual opening of the General Assembly would invariably attract a horde of businessmen and arms merchants, and we would hear from many of these people as well. Some called us for their own pleasure, but many others contacted us to sweeten a deal, repay a favor, or arrange for several girls to accompany a group of clients to a fancy restaurant or a nightclub.

Regine's, a private and opulent nightclub with branches in major cities throughout the world, was especially popular with the diplomatic crowd—and with the girls, who loved getting dressed up to go there for a night on the town. It was also a particular favorite of our Arab clients, which presented a bit of a problem, as it could be quite a challenge to find a cocktail dress that didn't violate their sensibilities. Many Arabs were not comfortable with a girl whose neck, shoulders, or arms were bare, or who was wearing anything sleek or overtly sexy.

We had our share of famous clients, but they trusted us to be discreet, a promise that I intend to honor. We also had many clients who weren't exactly famous, but were prominent in their fields, and whose names would be instantly recognized in the business community. These included corporate chairmen and presidents, investment bankers, theatrical producers, advertising executives, and restaurateurs.

We were proud of our clients and their achievements, and we maintained a "celebrity board" in the office, where we posted clippings from newspapers and magazines that described the various deals and projects these men had been involved in with their clothes on. It wasn't unusual for one of our clients to be profiled on the first page of the business section of the *New York Times* or on the front page of the *Wall Street Journal*. When the article described an important business deal, at least one of our girls generally had heard all about it during the planning stages and took a special pride in being in the know before the announcement.

It was understood, of course, that the celebrity board was strictly for internal consumption and was not to be discussed outside of the office. But the girls got a big kick out of these clippings, which served as a continual reminder that ours was the agency of choice for some of the world's most prominent businessmen.

As for our celebrity clients, they weren't much different from all the others, with two small exceptions: they tended to be better tippers, and those who lived in New York usually kept a well-stocked refrigerator. This is worth noting because many of our local clients lived alone and took all their meals in restaurants, so a girl who went over to one of their apartments would be lucky to find a dusty can of diet soda in the back of a cupboard. The celebrities often lived in more elaborate homes, with servants who made sure their larders and refrigerators were well supplied.

Among our celebrity clients was a hockey player who called us when he came into town. He was nervous before the game and eager to relieve the tension he was feeling. When Shawna arrived, he called room service to order a bottle of champagne and a Perrier. The champagne was strictly for his guest, since this man refused to touch alcohol the day before a game.

Another celebrity client was a prominent television personality. He was very depressed over the breakup of his marriage several years earlier and talked about little else. On the air he was upbeat, smooth, and funny, but in person he was self-pitying and morose—to the point where most of the girls who saw him were not eager to pay a return visit.

Then there was the well-known British rock musician who would ask us to have the girl bring over several changes of outfit, ranging from bathing suits to evening clothes. He had always wanted to be a fashion photographer, and he would take a camera—with no film in it—and pretend to shoot a series of pictures as he gave out directions: "Beautiful, baby, okay, now look to the left, smile, hold it, that's just *fabulous.*" Sometimes he would sleep with her, but not necessarily.

He and Camille really hit it off, and at one point he saw her every night for the week he was in town. A month later, when he was back in New York, he called us again to ask for Camille. This time, when she walked into his hotel suite, he was playing the tape of a song he had written for her. The following year it appeared on his new album, and one of the local FM stations used to play it constantly.

Christine once went to see another rock star, and when he learned that she was in the fashion business, he insisted that they spend the evening going through his closets, coordinating his various outfits and deciding what to get rid of. During her visit, girls were continually calling him on the phone, and just before she left, Christine asked him the obvious question: with all these girls throwing themselves at him, why had he called us? He replied that he preferred to be with somebody who would relate to him not as a celebrity, but as a person. "The girls who ring me up don't really care about *me*," he told Christine. "They're star-fuckers. They want me because I'm famous, so they can tell their friends they've slept with me. The girls from your agency are real people, and I'd much rather be with them."

I could certainly understand why a man would prefer our girls to groupies, but I was a little more surprised when we heard from a prominent fashion photographer who spent his days with some of the world's most beautiful and glamorous women. "I don't want to seem rude," I said to him one night on the phone, "but I'm curious. With all the beautiful women you see every day, most of whom would be happy to go to bed with you, why are you calling us?"

"It's very simple," he replied. "The models who want to sleep with me are only interested in one thing: what I can do for their careers. They're always trying to impress me, and being with them is no fun. The girls you send me are a lot nicer than that—and they're also more intelligent, which I appreciate."

Prominent or not, most of our clients were gentlemen, and that was far more important. As I've described, we encouraged this tendency from the very start, when the assistant would call the man "sir" and refer to the girls as "young ladies." Most clients, however, did not have to be told how to act. They had an ingrained sense of style and were accustomed to being gracious.

To be sure, some gentlemen came in unusual wrappings, like Lenny, a well-known pornographic writer who was associated with a particularly raunchy publication. Knowing his reputation, the girls were not eager to see him initially, in part because they were afraid that the details of their visit might eventually find their way into print. And the fact that his apartment was decorated like a New Orleans bordello did not make them feel any more enthusiastic.

But when they actually met Lenny, the girls were invariably surprised at his considerateness and generosity as well as his skill as a lover.

"But what about all that trash you write?" Debbie once asked him.

"Honey," he said, "that's what people want to read. We've all got to make a living."

The few clients who weren't already gentlemen would have to be trained. On one occasion, a new client was all over Barbara as soon as she walked in the door. Barbara promptly left.

"I don't understand why she did that," he told me later on the phone. I explained that our girls were used to sitting down, having a conversation, and perhaps enjoying a glass of wine before moving on to the next item on the agenda. Whenever it was necessary, which wasn't very often, I would speak to a client bluntly: "I'm not running this business for people who just want to get laid. If that's the only thing on your mind, call somebody else."

The great majority of our clients shared Barbara's attitude and preferred to get to know a girl before taking her to bed. Most of our girls had had little experience with men over thirty, and the new girls especially were relieved that most of our clients did not want to hop into the sack right away but preferred to talk first—at least for a few minutes.

We once had a complaint from a client who had been spending a very pleasant evening with Melinda, who had recently joined us. Half an hour into the call, being nervous and not altogether certain how to get the ball rolling, she suddenly stood up and said, "It sure is hot in here." Then she took off her blouse.

"Maybe I'm crazy," said the client, "but I found this a little abrupt, and it spoiled the whole mood of the evening." The next day, I reminded Melinda about paying attention to the subtle signals that most men gave off when they were ready to move into the more intimate part of the evening.

I don't think there was a single girl who worked for me who didn't ask, early on, "What about the weirdos?"

Generally, the girls were worried about men who might want to tie them up or would ask them to do something kinky. I would repeatedly and patiently explain that most of the so-called weirdos and perverts out there had a pretty good idea of exactly what "perversion" they wanted to pursue and were not likely to spend their money on a call girl who might not even understand what they were talking about. The men in this category who do use escort services call highly specialized agencies that cater to their particular whims. And of course, anybody who was obviously weird on the phone would not get past the assistant who took the call.

As for potentially violent men, they just didn't call an escort service like ours, which took the trouble to confirm a client's name, address, and phone number. Although the girls would run into an occasional unpleasant character, we never had a single incident of violence. Could it happen? Of course—just as you could find yourself in trouble while walking down the street. But given our cautious approach, the risk was minimal.

The majority of our clients were between the ages of twenty-eight and fifty, although there were exceptions at both ends of the spectrum. Fred, who was in his early seventies, was a sweet, grandfatherly type. He was retired, and every six weeks or so he would fly up from Florida to check on his real estate investments.

He invariably followed the same routine: he would stay at a private club in midtown, and one of our girls would meet him in the lobby at exactly five P.M. They would go to the Algonquin for drinks, the Four Seasons for dinner, and from there to a Broadway show, before ending up back in his room for a nightcap and whatever.

Because he was so courtly and charming, Fred was a great favorite with the girls. Approaching a door, he always managed to get there first—without ever seeming to rush—so that he could open it for her. At the restaurant, he would take her coat with a flourish and gently guide her to a chair. When the waiter came, he would suavely order for his companion and himself. All this was in sharp contrast to the men the girls knew socially, who had come of age during the 1960s when good manners were considered unimportant.

Still, not every girl was willing to see older men. Not only were men over fifty often out of shape, but conversation could sometimes be awkward with someone who was old enough to be your father. And, because everything slows down with age, it would sometimes take these men a little longer to become aroused.

Our youngest client was the teenage son of a very prominent investment banker, who used to stay in the bank's corporate apartment while he was on vacation from prep school. I suspect he was a virgin when he first called us. Jeannie went to see him, and after half an hour of conversation she disappeared into the bathroom. A few moments later she walked out in her stunning black lingerie, and with her long red hair and fair skin she must have presented quite a sight. Her young client, however, just stood there in shock. A moment later, a stricken look crossed his face. He moaned and ran into the bathroom, and it was some time before she was able to coax him out. Apparently this poor boy had been so turned on by the sight of a real, live, beautiful woman in alluring lingerie that the inevitable happened and the episode was over before it began. He was terribly embarrassed, but Jeannie was very understanding, and a little later in the evening she initiated him into the ranks of manhood. He called several times after that—always on school vacations—but he would never see anybody but Jeannie.

The men who became our clients called us for a variety of reasons. There were some who hoped that a high-class call girl would provide them with the ultimate sexual experience. Others were workaholics whose schedule and pace left them no time for a personal life. They would work for days without a break on a complicated project or a major deal, and by the nth day, when it was all over, they would realize that their lives were drastically out of balance. Still other clients, who did business with Hong Kong or Japan, kept ungodly hours, which made just about any kind of socializing difficult. They, too, might find themselves home at an early hour, having done nothing but work for ten days straight and with nobody to talk to.

More than most other cities, New York is filled with men whose lives are totally consumed by their work. Albert, for example, was a currency trader for a major bank. Because his business contacts were in London, Germany, and Japan, he kept irregular hours and maintained no clear division between work and leisure. He had a tiny, battery-operated computerized screen to keep him apprised of the latest fluctuations in the German mark or the British pound. He took it everywhere, and he used to glance at it constantly—even in bed.

While we certainly had a few clients who might have had trouble getting a date, many more were so attrative and successful that most single women in Manhattan would have killed to go out with them. So why didn't they have wives or girlfriends? Some of them did and used us anyway. Others called us between relationships. These days, even the most accomplished single people have very few dignified, comfortable ways to meet each other outside the workplace, which most of them consider off limits. For a man who could afford it, hiring a date was often easier, more direct, and less awkward than searching for a partner at a singles bar or among the classified personal ads.

It has been reliably estimated that single, heterosexual

women in New York outnumber their male counterparts by close to a million. But even so, this doesn't mean that it's easy for a man to find a companion. One effect of the man shortage is that single women have become far more ruthless in their pursuit of men, which doesn't always sit well with the objects of their pursuit. Clients would often talk to our girls about their love lives, and the girls heard one complaint after another about women who were too aggressively on the hunt or simply too eager to get married.

Some men actually hoped to find a girlfriend through our agency, and it often happened that a client would become attached to a particular girl and would request her again and again. Usually, when this happened, the girl would come to me and say, "Sheila, I think he's starting to like me too much, and I'm feeling guilty about taking his money." I was always proud of a girl when she told me this, because she was putting principle ahead of pocketbook.

This was the situation with Mario, a professional opera singer with a special interest in the occult. The first time he called we sent him Camille, and as soon as she walked into his apartment he read her tarot cards. They must have yielded a positive message because Mario never wanted to see anybody else. He would talk with Camille for hours at a time, and after a few visits, he asked her to marry him. At her request, we gently explained to Mario that his true love had moved to Phoenix.

In most such cases, though, we would generally tell the client that the girl had quit, and we'd encourage him to see somebody else. But we'd also have to remind each subsequent girl who saw him that if he asked about the first girl—which he often did—the official word was that she was no longer working for us.

For the unmarried man who could afford to call us, we offered the object of every man's fantasy—the "sure thing.'' He could depend on the fact that a girl we sent him would be attractive. He knew she would arrive on time and would be elegantly dressed. He knew that she would be able to carry on an intelligent conversation. And above all, he knew that she would be *there* for him. With a girl from Cachet, there would be no whining, no feminist rhetoric, and no expressions of concern about commitment or the biological clock. She would not be trying to impress him or check him out as a ''possibility.''

The client also knew that there would be no struggles over sex, that he could go to bed with her with no guilt and with no strings. Furthermore, he knew that there would be no pressure on him to perform under the covers, as the girl we were sending him was not that intimidating, multiorgasmic, insatiable new woman he kept reading about in *Esquire* or *Playboy*. She was there for his pleasure, not her own, and if he didn't feel like being the initiator, he could ask her to take over.

These considerations were especially important for the newly single man. Many clients who were recently divorced or separated were simply not ready for (or capable of) a full relationship with a woman, and some of them were very much afraid of the new woman who had come into being during the time they had been married. In a few cases, divorce had left some men feeling sexually inadequate as well, and the girls who saw them often functioned more as therapists than anything else.

But sex wasn't the only area where a recently divorced man might need help. John was a real estate lawyer who saw Claudette each week for one hour. When Claudette first went over there, his new apartment was virtually empty. Gradually, week by week, with her encouragement, John began buying furniture. Before long, Claudette was acting as his decorating consultant, suggesting a beige rug for the living room, a red kitchen table, and so on. It was almost predictable: as soon as John's apartment was completely furnished, he stopped calling us.

We had a few clients who called us primarily to show off, proud that they were able to afford the highest-priced call girls in town. With these men, the girls were not only the prize; they were also the audience. This type of man would always spend a great deal of time showing off his art collection, for example, being sure to mention the value of each painting. But it used to drive the girls crazy that the men who bragged endlessly of their wealth rarely gave them tips, and more than one girl was silently furious when she was handed four fifties by a man who expected to receive five dollars in change.

We also had several clients who used our service because they had physical disabilities. One man was blind, and several others were confined to a wheelchair. Bill, who had had been paralyzed from the waist down in Vietnam, would always keep a girl for two or three hours; he liked to talk, play chess or backgammon, or simply watch TV. For the last few minutes of the evening, he would have her undress down to her lingerie. They would lie together on the bed while he simply hugged her, ran his hands over her, and was held in return. Bill was a handsome, sweet, and loving person, but going to see him made most of the girls unspeakably sad. The first time a girl came back from seeing him and told me about his condition, we were both in tears.

Another client was very sensitive about his face, which was slightly disfigured, and he believed himself to be so ugly his appearance would frighten the girls away. He used to leave his apartment door ajar and wait in the bedroom for the girl to make her way through the darkened living room until she found him. When I heard about this, I decided to speak to him. "I know this is how you prefer to do things," I said, "but you have to understand that when a new girl comes to see you, it's very frightening for her to fumble her way through a strange, dark apartment. It makes her think she's going to see a crazy person." We agreed that if a girl had been there before, he could continue in his old way, but if she was there for the first time, he would open the door himself.

Our married clients called us for somewhat different reasons than the single ones. Many were lonely travelers—although a lot of single men, too, fell into this category. Others were stuck in bad marriages or were married to women who, for a variety of reasons, were simply uninterested in sex.

Frank was a banker in his late fifties, with whom Melody once spent a few hours. As she was getting ready to leave, he unexpectedly started crying. When he pulled himself together, he explained that his wife had been an invalid for the past two years, that it had been terribly difficult for him to call us, and that he had feared he would never make love again. All these pent-up feelings had collected inside of him, and now, suddenly, they burst into the open. Melody didn't feel right about leaving him when it was so clear that he really needed to talk, so she volunteered to stay another hour at no charge, for which Frank was extremely grateful.

The next time he came to town, Frank asked to see Melody again. This time, he took her to dinner at Windows on the World in the World Trade Center, where he told her that he had a son who had just turned thirty and was starting to think about marriage. Was there, Frank wondered, some way Melody and Frank junior could meet? "I realize that you're making a fair amount of money right now," he said, "but if you and my son became serious about each other, and you were willing to leave your job, I would be happy to make up the difference for the first year." Melody told Frank she was honored by his suggestion and would consider it, but she never took him up on his offer.

Stacey once saw a client from the midwest who owned a lumber business. Several months earlier he had undergone a prostate operation, and ever since, he had been reluctant to try to make love to his wife because, like many men in his situation, he was afraid he was no longer capable of having sex. He had never called an escort service before, but this was a chance to see if he could still function as a man. The experiment was a rousing success, and he was ecstatic with gratitude. "It was almost like I had given him his life back," Stacey told me the next day.

We had a number of residential clients who called us when their wives were out of town, and each summer there was a dramatic rise in the number of calls from men whose wives and children were safely ensconced in a summer house at the ocean or in the mountains. Jack, who owned an advertising agency, called us at least three nights a week for an entire summer while his wife and children were in the Hamptons. The night before they were due to return, he suddenly realized that there were three girls he had never seen. Unable to tolerate this omission, he decided to have them all over in one evening, one after another.

For the first couple of years, I didn't really understand why so many married men were calling us, and I unthinkingly bought into the conventional wisdom that most of them must have been having problems at home. But gradually I came to realize that a traveler's desire for the company of a woman who was attentive and loving wasn't necessarily a negative comment on his marriage. In fact, the closer he was to his wife, the more he was used to having somebody to talk to, and the more uncomfortable he might feel about spending a string of long evenings alone.

A man who is on the road for long stretches at a time can easily enter a different world. Suddenly his natural support systems don't exist, and he might do things he would never dream of doing back home. I'm not saying that I'd be entirely comfortable knowing that my own husband called an escort service when he was away on business, but neither would I consider it a sign that our marriage was in trouble.

Loneliness, of course, was not the only reason married men called us; many of our clients were also interested in a little variety in their love lives. This well-known phenomenon on the part of the male of the species has been termed the Coolidge effect, after a legendary incident in the life of Calvin Coolidge. As the story goes, President and Mrs. Coolidge had gone to see a government farm, where they were taken on separate tours. When the First Lady passed by the hens, she asked the manager how many times a day the rooster had sex. "Dozens of times," replied the official.

"Please tell that to the president," she said.

A few minutes later, President Coolidge passed by the hens and asked the same question: "How many times a day does the rooster have sex?"

"Dozens of times," replied the official.

"All with the same hen?" asked the chief executive.

"Oh, no, Mr. President," he was told. "It's with a different one each time."

"I see," said the president. "Please tell that to Mrs. Coolidge."

In addition to the Coolidge effect, a call girl who visits a man for a couple of hours presents a striking (and, I must admit, patently unfair) contrast to his wife: she's glamorous, she never criticizes him, she never has a headache, she's never too tired, she never wears curlers, and there's nothing that she absolutely *must* discuss with him because it's been bothering her all week.

Some of our girls were disturbed by the number of married men who used to call us. Most of them looked forward to being married someday and found it upsetting to see—not to mention participate in—such close-up evidence of marital infidelity. This may be why some girls preferred to see single men, although it may also have been that the single men were generally closer to their own age. On the other hand, there were girls who much preferred married men because they were more appreciative.

Most of the girls came to the realization that if their husband were away on business, they would much prefer that he call an escort service than have an affair. With a call girl, the limits of the liaison are clearly defined in advance, whereas a genuine love interest can be far more threatening. A couple of men did use our service with their wives' consent—in one case, a woman in her eighth month of pregnancy called us as a birthday present for her husband—but this was highly unusual.

I believe that women have to be more realistic and accept the fact that most men need—or very strongly want—a new sexual experience every once in a while. It's one thing to discover that your husband or lover has a girlfriend on the side, but if he's enjoying the *occasional* one-night stand when he's away from home, it doesn't mean there's anything wrong with you. It's just something that men enjoy every now and then.

Not every man, incidentally, asked to see a girl who was beautiful. One category of men consisted of the nerds we all remember from high school who always did well in class but were social misfits. Now, as adults, they were financially successful, but their essential nerdiness still remained. These men continued to be intimidated by the beautiful women who hadn't given them the time of day two decades earlier. Although they were now in a position to buy the favors they couldn't get for free, many of them preferred a woman who was not so beautiful as to make them feel uncomfortable.

But it wasn't only the nerds who were willing to see the less beautiful girls. Some men found a beautiful girl sexually intimidating; others believed that such women were vain, selfish, or not overly bright.

Bert, who served on the board of several corporations, had a one-track mind: brains. Whereas most clients would ask us about a girl's physical characteristics, Bert cared only for girls who were bright and well educated. "You know why I like him?" Kate once told me. "Because as much as he likes to talk, he also enjoys *listening*."

A man who could listen was always popular, and so, of course, was the man who enjoyed giving gifts. Peter, who ran a chain of dress shops in the south, would always prebook a girl a week in advance and ask for her dress size. As soon as the girl walked in, he'd say, "I have a present for you, and if you can find it, it's yours." The gift would be a new dress or a suit, although from time to time he would hide an envelope containing a thousand dollars in cash, which might turn up in the lining of a curtain or underneath a rug.

Another client, who imported ski parkas from the Far East, would always give one to the girls who saw him; whenever possible, we would send over somebody who skied. And a client who imported fine Italian handbags would always give those as gifts. But by far the most interesting benefactor was Art, the handsome and flamboyant owner of one of the biggest nightclubs in New York. In the fall of 1983, when Cabbage Patch dolls were all the rage and could not be found at any price, Art had *thirty* of them in his apartment, perched on every couch, chair, and empty space. At the end of the evening, he would invite the girl to take home the doll of her choice. Tara once returned from Art's place half an hour late; it had taken her that long to make a selection.

As if that weren't enough, Art also had a business connection with a premium brand of ice cream, and he always kept at least a dozen different flavors on hand in a separate freezer. Not surprisingly, he was one of our more popular clients, and Ginny, who was a real ice cream freak, once left me a note saying that if I ever owed Art a favor, she would be delighted to see him for free.

Alexandra once went to see an Arab client who sent her home twenty minutes later—with a tip of a thousand dollars. And after Margot spent the evening with a man who was about to move out of his apartment, he had his driver take her home in his limousine along with art prints, chairs, curtains, and lamps that he no longer wanted, but that Margot was delighted to have.

We also had our share of less exciting clients, and there were even a few men none of the girls would see a second time. Several of the men in this category had enormous sums of money and beautiful apartments, but were insufferably arrogant. Once, when I had to expel one of these guys from the service because nobody would see him, he tried to convince me that I must have made a mistake and that six different girls must have confused him with somebody else. I always felt sorry for these men because no matter how obnoxious they were, it must have felt terrible not to be able even to *pay* for a date—at least, not through Cachet.

If we could have voted on our least favorite client, the odds-on favorite would have been Charles the bikini man. The girls called him that because he always wore bikini underwear and because for some reason known only to him, the word "bikini" was enough to arouse him. The bikini man had been the wrestling champ of his high school, and in his own mind, at least, he still was.

He needed the girls to assure him continually that he was still as strong and as muscular at thirty-four as he had been at seventeen.

A complete narcissist, Charles had mirrors all over his apartment, and he would pose endlessly in front of a three-section mirror while his visitor watched and admired him. He kept a telescope on his balcony and binoculars by the window, and he used to tell the girls that he "knew" his neighbors were watching him—especially in bed, where he would always take time out to strike a few poses for his imagined audience.

At one point, we had a girl named Jessica who, because of her dull personality, was not one of our most popular escorts. But when the bikini man called and asked to see her a third time, my interest was piqued. Nobody had ever requested to see Jessica even a second time, so I asked her to tell me what was going on. "He's not that bad," she said. "I keep him happy by gushing over him as he poses in front of his mirrors. I tell him things like 'Oh, Charles, you're *sooo* sexy!' " He simply wanted to be admired, and once I realized that oohing and aahing was all it took, every girl who saw him knew how to make him happy.

Tony was a prominent tax attorney with a brilliant mind who liked to argue with the girls over almost any topic. He once spent ninety minutes fighting with Kate over options trading, about which she knew a great deal. During the course of this debate, Tony consumed an entire bottle of Scotch. As Tony became increasingly abusive, Kate threatened to leave. At this point, Tony quickly backed down and became very gentle. A few weeks later, he asked Kate to marry him.

Harold was another difficult client—not because of his personality, but because he kept half a dozen cats in his apartment. The first girl who saw him reported that the stench from the litter box was so unpleasant that she didn't want to go back. The next time he called, I sent over somebody else, but she had the same reaction. When he called a third time, I decided to warn the girl about the other two complaints and let her make up her own mind. She decided to take the call, but when she came back she told me that the kitty-litter problem really *was* pretty bad.

The next time Harold called, I explained to him that we couldn't send any more girls unless he got rid of the cats. I hated to give up a client as nice as Harold, but I had to be clear about my priorities.

Although I valued our clients, the real challenge of the business was to find enough nice girls to send to them. And once I had such a girl working for me, the best way to keep her was to ensure that her working life was as enjoyable and comfortable as possible. As I saw it, every girl had her own internal limit of how many unpleasant experiences she could tolerate before she couldn't do the job anymore, and it was my responsibility to keep those experiences to a minimum. Besides, it never hurt to let the girls know that the boss was looking out for them.

One of the more alarming experiences a girl ever had was when Marguerite went to see Doug, a new residential client. He seemed a little depressed and on edge, which she attributed to his being nervous. It was clear that he needed to talk, so Marguerite settled herself on the sofa as he began to tell her about his problems. Suddenly, somebody started banging on the door and calling Doug's name. When he didn't answer, the visitor tried to kick the door in. Fearing that this was a drug bust, Marguerite jumped up in alarm and ran into the bedroom. Finally Doug opened the door, and from the conversation she overheard, Marguerite realized that earlier in the evening Doug had called a suicide hotline, and now they were here to make sure he was all right. As he told her later, his girlfriend of two years had just run off with his best friend, leaving him doubly betrayed and alone.

A number of our most difficult clients were good people who had become overly involved with cocaine. Starting around 1982, there was a middle-class cocaine boom, and some of our younger clients were real enthusiasts. Cocaine is an insidious drug, and we witnessed the slow deterioration of some very sensitive and talented people. One client, for example, started off as one of our all-time favorites; two years later we refused to have anything to do with him. For several of these guys, cocaine brought about a real night-and-day change, and it was frustrating to watch it happen while being powerless to intervene.

We had one client who would often call when he was coked up, and there was always such desperation in his voice: "An hour? I can't wait an hour. I want somebody *now*." Being with the coke users was no fun, because you had to listen to their constant talking—usually about themselves—as well as their frequent paranoia and occasional belligerence. The main reason we were not open after one o'clock in the morning is because that's when most of the drug calls come in. It is also when most of the other agencies made the bulk of their money.

Most of our clients who used cocaine or marijuana would offer some to the girls. I wasn't so naive as to think I could forbid their joining in, so I talked to them instead about the need for moderation and discipline. Despite what the government and the schools would have us believe, millions of Americans use and enjoy illegal drugs without abusing them, just as millions of Americans are able to use alcohol in a socially acceptable manner. Drug use, in other words, is not the same as drug *abuse,* and my concern was ensuring that those girls who chose to use "recreational" drugs did so in a socially responsible manner. Needless to say, none of our clients or our girls used hard drugs.

It was absolutely forbidden for a girl to furnish or supply a client with drugs. Some of our clients in the corporate world were eager to try marijuana or cocaine, but they didn't know anybody who could get them some. Because our business had illegal overtones, they would sometimes ask the girls to help out. Now a prostitution arrest is one thing, but an arrest for drug dealing is far more serious. Some escort agencies are heavily involved in the drug scene, and more agencies are busted for drugs than for prostitution. If this problem had ever come up in our agency, I would have fired the girl on the spot.

Generally speaking, the girls much preferred marijuana smokers to cocaine users. Marijuana tends to produce a peaceful reaction, and the man who smokes it is likely to be funny and gentle when he is high. Cocaine, on the other hand, often made our clients abusive, argumentative—and ultimately boring, since they would repeat themselves over and over.

When it comes to sex, a call girl normally prefers a very different experience from the one she might enjoy in a more conventional relationship. Except for the men who were skilled lovers—and although there were more of these than you might think, there were fewer than the girls would have liked—the girls preferred a client who was, as they would say, "quick and easy." Because the job could involve a fair amount of wear and tear on a girl's body, the girls would complain whenever they saw a client who, in their terms, "really got his money's worth." We had a number of clients who were designated as "marathon men," including several who were known to satisfy themselves in private before the girl arrived in order to prolong the experience. While most women are interested in sexual techniques that help a man last longer, our girls were always exchanging advice on how to speed things up.

Men's bodies vary tremendously, and when a client was more generously endowed than most, some of our smaller girls would refuse to see him. As for the age-old debate as to whether size makes any difference to a woman's sexual fulfillment, most of our girls agreed with Ginny that "it's the singer, not the song."

When they're with a call girl, many men act differently in bed from the way they would with their wife or girlfriend. Some men would refuse to kiss an escort on the mouth, and others would use the occasion to experiment with new techniques or new positions. Still others, who might be very good lovers in another setting, would use the opportunity to lie back and have the girl do all the work.

New girls were invariably surprised to find that a number of our clients were so "quick and easy" that the intimate part of the evening came to an end almost before it had begun—although virtually all of these men would swear that nothing like this had ever happened before. Although the girls were secretly pleased when this happened, they were sympathetic enough to realize that it could represent a real psychological problem for the client and required some tenderness and understanding. It may be that our men were typical of the larger population and that premature ejaculation is even more widespread than is commonly realized. It may also be that our clients became enormously excited while they were waiting for the girl to arrive and were thrilled by the idea that a beautiful stranger was on her way to see him for the explicit purpose of making him happy.

Still, Cachet's style wasn't for everyone. Most of our clients appreciated the genuine good feelings and mutual respect that existed between the girls and themselves, but from time to time, when we telephoned a client after a girl had left, he would explain that he wouldn't be calling us in the future because our girls were "too nice." Occasionally, after an evening in which nothing sexual had taken place, the client would call us as soon as the girl left because he imagined she might get in trouble. "I just wanted you to know," a client once told me, "that the reason we didn't *do* anything isn't because I didn't like her, but because she was so *nice* that I just didn't want to." A client who was interested in a "dirty" or shameful experience—as some men are—was generally better off calling another service.

Considering the type of business we were in, ours was a very conservative operation. There were occasional requests for girls to appear in costumes: when Tricia told clients that she was an airline stewardess, some of them begged her to show up next time in uniform. Suzie was once asked to arrive in a cheerleader's outfit, which delighted her because back in high school she had been captain of the cheerleading squad. Over the years, requests for costumes included a girl who was dressed as a hooker, a teenager from the fifties with teased hair and bobby socks, a librarian, a nurse, and a shepherdess. One man asked for a girl to come dressed as a nun, but there were no volunteers.

On some of these calls, a man might want the girl to act out a fantasy with him, and if she had no objections, I didn't, either. A client once asked Melody to pretend she was his high school English teacher and that she was angry at him for not doing his homework. "It reminded me of an acting class," Melody said later, "a very boring acting class, because this guy wanted to repeat the scene at least a dozen times."

This kind of thing fell into the category of "light dominance," and if a regular client requested it, we would try to accommodate him. First, of course, we would explain his preference to the girl, so she would never end up in a situation she couldn't handle—or didn't like. We permitted verbal abuse and light bondage, but anything beyond that was referred to a woman I knew who worked as a professional dominatrix—much like Baroness Von Stern, whose house I had visited as part of my research before Lucy and I opened the business.

By and large, calls involving two or more girls and one client were about as exotic as we would get. These were known as "playing bridge," because we needed a code word on the phone, and rounding up another player for a game of bridge sounded fairly innocent.

The girls received an additional fee for bridge calls: the moment anyone in the room removed any article of clothing, each girl there would be paid an extra fifty dollars an hour—all of which they got to keep. (Other agencies, incidentally, do not charge the clients extra for these calls.)

At first, when I asked the girls if they would be willing to be intimate with another woman in the presence of a client, most of them refused even to consider it. But as they came to know the other girls, they would often change their minds. Playing bridge was not only more lucrative, but it was invariably more fun because you had a buddy there with you. As one girl put it, "When I'm alone with a man, it's a job. When another girl joins us, it feels like a party."

Besides, as the girls quickly discovered, making love with another woman could usually be dramatized. The implicit understanding among the girls was, "I'm not gay or even bisexual, you understand, but if the client wants us to pretend otherwise, I'm willing to go along with it—especially if I can make an extra fifty dollars an hour." In fact, when word got out that one of the escorts seemed to be enjoying these dramatizations a little more than necessary, most of the other girls refused to go on bridge calls with her.

Although some clients especially enjoyed watching two girls together, others preferred to join in on the fun. Sometimes the client simply wanted to be pampered by two or more women, with little or no interplay among the women and, in a few cases, with no overt sexual activity at all.

We had one client, a very wealthy man who ran a large industrial corporation, who would routinely ask for five or six girls to come to his hotel suite. He never had sex with any of them and never asked them to be intimate with each other. Apparently he just loved having them around in their lingerie, drinking champagne, laughing at his jokes, and generally making him feel like a sultan. Not surprisingly, most of the girls clamored to go on these calls, but I had to be careful not to send anybody who was overly shy or who refused to share the spotlight.

Because the men would often discuss their fantasies with the girls, and because being with two women at once is the most common of all male fantasies, the idea of bridge would often arise during a call. If the timing was appropriate, and the girl was so inclined, she might suggest that the client call the office to check on who else was available, or she might say, "There's another girl who works for Sheila, and every once in a while she and I will play together. Would you like me to see if she's free tonight?" I always suggested that the girls who played bridge find themselves a partner they enjoyed working with. In some cases, girls who worked as a team at bridge would actually choreograph the moves in advance so that the erotic interaction between them would seem more realistic.

But if the client suggested inviting over another girl, and the girl he was with was not interested, she would say, "That's not my cup of tea, but the next time you call, why don't you say that you're interested in playing bridge tonight." This suggestion carried the additional advantage of letting the client feel he was in the privileged position of knowing our secret code, and some men found the combination of secrecy and sexual fantasy irresistible.

From time to time, a client would ask us to send a girl on a call to himself and his wife—or his girlfriend. In this situation, assuming the girl was willing to go, we would charge twice our hourly rate because the escort had to be available for two different people at the same time. This kind of request was rare, but when it did happen, I would always caution the girl to be especially sensitive to the feelings of the other woman. Such an arrangement is almost invariably the man's idea, and even when his wife or girlfriend goes along with it, they often do so with a great deal of ambivalence. On at least half these calls, nothing sexual would happen because the man's companion was so obviously uncomfortable that the escort would take the client aside and point out that proceeding with his plan would not be in his best interest.

A few clients used to play bridge regularly, while others might do so only once a year, for a very special celebration. But although bridge calls were expensive, they would often last for several hours. More than one man told us that an evening he spent with two of our girls constituted the greatest sexual thrill of his life. I wonder how many other entrepreneurs could boast of such satisfied customers?

Chapter Ten

*B*y early 1984, as we entered our fifth year, I realized that I couldn't spend the rest of my life in the escort business. I was now in my early thirties and starting to think more practically about my future—which would, I hoped, include marriage. As much as I loved my job, I had to acknowledge that the kind of man I was likely to fall in love with would never marry the owner of an escort service. I could probably get by with having an episode like this discreetly tucked away in my past, but only if it was clearly over and done with. If I didn't want to remain single forever, I would sooner or later have to return to a more conventional line of work. In other words, it was time to think about resuming life as a regular person.

At the same time, I had no interest in being a regular *poor* person. Over the past four years I had pretty much spent my money as it came in, without looking very far down the road. By the fifth year, however, I had resolved that it was time to concentrate on saving my income and investing it for the future. At some point, I expected to enter a more socially acceptable line of work—either by starting my own business or working for an established one—and no matter which path I took, it might be two or three years before I started earning a decent living. The only practical thing I could do, then, was to make sure I had a healthy amount of money saved up.

By this time, I was developing an interest in financial planning and investing. I had read several books and many articles on money management and realized that with enough research I could probably make my own investment decisions. I didn't need an MBA to build up a nest egg, any more than I had needed one to go into the business in the first place.

I decided I would stay in the escort business until 1990, investing my money rather than spending it. Until now, I had been far too careless about my finances and had spent nearly everything I made indulging my every whim, especially with respect to clothes, my biggest weakness. Although I usually bought elegant, classic pieces that could be worn forever, each season I would splurge on several trendy outfits, knowing full well that in another year they would probably look dated. I also spent rather freely on fine accessories like leather handbags and unusual jewelry and justified the high prices to myself with the logical excuse that a woman who pretends to be in the fashion business should at least dress the part.

I want to be clear, however, that I was "rich" only by the most modest of standards. Because of all the publicity I have received, and because after the bust the press started referring to me as "the Million Dollar Madam," people always assume I was really raking it in. A fair amount of money was indeed flowing into the business, but almost as much was flowing right back out. My expenses were enormous, including a considerable advertising commitment, astronomical phone bills, salaries for the assistants, rent for the office, printing costs for brochures, and so on.

On the supply side, our income was subject to a

number of severe limitations. Although we accepted Mastercharge and Visa, we were never able to make an arrangement with American Express, which refuses to do business with escort services. (Because American Express is the credit card of choice for most corporate expense accounts, I was dying to work something out with them, but I was never successful in doing so.) We also missed out on a considerable amount of business because of our restrictive policies, such as not sending the girls outside of Manhattan, or to any but the most select hotels, or to clients at their offices. And we certainly paid a price for not accepting clients after one A.M., which in the escort industry is the equivalent of closing a Manhattan restaurant at nine in the evening. Finally, the fact that we were so selective about the girls we hired and the clients we accepted served to limit our income even further.

Now I don't want to plead poverty here. We did manage to turn a profit, and although I was far from wealthy, I was certainly comfortable. As long as I wasn't extravagant, I could usually afford the things I wanted that made life more enjoyable. I'm not talking about diamonds, Rolls-Royces, or exotic vacations; my most expensive splurge came in 1984, when I spent two thousand dollars for a couple of weeks at an exercise spa in Vermont.

One financial option I did not consider was to marry a rich man or look for a sugar daddy who would instantly solve all my financial worries. I don't have anything against rich men—far from it—but I could never feel secure knowing that someone else had that kind of control over me.

Actually, I consider myself exceptionally lucky when it comes to men, and over the years I've had some sweet and sensitive boyfriends. I'm still close with several of them, and I've always thought that women were foolish to eliminate ex-lovers as potential friends merely because the romantic part of the relationship was over. A former boyfriend is somebody who has known you well and cared about you, and if that's not a good basis for a friendship, I don't know what is. Besides, when you fall in love with somebody, you presumably find a lot to admire in his character or personality. Even if the love affair is over, you can still appreciate those same qualities that attracted you in the first place.

Despite the business I was running, my personal sexual ethics have always been very conservative. Some people are surprised to hear this because they assume that a woman who ran an escort service must therefore believe in free sex. But nothing could be further from the truth. It's not free sex I believe in, but free *choice*. If a man chooses to call an escort service, and a girl is willing to see him, I am more than happy to help make that transaction as pleasant and as uplifting as possible. But when it comes to my own life, I am monogamous and rather old-fashioned. This is *my* choice. When I enter into a relationship, I am committed to that relationship for as long as it lasts.

Instant intimacy just isn't something I'm comfortable with. I tend to maintain a certain reserve with new people, and I don't even like it when somebody I have just met in a business setting feels free to call me by my first name.

Nor do I care for the European (and increasingly American) custom whereby two acquaintances of the opposite sex (or even the same sex, for that matter) feel obliged to kiss each other if they've been apart for more than twenty minutes. And I certainly don't feel that any man "deserves" a good-night kiss—much less anything else—at the end of a date. In the context of a close relationship with a man I know well, I am warm, loving, and affectionate, and like many women, I find it easier to give love than to receive it. But to be blunt about it, recreational sex has never appealed to me.

That's why I don't feel altogether comfortable with today's singles scene, where one of the unwritten rules seems to be that you either sleep with the man by the third date or you stop seeing him. I've always had a hard time with that notion, because for me, the third date is absurdly early to make that kind of commitment—even with somebody I'm crazy about.

I suspect that many other single people, men and women alike, feel the same way, although not all of them successfully resist the pressures to jump into bed. Some women sleep with men they hardly know because they're afraid of being rejected or because it's the only way they know to be held and hugged in a man's arms. And some men try to sleep with women because they think the woman expects it or because sex is a quick and easy way of finding out where they stand with her. But there are other ways to let somebody know you're interested. I've always found that words will do the trick very nicely. If I want a man to know that I'd like to pursue the relationship, I'll look him in the eye at the end of the evening, take his hand, and say with a warm smile, "I had a very nice time tonight, and I'd really like to see you again." They always get the message.

Before I went into the escort business, I always had a steady boyfriend. But as I matured, I realized that I had become a little too dependent on men. Some people never learn how to be alone, which is one reason escort services remain in business. This phenomenon is even more serious for women, however, and over the years I've seen many of my women friends remain in bad relationships with men who clearly weren't good for them simply because they were convinced that having a man around—*any* man, really, no matter how flawed—was still preferable to being on their own.

When a woman is overly afraid of being alone, she is bound to make bad choices when it comes to men. Like many women of my generation, I have made a conscious effort to be independent and not to need a man to give meaning to my life. If I *want* to be with a particular man, that's fine, but it has to be out of choice rather than necessity and out of positive feelings about myself and him, rather than from any fear I have of being on my own.

At the same time, it's all too easy to swing back in the other direction. I have known many women who are overly critical of every man they meet. When my girls would come to me for advice about their love lives, I often found myself helping them distinguish between a man who simply wasn't good enough for them and a man who didn't happen to measure up to their lofty and often unrealistic standards.

Listening to the girls, it struck me that without even knowing it, they would often compare the men in their lives to their female friends. "But that's not fair," I would tell them. "Keep in mind that most men are years behind us in terms of their emotional maturity, their self-awareness, and their ability to give. If you insist on judging men by the standards of women, you're never going to be happy."

Like most advice, this was easier to give out than to live by. At one point, I spent a year with a man who was so self-absorbed he never even noticed that I didn't talk about my work. To make matters worse, I put up with this ridiculous situation. "How's business?" he would ask, referring, of course, to my mythical accessories company. "Fine, thanks," I would reply, and we'd move on to some other topic, as he never wanted to pursue the matter any further. In retrospect, there was at least one distinct advantage to our relationship: because he never asked any questions about my work, I never had to tell him any lies.

I hate to lie, and during the years that I led a double life, I would go to great lengths to avoid doing so more than was absolutely necessary. Whenever I was with friends who didn't know about my real job, I preferred not to say much about my work. Keeping my secret was less difficult than I had expected, however, because I found that most people are so busy talking about themselves, and so appreciative when they find a good listener who pays attention to what they're saying, they can go for years without realizing you're not disclosing very much. Whenever questions came up, I would give broad, general answers and soon steer the conversation back to the other person's work or to some other safe topic.

When my friends raised specific points about the accessories business, I would respond as truthfully as possible—but about the escort business. If somebody wanted to know which stores I bought for, I'd reply that my clients were scattered all over the country. Did I visit the stores? No, the clients came to New York, and we did a lot of work on the phone.

I did tell the truth to a handful of friends, but I had to be careful to select people who were paragons of discretion and whose sensibilities would not be offended. I've always had good relationships with gay men, and I found it easy to let these friends in on my secret. They were always very supportive, perhaps because, like me, they too were living outside the moral code of bourgeois society.

On the other hand, I certainly couldn't reveal my secret to anyone at the Society of Mayflower Descendants, for example, where I continued to attend meetings and parties. I was far too busy to undertake the enormous effort of applying for membership. Even though my great-grandmother had been a member, under the rules I would have to go through the lengthy application process myself. Still, I continued to be welcomed by the members, who were delighted whenever a young person showed any interest in attending the meetings.

Some people have been surprised to learn that a woman of my profession should care about the Mayflower Society, but why not? It's my heritage, after all, and where is it written that Anglo-Saxon Protestants aren't allowed to have roots? Besides, I genuinely liked the people who attended these meetings, and they seemed to like me, too. Among other things, these people helped me to expand my social horizons by inviting me to parties and occasionally offering to introduce me to their sons or nephews. I wasn't meeting new people through work, and this was an enjoyable way of making new and interesting acquaintances.

Men come and go, but girlfriends are with you forever. During this period I kept up close relationships with several of my women friends, who had no idea about the real nature of my work. We would often meet for dinner or an occasional movie, and I spent many a Thursday evening and Saturday on shopping trips, helping my friends pick out new clothes. They, of course, had no idea that I did this regularly as part of my job, but I didn't mind because I've always loved the fashion business and I never get tired of going to Saks Fifth Avenue.

I had one very close male companion—David, who had been a longtime boyfriend of an old friend of mine. She, apparently, did not subscribe to my theory about the value of old boyfriends, but just because David and Leslie were no longer together didn't mean that I had to drop my friendship with either of them. David ran his own consulting business, and I'm sure he could have given me some good business advice, had I told him the truth about what I did. But I always felt he would have disapproved strongly, so I kept quiet about my real occupation and we talked about other things.

Naturally, I kept in touch with my real family, but we were never close. My brother had grown up and become a corporate executive, but ever since I went off to boarding school at the age of fifteen, when he was twelve, we'd never really had a chance to know each other. I would see him at Christmas and Thanksgiving, and at family weddings, but that was about it.

I saw my mother slightly more often. Every year on my birthday she'd come to New York City and we'd have lunch out before going to the costume exhibit at the Metropolitan Museum of Art. I didn't have to lie to her because she never asked specific questions about the accessories business. Mostly we talked and gossiped about the family. She had remarried—to an Austrian conductor and music teacher, a very fine person—and I was pleased that she was no longer alone.

I was almost never in touch with my father. But once, when Granny Sydney insisted that we ought to see each other more often, he called me before his next business trip to New York and asked me to make dinner reservations at a restaurant of my choice. He was charming that night, and when he asked what I was up to, I decided I had nothing to lose by telling the truth. "You used to say that you didn't care if I became a ditch digger, so long as I was a good one," I began. "Well, believe it or not, I happen to run an escort service. Actually, it's the best one in New York."

I was afraid he would be upset, but to my surprise and relief, he was fascinated. Like everyone I had told, he had a million questions.

"When did you start?"

"How many girls work for you?"

"What does it cost?"

"Aren't you worried about the police?"

"What are the clients like?"

"Where do you find the girls?"

He found the whole story amazing, but the one thing he just couldn't get over was that we accepted credit cards.

"How long are you planning to stay in business?" he asked.

I told him about my five-year plan and how I hoped to find another, more respectable job when I left Cachet.

He was very optimistic. "You're actually running a company," he said, "and that's great experience. You're doing something naughty now, but look at all the skills you're picking up. I'm sure you'll be able to draw on all of this when you go into another line of work." It wasn't what I was expecting, but I was relieved that he wan't angry or critical. He was also the first person to point out to me that I had picked up some useful business skills that could be put to good use in some future enterprise.

My main circle of friends consisted of a group of people with whom I spent summer weekends in West-hampton, a popular seaside community on Long Island. Together we shared a large, rambling, nine-bedroom wooden house with a huge wraparound porch, which was part of a loosely knit community of about thirty such houses. Most of the house members were young professionals who escaped from the city every week to play tennis, lie on the beach, and socialize—except for a few type-A men who insisted on bringing along their work.

For me, socializing was a welcome contrast from the high-pressured singles scene back in the city, and the summer house was a lot like a coed dorm, where the people in your own building are generally considered off limits as romantic partners. As a result, there was a warm, easy camaraderie among the men and women in each house, which was a great relief and a refreshing change from life in Manhattan, where there were few opportunities for casual, uncomplicated friendships with members of the opposite sex.

The men in each house regarded the women as sisters, and they were protective toward us and sweetly suspicious when men from other houses came courting. With two or three house members sharing a room, finding a place to be alone was difficult. People met in the casual atmosphere of the beach and would get together later, for more serious purposes, back in the city.

There were parties every Saturday night, and during my first year out there a couple of other new girls and I couldn't understand why nobody ever asked us to dance. We were sitting around the kitchen one night, wondering what we were doing wrong, when one of the veterans came in and explained that these men were so used to being chased after by the women, who greatly outnumbered them, that they had grown used to being passive and letting the women do the initiating. It was awkward at first, but once I accepted this reality, I had a much better time.

I really looked forward to these weekends, which provided a perfect opportunity to escape the pressures of the business. I had full confidence in Jaime, Liza, and Ashley, who were running the store, and I knew that if ever there was an emergency, they would call me.

The subject of what I did for a living rarely came up, but when it did I gave my usual cover story. Because of my work at the May Company and with The Cutting Edge, I knew enough about the business to hold my own when anybody asked questions. But almost nobody did, as most of the people in that group were in banking or advertising. I did get a scare one year, however, when a woman joined our house who turned out to represent a large handbag manufacturer. Fortunately, she showed little interest in talking to me about business and did not—as I had feared she might—pressure me to come down to the showroom to "shop the line."

The focal point of our group in Westhampton was a private beach and tennis club. At one point, I applied for membership in the club and was accepted, but a few days later one of the board members called and advised me to decline the honor. Apparently, the roommate of a girl who had once worked for me and who had somehow learned my name was a good friend of the woman on the board, and because my name was so unusual, she had figured out who I really was. If I declined the offer of membership, I was told, nobody would be the wiser; but if I didn't go along, they would be forced to go public with my secret. They still permitted me to visit the club, but they drew the line at allowing a madam to be a member in good standing.

I really loved my business, and the experience of writing this book brings back many of those good feelings. Two or three years ago, I would have given a lot for the privilege of being so open about what I was up to. It's not easy to keep a secret when you're proud of what you've done, and I had a great deal to be proud of—including our reputation for quality and integrity, and my ability to run such a complicated operation. Had we been a large enterprise like Abraham & Straus, such diverse areas as personnel, advertising, training, operations, and accounting would each have been handled by different departments. But here I was, without a standard college education—much less an MBA—operating a successful and complex business simply by following my instincts, utilizing my experiences, and keeping my eyes open.

From all the available evidence, nobody had ever run an escort service like this one. We were the best in the business—how often in life do you have the opportunity to make that claim? It was very frustrating to have to keep it a secret.

Still, it wasn't as if nobody knew. The girls who worked for me were certainly well aware of our reputation, and so were the girls who worked at other agencies and came to me for job interviews. The clients knew, too, and they would often compliment both me and the girls on the quality of our operation. That's why I always enjoyed answering the phones, even after I had hired the assistants to help me out in the office. Night after night, successful and discriminating men from all over the world used to tell me how much they liked and respected my business and how they appreciated the way we treated them. Several of our clients who were on the road a great deal let me know that they were so impressed with Cachet and Finesse that they no longer called other escort services in other cities because the contrast was just too dramatic. I'll never forget the client who said that after doing business with me, he wouldn't ''lower'' himself by calling anyone else.

These compliments were enormously gratifying, but they didn't entirely compensate for my not being able to talk about my work when I was with friends. These days, regrettably, work is what people talk about when they meet, and to a large extent, at least initially, you really are judged by what you do rather than who you are. I felt constrained not to be able to refer to my career when everybody around me was talking about theirs.

It was even more frustrating to talk on the phone to some of the most eligible bachelors in New York and not be able to meet them. This, of course, was my own decision. But some of these men were always asking the assistants and especially the girls about the mysterious Sheila who was behind this well-run operation. "Say anything you want about me," I would tell them, "as long as none of it is true." As a result, there were probably hundreds of men scattered across the nation, each carrying around in his head a slightly different fantasy of who Sheila Devin really was.

I never really thought of myself as a "madam," although in retrospect that's really what I was. There has always been a mystique about madams, a curiosity about them on the part of others, and that was certainly true among our clients. John Steinbeck once wrote that a madam combines "the brains of a businesswoman, the toughness of a prize fighter, the warmth of a companion, and the humor of a tragedian."

Thanks, John, I appreciate the compliment. To capitalize on that mystique and also to personalize our image, I told both the girls and the assistants to drop Sheila's name regularly in their conversations with the clients. I wanted the men to know there was a strong hand at the helm and that even though some of our personnel might change over time, top management was stable and consistent.

The biggest difference between me and a traditional madam was that I didn't meet the clients. For one thing, I didn't want the risk of running into a client in my social life, where it would be all too clear that the woman he knew as Sheila Devin had a separate existence as Sydney Barrows. For another, I was young and reasonably attractive, and I didn't want to go through the ordeal of having the clients come on to me. It was bad enough on the phone, where, sight unseen, some of our clients would occasionally offer me considerable sums of money to sleep with them. For some men, apparently, the prospect of bedding the madam herself represented an irresistible challenge. When I graciously declined these propositions, the men would often act wounded, and more than one client was convinced that if he only offered me enough money, I would surely say yes.

I suspect that a few of these men may have had in mind the classic joke about the man who goes up to an attractive woman and asks, "Would you sleep with me for ten thousand dollars?"

"I might consider it," she says with a smile.

"And would you sleep with me for ten dollars?" he asks.

"What do you take me for?" she replies indignantly.

"My dear lady," he replies, "we've already established *that*. At this point, we're only quibbling over the price."

Chapter Eleven

As 1984 approached, I was optimistic that this was going to be our best year ever. In retrospect, I couldn't have been more wrong. Everything that could have gone wrong did—and much more, too.

In December 1983, a couple of weeks before Christmas, a man called and told Liza he was a retired police officer who was soliciting donations for the retired policemen's association. Were we interested in making a contribution?

Liza suspected it was a hoax, but she wasn't sure and didn't want to take any chances. "It's not up to me," she said. "I'll have to check with Sheila." The man thanked her and said he'd call back the following evening.

Like Liza, I wasn't entirely sure what to make of this request. Assuming the caller was legitimate, this was our very first interaction with a police officer. There seems to be a widespread belief that escort services routinely pay off the police, but that certainly wasn't the case with us, and I have never heard of any other escort agency in New York doing it, either.

On the assumption that our caller was telling the truth and simply hadn't understood exactly what kind of business we were, I told Liza to get the name and address of his group and that I'd send a contribution.

"Why not?" I said blithely. "It'll look good at my trial." Liza, a firm believer in such concepts as karma and fate, was not amused.

Whoever he was, the man never called back. Looking back, I wonder whether his inquiry was an attempt by the police to learn more about our decision-making On the other hand, he may well have been legitimate; I'll never know.

A couple of weeks later, Ashley approached me nervously. "You might think I'm crazy," she said, "but last night I brought down a bag of trash, and today it wasn't there. I know which days the trash is picked up, and today isn't one of them. I wouldn't have mentioned this, but the exact same thing happened last week. Do you think somebody could be stealing our trash?"

As wild as the idea sounded, it certainly was a possibility. From that day on, I had the assistants tear all of their notes and paperwork into tiny pieces, and a few weeks later I bought a paper shredder. It was a big expense for a small business, and for some reason shredders were nearly impossible to find. But how could I put a price on our security?

This, of course, was one of the most difficult parts of the business: somehow I had to determine when a little paranoia might actually be justified.

The incidents mounted. Shortly after the case of the missing trash, Kelly told me that she had noticed two men standing outside the door of our building, keeping an eye on who was going in and out. Kelly's brother was a police officer, and she was convinced that these were plainclothesmen. "They tried not to be obvious about it," she said, "but I know when I'm being watched."

Half a block from the office, on the corner, there was a gay bar, and some of the regulars used to stand outside and chat with the girls while they waited for cabs. One night, one of the men told Kate that he had seen several police officers snooping around and observing the girls coming in and out of the building. This news came a day or two after Kelly's report, so we were clearly being monitored.

What happened next was considerably more disturbing. As careful as I was about whom I hired, there would occasionally be a girl who didn't work out. Elise was both pretty and sexy, which made her easy to book. She was also very young; she had just turned twenty, but she could pass for sixteen. Petite and busty, with long, beautiful hair, she was a real Lolita type, which made her especially appealing to our Arab clients.

The problem with Elise was that she insisted on wearing vintage clothing and refused to spend any money on her wardrobe. On the rare occasions when she put on something more contemporary, it would invariably be a real *shmattah*—a cheap polyester dress. This infuriated me, for not only was she disobeying one of our basic rules, but there was no excuse for her penny-pinching. In addition to earning a great deal of money with us, Elise lived at the Y, which meant she was spending next to nothing on rent. But I just couldn't get her to part with four hundred dollars for a nice outfit and matching shoes, even though she often took home that much money in a single night.

On several different occasions, I tried to explain to her that she could be even more successful if only she would make a small investment in her wardrobe, that all she really needed was a nice suit with a couple of blouses and a pretty dress. With the outfits she insisted on wearing, I couldn't send her to our more sophisticated clients, who might have wanted to take her to one of the better restaurants or nightclubs in town. But Elise paid no attention, in part, I suppose, because we would sometimes end up sending her on those calls anyway, as she was so often exactly the kind of girl our clients wanted to meet.

Despite my complaints, her behavior started growing worse. She began to show up late for appointments, and several girls reported that she was always nodding out on what they suspected were Quaaludes. Before long, the other girls refused to go on calls with her because she was unreliable and spacey, and they were concerned that her negative image reflected badly on them. Elise also made them angry because they had gone to considerable trouble and expense to live up to our classic, elegant look, while she insisted on dressing like a refugee. Before long, the assistants were complaining as well. "If you don't fire that girl," Liza told me, "we're just not going to book her anymore."

Firing Elise was the obvious solution, but I've always found it hard to fire anyone who worked for me. Even when it was clear that I had to let a girl go, I would procrastinate, and once I actually asked Ashley to do the dirty deed for me. In Elise's case, what finally pushed me to act was that one of our clients told Jaime that Elise had complained to him about my strictness and said that I was driving her crazy with our rules. That did it: putting down the agency in front of a client was something I wouldn't tolerate.

"I hate to do this," I told Elise on the phone, "but you're obviously unhappy working for me, and I think you'd be better off somewhere else."

She was furious: "I bring in the money, so what do you care?"

"I care because this is my business, and I have a certain way of doing things. The reason we are what we are today is because my system works. You obviously think your way is better than mine, so why don't you go work for someone else?"

Which she promptly did. She joined up with an outfit

that billed itself as "the most costly escort service in New York." That was about the only thing this agency could brag about, for it was known as one of the sleaziest places in town.

I guess you could say that Elise paid for her crimes after all, for during her first week at the other agency, she and two of her fellow escorts were arrested at a midtown hotel. By coincidence, one of the other girls was a friend of Claudette's, which is how we subsequently learned what really happened that night.

Apparently, Elise's new employer also operated a house, where all of the escorts were required to work two nights a week. The police were intrigued by this complex operation, and they asked the girls a great many questions. As the new kid on the block, however, Elise wasn't able to provide many answers. So in an effort to please the arresting officers, who thought she was holding out on them, she started talking—about *us*. And to make her story appear more interesting, she apparently built us up to be considerably larger and more elaborate than we actually were. At the time, the police did not act on Elise's information, but our luck would not hold out forever.

Meanwhile, on another front, we were starting to run into problems with our landlord. Back in November, he had offered me a renewal on our lease, which I had promptly signed. But at the very end of February, just before the new lease was about to take effect, I received a formal notice that he was bringing a suit against me for operating a business out of a residence.

Our original landlord had known about us all along, but he was an easygoing fellow and never gave us any trouble. As long as we paid the rent on time and nobody complained, he left us alone. But when his son-in-law came into the business, the younger man probably started thinking about making the building more profitable. Our apartment was rent-stabilized, which meant that the landlord was allowed to institute a limited rent increase only when the lease expired, when he made improvements, or when a new tenant moved in. We were paying far less than half of what he could have charged for that apartment, which gave him a compelling interest in getting rid of us.

This sort of tactic goes on constantly in the world of Manhattan real estate, where apartments are so scarce that would-be tenants have been known to buy the early edition of the newspaper in order to read the obituaries—where they might learn of the imminent availability of a vacant apartment. City landlords are constantly complaining to the police about tenants they want to expel, and in the case of women, accusations of prostitution are fairly common.

Although the girls had always done their best to keep their comings and goings quiet, it was impossible to be completely discreet when people were coming in and out of the building all through the evening and late into the night. To be absolutely certain that we weren't disturbing anyone, I had canvased most of the tenants. "I keep late hours," I told them, "and I often have friends over. Please let me know if you hear any noise or if they disturb you in any way, and I'll speak to them about it."

But there was one neighbor I couldn't placate. She had the unpleasant habit of leaving her trash out in the hall, and when I couldn't stand the mess any longer, I finally called the landlord to complain. What a mistake! Many of the tenants had probably figured out what we were really up to, but this was New York after all, where people tend to mind their own business. Most people, that is. The garbage lady was so angry at me that she went to the landlord and told him I was running a business that probably involved prostitution.

A few days later, the landlord served me with a "notice of eviction," which meant that I had to appear in landlord-tenant court. He charged that I was violating the terms of my lease by running a business out of my apartment; I responded by denying everything. My lawyer assured me that I was in no real danger unless the landlord was somehow able to prove that I was indeed running a business. He believed he could prove this by inspecting the premises, and to substantiate my innocence, I agreed to an inspection at ten in the morning on the following Monday. This way, he could see for himself what was going on in the apartment.

Personally, I found the prospect maddening, but the businesswoman in me knew that the problem was far from insurmountable. I arranged for a young electronics whiz, a friend of Claudette's who had previously worked for the phone company, to come to the office late Sunday night, after we had closed, to dismantle our entire phone system. With the help of a woman who lived across the hall, with whom I was friendly and who knew what we were up to, he and I carried all our records and all the telephone equipment into her apartment. At seven-thirty in the morning, just after my neighbor had left for work, my young associate and I moved over a mattress and some sheets from her place into the office. With a little creative decorating, we soon transformed the place into a modest but adequate facsimile of a residence. At nine forty-five, I sent Mr. Wizard out to have breakfast and told him to come back in an hour.

At exactly ten o'clock the landlord knocked on the door. He walked into the apartment, took a quick look around, and started to leave. "Wait a minute," I said sarcastically, "don't you want to see the bedroom? Don't you want to inspect the closets?" We had gone to a great deal of trouble to fix the place up for his visit, and I didn't want all our work to go for naught. More important, I didn't want the landlord to be able to claim, later, that he hadn't undertaken a complete inspection. As it happened, he came, he saw, and he left without a shred of evidence against us. It must have infuriated him.

One night, a week or so later, Liza answered the phone and was surprised to hear a man's voice on a phone line that was reserved for the girls and that none of our clients even knew about.

"Where did you hear of us?" she asked.

"Are you kidding?" said the caller. "I saw your sign on the street."

Assuming it was a crank call, Liza simply hung up.

Half an hour later, another man called on the same line and told Liza that he had read about us on a sign at Seventy-eighth and Broadway. Then a third caller said that he had seen our sign at Eightieth and Columbus.

At that point, Liza decided to call me at home. Although I found her story puzzling and vaguely upsetting, I didn't really pay much attention to it. Obviously something funny was going on, but I assumed that some wise guy had nothing better to do than harass us all evening on the telephone. The idea that there might actually *be* signs on the street was too ludicrous even to consider. I instructed Liza not to book any new clients for the rest of the night and told her I'd speak to her tomorrow.

The next morning, as usual, I walked over to the office. As I turned onto our street, I suddenly noticed a crude, handwritten sign taped to a lamppost:

SYDNEY BARROWS
aka
SHEILA DEVIN
Founder and Madam of
FINNES [sic], CACHET
Invites You to Try Her Girls
For 1984

Beautiful, Inteligent [sic] girls: They do
anything you wish.
Homes
or
Hotels

At the bottom of the sign were several of our phone
numbers—including the unpublished ones, as well as my
home number, my home address, and the address of our
office.

I was stunned and horrified. All I could think about
was that I had a number of friends in the neighborhood
and some of them might have seen this announcement
on their way to work that morning. I tore it down and
spent the next four hours on a systematic search of
every block on the West Side between Fifty-ninth Street
and Ninety-sixth. I found four more signs, three of which
were on our block, and I prayed that none had escaped
my eyes.

But what about the East Side? And who else might
have seen the signs? And how could I be sure that
somebody wasn't handing them out in Times Square?
And did this mean we were going to be robbed? My
heart was pounding all morning, and I have never been
so frightened in my life.

We never did learn who had put up these signs. But
whoever was responsible for this little joke, it was a
tremendous violation of my privacy as well as a powerful warning about our vulnerability. Despite all the precautions we had taken, we were suddenly exposed to
the whole world. Our address, especially, had always
been a well-kept secret. And now, I feared, that secret
was in the wrong hands.

Hoping it wasn't too late to take protective measures, I
sprang into action. I had an old friend whose father, a
former vice-squad sergeant named Marty, was now work-

ing as a private investigator. I called Marty and hired him as a consultant. Suddenly, I had a million questions: How much danger were we in? What new precautions could we take? What were the warning signs that a bust might be imminent? What kind of documentation did the police need in order to bust us? And if we *were* busted, what was the most likely scenario?

Marty knew a lot of the answers—and more. In the event of a bust, he told me, the police would be looking for client books and records, so we immediately started maintaining a second set of books—just in case. I had already had a carpenter install a secret compartment in the fireplace where we hid the real records. Now only the assistants were allowed to know where the hiding place was: after my experience with Elise, I didn't want to take any chances. From then on, when it was time to close up the office at the end of the night, any girl who was still there had to wait in the hall while the assistants hid the books.

Marty also explained that the police could not break into the office without prior evidence that a crime was being committed, and the only way they could gather that evidence was to actually bust some of the girls for prostitution. The only way to do *that*, as we already knew, was for an officer to pose as a client.

The solution was obvious: for the time being, we would accept no new clients unless they had been personally recommended by old ones. To avoid scaring away any potential new business during this period, we told callers that we were temporarily understaffed and that for the next few weeks we felt that it was only fair to give priority to our old clients.

What we hadn't counted on, however, was the impact that this seemingly innocuous announcement would have on the men who called us. It was absolutely unheard-of for an escort service to turn down business, and this new "policy" made us sound more exclusive and alluring than ever. If they take such good care of their old clients, a caller would think, I'd sure like to become one. We were in the dream situation of having more business than we could handle, and it was terribly frustrating to have to turn it down.

I called the girls together to tell them that Elise had "given us up," as they say in the law-enforcement world, and that we were clearly being watched. I didn't mention the signs, however, which would have terrified them, and about which they could do nothing in any case. "We're all in this together," I said, "and we've got to be more careful than ever. It's extremely important that you tell me everything you notice or hear about that might possibly lead to trouble. So *please* tell me if someone you know is dissatisfied. Anyone could turn out to be another Elise, so let me know what you see and hear, even if you have to leave me an anonymous note."

I continued, "Pay close attention to gossip and rumors, both from clients and from friends you may have who work for other agencies. The only way we learned that Elise squealed on us is that a friend of Claudette's was there, and she passed it on. So please keep your ears open and your mouth shut.

"Now as you know, in order to be arrested for prostitution in New York, all you have to do is *agree* to commit a sexual act for money. You never actually have to do it. You also know that the assistants never talk about sex with the clients, and that you are never supposed to talk about money. So at least in theory, you can't be arrested. Still, with everything that's been going on, I want you to be especially careful."

There were some questions: "Is it true that a cop isn't allowed to get totally undressed, and that if a man leaves his socks on, then he's probably not a legitimate client?"

"That's a common fallacy, and it's not true."

"If you ask a man if he's a cop, and he denies it, then is it true that he can't arrest you even if he is?"

"I wish that were the case, but it's not."

"Is it true that if a cop has sex with you, his testimony is invalid?"

"Yes, because that would mean that he, too, has committed a crime. But remember, he can arrest you just for *agreeing* to have sex for money."

The girls were clearly scared by the topic of the meeting, and they asked more questions than usual—in part, I think, because the longer the meeting ran, the more secure everybody felt. Until now, the operation had run so smoothly that we had all grown complacent, and we had temporarily lost sight of how vulnerable we really were.

As a further precaution, I hired Marty to sniff around and see if we were actually being investigated. Several weeks later, he called one night and asked me to meet him at a restaurant on Sixth Avenue. (Like many detectives, Marty would never talk on the phone.) He had checked around with his buddies on the squad and had turned up no evidence that we were in trouble. "But that's no guarantee," he warned. "There might be an investigation going on that my friends don't know about. It's also possible that they're hiding something from me."

Still, his report came as a relief, and as soon as he left the restaurant I went to a pay phone to call Ashley. "The coast is clear," I said. "You can book new clients."

"Good," she replied, "I've booked three already."

I was annoyed: "How *could* you?"

"It's all right," she said. "They all came recommended, and from American clients, too."

Now this was unusual, because American men rarely recommended us to their friends. For one thing, they don't usually have close male friendships. For another, most American men just can't admit that they "pay for it." European men, however, talk about sex much more openly with each other, not only because their friendships with other men tend to be more personal, but also because they come from a society where escort services are legal. For our European clients, tips about escort services were similar to tips about a new restaurant or an unusually good hotel.

According to Ashley, two of our new clients were booked for eight P.M., one with Denise and the other with Kelly. The third was booked an hour later with Corinne. At nine-ten, Ashley noticed that neither Denise nor Kelly had called in to say they were leaving—or that the client had asked them to stay longer. Following our procedure, she called the hotel room where Kelly's client was registered. There was no answer, so Ashley then called the front desk, verified his room number again, and put through another call. Again, no answer.

Ashley was nervous, but Kelly wasn't one of our more reliable girls, so Ashley assumed that she and the client had stepped out for a drink. She then called Denise, who was a stickler for detail, and when nobody answered there, either, Ashley turned pale. It was now nine-thirty, and she decided to call Corinne as well, to make sure that everything was all right. Here, too, nobody answered.

Both the escorts and the assistants had been given a special number to be used in case of emergencies. This number rang at an answering service, which had instructions to call me immediately with any urgent messages. If they couldn't reach me at home or at the office, they would track me down on my beeper. In four years, I had never received a single call from this service, and I can only imagine that the people who worked there thought of me as the least popular lady in all of New York.

Ashley tried me at home, and when nobody answered

she called the emergency number. "I want to leave a message for Sheila Devin," she said. "Please tell her that Ashley called, and that we've been busted."

Then Ashley called Risa Dickstein, my lawyer. When nobody answered at Risa's, she called Peter Fabricant, the backup attorney who would represent the girls. Peter thought that Ashley was overreacting, but he did agree to check with the police, who told him that Corinne was being held in one of the precincts. But there was still no sign of Denise and Kelly.

It had been difficult enough to track down Corinne, because the police kept moving the girls from one precinct to another. But Denise and Kelly had temporarily "disappeared" for another reason: to keep things simple, I had told all the girls to use "Fisher" as their last name. After Corinne had told the police she was Corinne Fisher, the two other girls realized that they couldn't use the same name, so they invented new ones on the spot. This made it impossible, at first, to find them.

As soon as Ashley learned that Corinne had been arrested, and that Denise and Kelly were almost surely in the same boat, she called every girl who was still out with a client. Interrupting several couples at awkward moments, she told the girls that she was leaving the office because she wasn't feeling well and that they should simply go home when the call was over. She then hid all of the books and records and closed up the office early.

Kelly, Denise, and Corinne had indeed been busted. Each of the officers who booked them, posing as a new client, had told Ashley that he had been referred by men whom Elise had seen shortly before I fired her.

Denise's guy had been very nervous, and he took so long to make the arrest that he finally received a phone call from one of his colleagues. Finally, with profuse apologies, he showed Denise his badge and arrested her.

Kelly's client actually had sex with her, which completely invalidated his testimony when his affidavit was reviewed by a judge. When three other officers burst into the room, Kelly jumped out of bed without a stitch of clothing to confront them.

"What do you think you're doing?" she demanded.

"We're arresting you for prostitution," one of them replied.

"How *dare* you?" she shouted. "Me? Prostitution? What are you talking about?"

Corinne's client had posed as an executive from Fortunoff. To prepare for his assignment he had spent a day at the company, memorizing details about the various stores in order to sound more credible.

During his conversation with Corinne, he said to her, "Listen, my wife hates oral sex. Do you think I'm sick for wanting to do it?"

"No," said Corinne, "It's perfectly normal."

"Does that mean that we could do it together?"

"Of course we can," she replied.

At which point he arrested her.

Just before the girls were taken away in the police car, one of the officers in the front seat turned around and said to Denise in a threatening tone, "You can tell Sheila Devin that Sergeant Elmo Smith is out to get her, and that pretty soon she's going to be sitting right where you are."

At the time, none of us knew the name Elmo Smith. I only wish I could say the same thing today.

The police kept moving the girls around, taking them first to a precinct, then to central booking, and finally to the courthouse. Because of a clerical error, their names were not on the court calendar, and it wasn't until the following night that we were able to bail them out.

As soon as it was clear that three girls had been busted, the lawyers advised me that the police might well be looking for me. By a stroke of luck, a good friend of mine was out of town for a month. I tracked him down and told him there was a bad leak in my apartment; could I stay in his place for a couple of weeks? He had no objection, so I was able to lie low until the whole thing blew over.

I spent the whole time on the phone. First, I had to console the three girls who were busted and arrange for their legal defense. (When the girls were first hired, I had promised to assume their fines and legal costs in the event that they were ever arrested as a result of their work for me.) I also had to keep in touch with all the other girls, who were suddenly out of a job and who hadn't ever really expected that we would be busted. I hadn't expected it, either, but I had always known that it was a possibility, and I fully expected that we would be back in operation within a few weeks.

But before we could open the office again, Denise, Corinne, and Kelly had to return to court to face prostitution charges. Kelly's case came up first, and the judge quickly dismissed it. At that point, one of the prosecutors ran up to the bench. "Your Honor," he said, "the police have been engaged in a major undercover operation, and we need more time on this case."

The judge made it clear that she didn't consider a prostitution case to be high on her list of judicial priorities—especially compared to the real and violent criminals who appeared before her. "Undercover?" she said sardonically. "I can just imagine."

"Really, Your Honor," said the prosecutor. "These girls are part of a major prostitution ring."

Reluctantly, the judge agreed to postpone the case for two weeks.

When the girls returned to court, the judge dismissed all of the charges. Not only are first offenders treated leniently in prostitution cases, but there was nothing in the girls' dress or demeanor to suggest that they were really prostitutes. The judge found the charges so ridiculous that she even gave the assistant D.A. a little lecture: "Can't you see that these are nice women? And don't you people have anything better to do than to arrest these people and ruin their lives?"

Until the case was settled, we had no choice but to close the office and turn off the answering machines. When we opened again at the end of April, we decided it would be foolish to scare the clients by telling them about the bust, so we explained instead that we had been having problems with the landlord—that much was true—and that he had illegally changed our locks.

We were thrilled to be back in business and earning money again. But only three weeks later we were hit with another disaster when Jason, a manufacturer from the south and one of our original clients, called up and said, "You better check the girls, because I just found out that I have gonorrhea. I think I picked it up three weeks ago when I was in Florida, and I saw several of your girls when I was in New York."

Strange as it may seem, this was the first time we ever had to worry about a sexually transmitted disease. And it wasn't just us, for despite what the public seems to believe, most escort services have never experienced health problems.

I immediately sent all of the girls to the doctor for tests. Most of them used my own gynecologist, who was very understanding toward working girls. Three girls showed a positive result, and all three had recently been to see Jason.

"I'm going to prescribe penicillin for everybody," said the doctor.

"But I thought only three girls were infected," I said.

"Only three that I can be sure of," he said. "But

these tests have an accuracy rate of only forty percent, so I'd rather not take any chances."

I called my local pharmacist. "Please don't ask any questions," I said, "but my doctor is going to call and give you an identical prescription for twenty different girls." The pharmacist told me later that during one three-hour period the next afternoon, twenty lovely girls, who all seemed to know each other, trooped into his store for their penicillin, and that this was the most exciting thing that had happened in the fifteen years he had been in business.

I wish that had been the end of it, but in the two weeks since those three girls had seen Jason, they had each seen at least half a dozen other men. And these men had been seen by some of our *other* girls. In our business, it doesn't take much before you have a full-scale epidemic on your hands—or wherever.

We kept the office open, but the assistants told every man who called that we were totally booked because a contingent of diplomats had reserved all our girls for the entire week. Meanwhile, we went back and pored over our records to retrace everybody's steps. We identified over a hundred clients who were at risk, and the assistants started calling them.

It was unprecedented for us to call clients, especially for something like this, but the situation was so serious that we had no choice. If a women answered, we would hang up immediately. If the client answered, we would ask if he had noticed any problems recently.

"Like what?"

"This is difficult to talk about, but we feel an obligation to tell you. We have had a bit of a health problem; one of our girls was exposed from a client who had seen someone in another city. All of our girls have been treated, and you may want to see a doctor as well."

Because gonorrhea has a three-week incubation period, we explained that if the client planned to call us again in the next twenty-one days, he would have to show us a clean bill of health from his doctor. This was, of course, an incredibly awkward phone call to make, but it was clearly the only right thing to do.

A few clients were outraged, and we never heard from them again. But most took it very well, although it was obviously a shock, especially when they realized that we could have gotten away without calling them. One man asked us to tear up a check he had made out to us the previous evening. "My wife just told me that she's infected," he said. "I'm going through a lot of problems on account of this, and I think you owe me one." I agreed.

The problem was equally hard for the girls, especially those whose boyfriends didn't know what they were really doing three nights a week. Two girls quit on the spot. Others concocted elaborate excuses: Montgomery "admitted" to her boyfriend that she and her roommate had been intimate and that her roommate had received a call from her boyfriend saying that *he* had it. Given the choice, it was obviously easier for Montgomery to say she was bisexual than to admit to being a call girl.

About six weeks later, just as we were getting back on track, Jason called a second time to say that his wife had just been to the doctor, that she had gonorrhea, and that she must have passed it back to him. Apparently, he hadn't ever told her about the problem in the first place. Unfortunately, Jason had recently been to New York, where he had seen four more of our girls.

This time the problem was more serious, and I had to take more drastic measures. I knew that some of our clients occasionally called other agencies and that if they had contracted gonorrhea from our girls back in May, they might well have given it to the girls at other escort services. And this, in turn, meant that we would keep getting it back. By now, it probably really *was* an epidemic, which meant that the only way to solve it was by a concerted, cooperative effort among all the agencies.

During the years I was in business, I was occasionally in touch with my counterparts from several of the better agencies in town. Whenever a client bounced a check, for example, we would quickly pass the word so that nobody else would get burned. From time to time, one of the other owners would call to warn me about a client who had tried to rough up a girl or who had refused to pay, and we would always post a big sign on the wall and enter him on our "do not send" list—just in case. But mostly we called each other to warn about girls—girls who stole money and girls who stole clients. Although both situations were fairly uncommon, over the years I was surprised to find that I was ripped off more often by girls than by clients.

Now, despite the nasty things I've said about the other agencies, I honestly expected that in a crisis of this magnitude, they would take the problem seriously and work together with me to solve it. But I was shocked by some of the things that my colleagues told me over the phone, and I promptly wrote them down in a notebook:

"These girls are old enough to know what they're doing. If they get into trouble, it's their own stupid fault."

"Nobody has called to tell me they've had a problem, so I'm not concerned."

"These guys know the risks they're taking, and I can't feel sorry for them."

"Listen, I've got enough to worry about. I can't take the time to worry about this, too."

"It's all part of the business."

"You shouldn't get so involved, Sheila. These girls don't worry about you."

And then my absolute favorite, which I still can hardly believe: "My girls know better than to bother me about something like this."

To my chagrin, not one of the other owners would agree to even *tell* their girls that there was a problem going around, let alone encourage them to seek any treatment for it. The only thing I could do, then, was to be as honest as possible with my own clients.

Rather than discuss the matter on the phone, I drew up a form letter that each girl would give to her client at the beginning of her visit. I hated to put any of this in writing, so the challenge here was to be as clear as possible without being overly explicit:

Dear Friends,

I have just become aware that New York City is in the throes of a rather serious "health problem," and that this problem is affecting many employees and clients in our field. I have spoken to several people who head up businesses similar to mine, as well as to our doctor and the NYC Board of Health, and all of them have confirmed that we are currently in the midst of a minor epidemic. I have taken steps to ensure that all of my staff is completely healthy, but I was unable to elicit the same concern or action from any of the people who run other services.

In order to protect the health of my young ladies and my other valued clients, I would like to ask you to seriously consider using protective measures until this problem clears up. Should you call upon the services of a similar business while you are in town, I would strongly suggest you take these same precautions, because as of this writing, none of them have ensured—or plan to ensure—that their staffs are healthy.

I hope you can appreciate how very difficult it is for me to write this letter. My old friends know how conscientiously I have worked to set and maintain high standards, and I would like to take this opportunity to thank all of them for their support and trust over the years. And I would like to welcome any new friends with the assurance that I will continue to provide the finest quality service possible, both now and in the future.

Respectfully yours,
[signed] Sheila

The letter would be given to all of our old clients and to a new client only after he was determined to be safe on other grounds. I realized this would be awkward for the girls, but I saw no practical alternative. "Don't be afraid of being embarrassed," I advised them. "In fact, the more embarrassed and uncomfortable you act—and you won't have to do much acting—the more sympathy and cooperation you'll get."

In a memo, I reminded the girls to be sure they had a supply of condoms and urged them to buy the finest quality available. "It's bad enough we're asking this favor," I noted, "without your showing up with brand X." Naturally, a girl had the option of leaving if the client refused to go along with this request.

Although I told the girls about my conversations with the heads of the other agencies, I asked them not to be heavy-handed about putting down the competition in front of the men, in part because I didn't think the clients would believe them. Instead of dwelling on the negative, I suggested that they might want to accentuate the positive by stressing how fortunate they felt to be working for a place that really did care about both the girls and the clients. I also asked them to keep me posted on the clients' reaction to the letter and to let me know if any of the language seemed offensive or inappropriate. If so, I said, I would be happy to rewrite it.

I still had to decide what to do about Jason. I greatly appreciated the fact that he had called us in the first place to tell us about the problem, but when he neglected to tell his wife, and when he was reinfected by her and passed it around a second time, I was furious. If a married man is going to sleep with somebody other than his wife, he has to accept the possibility that there may be adverse consequences. It was actually a lucky thing that she had developed a noticeable sore, or we might never have known where the second round came from.

By not telling his wife about the problem, Jason had shown an irresponsible disregard not only toward our girls, but also toward the other clients, whose wives were not likely to take this sort of news very well. This was the type of problem that could conceivably break up a marriage or, at the very least, cause an enormous amount of hurt and mistrust.

That's how I felt about Jason, but I still wasn't sure what to do. The logical option was to make him a DNS—a "Do Not Send"—but I decided against that because I didn't want him to conclude he had made a mistake by being honest. Instead, I asked the assistants to let him know that the girls were so upset about what had happened that they all preferred not to see him. At the same time, I also told them to voice our appreciation for his forthrightness.

Several months earlier, before all of these problems had overwhelmed us, I had planned to throw a fifth anniversary party for the girls. There was a lot to celebrate, and I had looked forward to giving out funny little prizes to honor, for example, the girl with the highest heels, the girl who spent the most time in the office, and the girl who most often called us collect from a phone booth because she never carried any change. But with the bust in March and the health problem shortly thereafter, I couldn't afford to throw any parties.

One Sunday in August, Ginny, whom I had recently hired as my personal assistant, asked me to meet her for brunch at an East Side restaurant to go over some paperwork. When I walked in she brought me upstairs, where I was greeted by a gaggle of girls yelling, "Surprise!" and throwing confetti. I had been unable to give a party for them, so now they were throwing one for me.

There was food and drink and genuine merriment. An hour into the festivities, I was momentarily terrified when a uniformed policeman walked in. Fortunately, it was a gag: in reality, he turned out to be a male stripper the girls had hired as a joke.

After he had finished his little routine, he turned to us and asked, "So what kind of business are you all in?"

There was an unusually long silence. Finally Melody said, "Us? Oh, we're in the entertainment business."

At the end of the party, the girls presented me with a beautiful set of wineglasses for the office. "You've always been generous with food and champagne," Liza announced. "But enough already with those damn plastic cups!"

Several of the girls gave short performances. Melody performed a monologue from the play *Tribute,* in which a call girl addresses her clients, who have thrown a banquet in her honor. Suzie did a rendition of "I Enjoy Being a Girl," but with all the champagne she forgot most of the words.

Ginny got up and told a few off-color jokes, including one that got a good laugh: "I hear the post office is going to issue a new stamp to commemorate prostitution. It's going to cost thirty cents—forty if you want to lick it.''

And Liza stopped the show with a song called ''Old Friends'' from the musical *I'm Getting My Act Together and Taking It on the Road*.

I found the party enormously gratifying. I was especially moved that nearly all of the girls were there, and on a beautiful Sunday in August, too. Sometimes you wonder whether people appreciate all the things you do for them, and then something like this happens and you feel happily foolish for ever having had any doubts.

Chapter Twelve

With our "health problem" under control, I could now turn my full attention to finding a new office. We had temporarily overcome the legal difficulties with our landlord, but there was no reason to believe that he was going to abandon his ongoing attempt to evict us. As long as we remained in our old location, we were living on borrowed time.

Ideally, I would have liked to close down the business until we could reopen in a new location. But for simple economic reasons, this was impossible. Our bank account was severely depleted because we had already been forced to shut down three times in the past few months—for six weeks after the March bust and twice more in the early summer due to the health problem.

But expenses don't close down when you do, and ours continued relentlessly. There were legal bills from the March bust, as well as rent, telephone expenses, and office supplies—not to mention our considerable advertising commitment. I had opted for yearly contracts to save money, so we were obligated to pay on a monthly basis whether or not we were actually open for business.

Although we couldn't afford to shut down, we could— and did—step up our security. This time we added a wrinkle: if a new client called us from a hotel, the girl who saw him would insist on seeing his airplane ticket. If the client was local, we didn't have to worry because Marty had already assured me that the police never used private apartments for prostitution busts.

If ever there was a task I wasn't looking forward to, it was searching for a new office. Trying to find an apartment in Manhattan is difficult under normal conditions, but it's even more of a challenge when you can't quite explain to the real estate broker that you prefer a building without a doorman (they notice everything) and that you'd like a place on the first floor, preferably in the front, to minimize your exposure to the other tenants.

There were other considerations as well: in order to retain the same phone numbers, our new office had to be within a few blocks of the old one. Finally, we couldn't afford more than a thousand dollars a month in rent, which in Manhattan is not a lot for a one-bedroom apartment. With all of these conditions, plus New York's notorious 2 percent vacancy rate, it wasn't going to be easy.

It would have been easier, of course, if we could have considered a commercial space, but that was not a realistic option. First, commercial landlords can raise the rent as often and as high as they wish, and the tenants have no recourse but to accept the situation. Second, in some commercial buildings you can't get in after certain hours, which would have been intolerable for us. Finally, we needed a kitchen as well as a shower, which left us with no choice but to rent an apartment.

One of the landlords I met along the way showed me several apartments. Because he seemed like a reasonably liberal and open person, and because I knew I couldn't risk another landlord problem, I swallowed hard and told him the truth: I was running an escort service. I stressed that we were open only a few hours a day and that only a handful of girls would be coming to the office each night. I said nothing about sex, but I could see that he knew how to read between the lines.

He took me over to a fabulous ground-floor apartment on West Seventy-fourth Street and told me I could have it for $575 a month—provided that I also came up with a $7,500 "finder's fee." At that point we didn't have this kind of money, but I knew this place was a real find and I had to grab it. So we made a deal: I would pay him $5,000 in cash, and he would take out the rest in trade—at the wholesale rate.

I had never made this kind of arrangement before, but I was desperate for that apartment. Besides, it didn't seem like that much of a burden—only a total of twenty-five hours with the girls, for which I would, of course, reimburse them. As it turned out, however, the girls were not crazy about the plan because the landlord was a far cry from the sophisticated, urbane, courteous men they had grown accustomed to. He was interested in only one thing, which made them feel cheap. Worse, he used to meet them at a seedy, semifurnished apartment until I objected, at which point he switched over to a friend's place. All in all, it was not an episode I was proud of.

Having learned my lesson at the old office, I went to great pains and expense to make sure that in our new place we wouldn't call attention to ourselves. With the girls talking and watching television late at night, it was important that the office be completely soundproof. I began by having the ceilings lowered and adding six inches of insulation along the wall we shared with the other ground-floor apartment. Because there were also two basement apartments beneath us, I installed wall-to-wall carpeting with a thick pad underneath. I brought in a carpenter to build three new desks with hidden compartments, and I also used the occasion to install a completely new telephone system with a custom-made answering-machine setup. To pay for all of this, I liqui-dated my personal cash management account at Paine Webber and put my long-term savings plan on hold.

On the second floor of our new building, a small modeling agency was being run out of somebody's apart-ment, which meant that the other tenants were accus-tomed to seeing pretty young girls coming in and out the front door. This would be helpful in the afternoons, but after six P.M., when the modeling agency closed, we'd be on our own.

The girls loved the new office, which was cleaner, larger, and airier than the old one. It also seemed to be more secure—a point that was driven home to us in our final weeks at the old place. One night, while Jaime was trying to call back a client, she heard a crackling noise on the phone, followed by a male voice saying, "Shit, I can't get the damn thing connected." For months we had been worried about our phones being tapped, but this was virtually an announcement that we were being bugged.

I got in touch with Marty immediately. "Sorry," he said, "I don't do phones." Instead, he referred me to John, a colleague who specialized in detecting wiretaps. Most of John's business came from corporations that were trying to prevent industrial espionage, and he had several dozen clients whose phones and offices he would sweep on a monthly basis.

The next afternoon, John came over to the office and hooked up his testing equipment to our phone lines. By measuring the strength of the electrical current in the wires, he was able to determine whether somebody had tapped into our lines. According to his meter, four of our ten lines registered dramatically low readings, which was almost a sure indication that somebody was listen-ing in. John then attached his machine to each of these lines and sent volts of electricity shooting back through the wires, so that any tape recorders that might be monitoring our conversations would be temporarily disabled.

When all this was done, we went over to check my own apartment, where John discovered that here, too, there was a tap on the line. Together we went down to the basement, where he located my phone line among those of the other tenants. "There's your problem," he said, pointing to two little wires that led up the wall and into a portion of the basement that was locked.

"That's it?" I said. "Let's cut the wires."

"No way," he said. "If this is a legal police tap, you could be arrested for tampering with it. Besides, if you cut the wires, they'll just be back tomorrow to replace them. The important thing is that now you know they're listening."

Believe me, it wasn't easy to walk away from those wires. From then on, whenever I had to make a sensitive phone call, I went down the hall to the apartment of Jimmy Roe, a neighbor with whom I had long been friendly. Jimmy and I kept a key to each other's apartments, so even when he wasn't home I had access to his telephone.

A few days later, still at the old office, we started receiving calls for a girl who lived downstairs in our building, and she started receiving ours; somehow, the lines had been switched. Here again I was lucky, for she and I happened to be friendly, and she had been vaguely aware of what we were up to. Still, she couldn't have been too pleased to have strange men calling her at midnight, wanting to know if she accepted credit cards.

We called the phone company to report the problem. Three days later, when the repairmen finally came over, one of them came up from the basement and asked if we had been trying to fix the problem ourselves.

"What do you mean?" I asked.

"Somebody has been down there, fiddling with the wires," he said. I just gave him a blank look.

We had always been exceedingly careful about what we said on the phone, but after these latest developments I initiated a policy of active disinformation. "How was dinner?" the assistants would ask the girls who called in. "Was his wife there? How were his children?" The assistants got a kick out of this improvisational theater, and so did some of the girls. But under the pressure of all the ringing phones, we soon became lax about the charade and reverted to our old habits.

We moved to our new office in July, and the telephone problems stopped immediately. But the dispute with our old landlord was still going on and unfortunately, once you're part of the legal system, the process has a life of its own. Although we had moved out of the old apartment, I still had a lease and was hoping to sublet the apartment to a friend who had recently moved to town. On September 10, 1984, I was required to appear once again in housing court.

While I was there, I was vaguely aware of a tall man in an off-white linen suit. He was sitting with the landlord and the landlord's lawyer, and he seemed to be paying particular attention to me. During the proceedings, as the lawyers were drafting a settlement that would have let me pass on the apartment to a friend, he wanted me to admit in the document that I ran a prostitution ring. Risa told him he was crazy. She also wondered why he was so interested in this particular topic, and she asked the landlord's lawyer to kindly identify the members of her party. The landlord's lawyer assured us that everybody in the group, including the man in the linen suit, was associated with her law firm.

The negotiations continued all day. Late in the afternoon, the agreement was completed; I had won the sublet right, and our case was finally called. All of us were sitting at the counsel's table, and the two lawyers were discussing the final settlement language with the judge.

While this dull but necessary legal talk went on, my eyes started to wander around the room. I noticed that the suspicious stranger was now seated at the back of the courtroom, still watching me. If he really was part of the legal team, I wondered, why wasn't he up here with the rest of us?

I asked Risa to find out who he was and what he was doing there. "Your Honor," she said to the judge, "we realize that this is an open courtroom, but we would like to know who that gentleman is."

As soon as he heard her question, the mystery man shot out of the room.

"Who was that man?" the judge asked the landlord.

"Do I have to tell you?" asked the landlord.

"Yes, you do," the judge replied.

"He's my best friend," said the landlord.

"And what's your best friend's name?" asked Risa.

"Do I have to answer that?" the landlord said.

By now the judge was visibly angry. "I have the power to hold you in contempt," he warned.

"He's Sergeant Elmo Smith of the New York City Vice Squad," said the landlord.

Click!

For some reason I no longer remember, Risa asked me to leave the courtroom and wait for her outside. I soon spotted Sergeant Smith at a phone booth, and I hid behind the concession stand until he finished his call—which I wasn't able to hear. I decided to follow him out of the building to see what he was up to. As I watched, he walked up to a decrepit-looking young man who was loitering on the corner. They talked for a while, and then Smith crossed the street and spoke to what I assumed was another undercover officer in a van. Five minutes went by, and then the two of them walked off together.

Presumably, Sgt. Smith had come to court that day to see who Sheila Devin really was and to try to get a legal admission from me. He and his cohorts had probably intended to follow me as I left the building. But now that the jig was up, he seemed to have abandoned his plan to follow me—at least for now.

Risa, however, was not so sure. When we returned to her office, she told me that Elmo Smith might be planning to follow me home to see where I lived or where our new office was. I called Jimmy Roe, my neighbor down the hall. "This is an emergency," I said, "and when there's time, I'll explain everything. But right now, I need to ask you a huge favor. Would you please go into my apartment and bring me a change of clothes so that I can come back home without being recognized?"

Jimmy was wonderful. He immediately dropped the hundred other things he had to do that day and told me to meet him at the Performing Arts Library in Lincoln Center. Not only was it near our apartment building, but if anybody was following me there from Risa's office, the Lincoln Center complex had so many exits it would be easy to slip away unnoticed.

Five minutes after I arrived, Jimmy showed up with a shopping bag. I couldn't believe it: he had picked out a complete outfit, consisting of a pink jumpsuit, matching shoes, socks, and a handbag. He had even brought appropriate jewelry and a hat! When I emerged from the ladies' room with my hair in pigtails and my mouth outlined in bright red lipstick, I looked like an outtake from "I Love Lucy."

Jimmy and I walked home together, but Sgt. Smith and his smithereens were nowhere to be seen. I must admit that I was a little disappointed. Here I had gone to so much trouble to make a good entrance—and the theater was empty.

The next day, Risa filed an official complaint against

Sgt. Smith, claiming that he had spent the entire day in civil court, on taxpayers' time, pretending to be a lawyer. Had I been a suspected terrorist, perhaps his actions would have been justified. But if Smith was merely helping a landlord get rid of a tenant in order to raise the rent on an apartment, then his behavior was highly inappropriate. The counsel for the police department assured Risa that he would look into the matter.

Risa also checked around with her contacts and dug up some information on Elmo Smith. He had started out in the 1960s as an undercover cop and had infiltrated leftist groups. In 1965 he infiltrated a small radical group which planned to blow up several national monuments—including the Statue of Liberty. According to one report, Smith was decorated for his actions in the case. But other sources claimed that he had been overzealous and that because of him, some defendants had been acquitted. In any event, he was later transferred to the vice squad, which in police circles is contemptuously referred to as the "pussy posse."

By early October, we were comfortably settled in our new office and starting to enjoy our traditional busy season. In anticipation of the opening of the U.N. General Assembly, I had recently hired several new girls and two new assistants. Between the new girls, the new office, my worries about Sergeant Smith, and the need for a more stringent policy on new clients, it was time for a general meeting.

Because the meeting was mandatory for all the girls, I scheduled two sessions, at four P.M. and again at six, so that everybody could attend. I began by introducing each of the new girls, as well as Claire and Lorraine, the new assistants. When that was taken care of, I quickly ran down the lists of items on my agenda.

"Now that the summer is over," I began, "some of you will be needing new coats. Keep in mind that the

Columbus Day sales are coming up this weekend. You'll find that Saks and Macy's have the best selections.

"I also want to remind everybody that New York will soon be experiencing its annual stocking shortage. As some of you know, so many people buy stockings for Christmas that they generally clean out the stores. Because all the stores take inventory in January, they don't usually reorder until February—when all the stockings disappear again because of Valentine's Day. So if you don't pick up extras soon, you might not find any for quite a while.

"Some of you may have noticed that we've been running low on champagne, so I'm happy to tell you that I've just ordered four cases of Dom Pérignon, which should be delivered within the week. That's the good news. The bad news, for you new girls, is that the champagne is for the clients, not for you. If you're lucky, you'll get to drink some of it. As most of you already know, we always bring a bottle of champagne to a good client on his birthday, or to thank an old client for sending us somebody new."

Some of our clients had been complaining that a few of the girls had been wearing too much makeup, so I took a few moments to review some basic cosmetic tips. These were points I had covered in each girl's reinterview, but I had given them so much information back then that they couldn't possibly remember it all. At the meeting, I advised the girls to use soft-colored blush and a lipliner pencil, and I made a special point about the importance of neutral eye shadow. "Nobody looks good with pink eye shadow," I said. "Or even blue or green. If God had wanted you to have green eyelids, He would have issued them to you."

When these tips and announcements were out of the way, I devoted the rest of the meeting to our new security arrangements:

"Most of you already know how to deal with hotel security, but let me go over a few points just to be safe. Above all, you don't want to look suspicious. So if you have long hair, you might want to pile it up under a hat and perhaps put on a pair of glasses so that you don't look so attractive. Another possibility is to keep your good shoes in your briefcase and walk into the hotel in a really ugly pair of flats, or in canvas, Chinese-style sandals. Believe me, nobody is going to follow a women who wears those.

"Another good ploy, if you're coming into the hotel between, say, ten-thirty and midnight, is to carry a *Playbill* with you. Please make sure it's from a current show. But the best thing you can carry is a briefcase—in case any of you still don't have one—because ever since large numbers of women started traveling on business, escorts who carry briefcases have had almost no problems.

"Sometimes, if they suspect what you're up to, they'll follow you into the elevator to see where you're going. If you get into an elevator and a man follows you, wait for him to press the button first. If he doesn't press any button, get out of the elevator. If he gets out, too, go right up to the front desk and say, 'Excuse me, but I have a business appointment upstairs, and I'm running a bit late. I'm a little nervous about getting in the elevator because there's a strange man who keeps following me. Could you call a bellhop or somebody to escort me up?' If that doesn't throw them off, nothing will.

"If you do get stopped by hotel security, don't get all indignant and huffy, because that's what they're expecting. And don't act guilty, either. Act bewildered, as though you don't understand what's going on. If you can speak a foreign language, this is the time to start jabbering away. Be sure to drop in a few English words like 'diplomat,' 'embassy,' and 'United Nations.' These people all have immunity, and if the hotel personnel believe you're part of that world, they won't bother you.

"In most cases, they'll threaten to call the police if you don't cooperate. As soon as you hear the word 'police,' you sould say, 'That's a terrific idea. Yes, I *insist* you call the police, because I want to tell them how you're keeping me here against my will.' That should change their minds.

"Now I want to say a few words about the possibility of entrapment by police posing as clients. As you know, any new client is a potential undercover policeman. It's relatively easy for these guys to get a fake driver's license and a credit card, but they're not likely to bring along an airplane ticket. So you must be sure to ask any new out-of-town client to show you either his plane ticket, a train or bus ticket, or rental-car papers. Unless he's obviously foreign, he should also be able to show you his driver's license. If you have any doubts, ask to see a credit card, too. If he's a residential client, though, you don't have to worry, because I have it on good authority that the police never conduct a prostitution bust in a private apartment.

"As you all know, you can be arrested merely for *agreeing* to have sex for money, so never give any indication that you're going to accept a payment. If he tries to offer you money at the beginning, don't say, 'Oh, I'll take that later,' because that means that you're eventually going to take it and that's still enough to get you in trouble. Instead, say, 'Oh, no, put that away.' In the event that he has a tape recorder going, you can always tell the judge that the client was exposing himself.

"If he has a plane ticket, but you're still suspicious, look around to see if he has any clothes in the closet—or any luggage. If you're still unsure, tell him you have to blow your nose, then go into the bathroom and check around to see if he has any toiletries. Keep a special watch for paper bags or takeout coffee cups, because on a stakeout the police bring in their own sandwiches and coffee. Real businessmen who stay at hotels always order room service, so that's a dead giveaway. Another clue is his socks: most legitimate clients wear thinner socks rather than the knitted, heavier kind.

"Now I cannot emphasize enough how incredibly important it is that these policy requirements never be revealed to anybody who doesn't work for us. That goes for old clients, too, who may simply be curious as to how we avoid trouble, and for girlfriends who may work for other agencies. You know how people talk, and as soon as the opposition knows our battle plan, they can get fake tickets, credit cards, or whatever they need to entrap us.

"That's why we never alert a new client ahead of time that we're going to be asking to see any ID, tickets, or anything else. On the contrary: you should always give him the impression that these precautions are *your* idea, and that they have nothing to do with our policy. That way, if you do end up with a police officer, he'll just assume that he's had the bad luck of ending up with a girl who's paranoid, and that he'll be able to get us next time.

"If a client has no tickets and no rental-car papers, there's a *very* strong likelihood that he's an imposter. If that's the case, don't even consider asking to see any identification; just get yourself out of there. Above all, don't explain to him that if he could only show you a certain document, you could be sure that he's not a cop, because then he'll come right back the next day with the correct 'proof.' Remember, they can't form a counterintelligence operation against us unless they are aware of what measures we're taking.

"As you know, our phones have been tapped in the recent past, so you must always be extremely careful about what you say on the phone. Obviously, there's no point in having code words if you use them in such a way that it's obvious what you're talking about. For example, one of you left the following message on the answering machine: 'I can't work tonight because I got my migraine and it will probably last until Thursday.' Come on; these guys are not stupid! Never say anything on the phone that you wouldn't want your mother to hear at your trial. Because these tapes really *could* be played at somebody's trial—maybe yours, maybe mine. So let's be careful out there, okay?

"In the awful event that the police come to the office and you're there when it happens, do your best to put any incriminating evidence in the shredder. They will probably try to force their way in, and if they do, everybody should be sitting in the living room to make it harder for them to identify the assistants. I've also given the assistants another working name to be used in case of a bust, so that their names will not sound familiar in case the police have already spoken to them on the phone.

"Now I hate to talk about this next item, but we do have to cover every possibility. If for any horrible reason something *does* happen and you find yourself in legal custody, it's okay to recognize or let on that you know any of the other girls who may also be in legal custody. However, under no circumstances must you *ever* let on that you recognize me or any of the assistants. That's because we would be charged with promoting prostitution, which is a felony, and we would risk going to jail. Prostitution, as I'm sure you know by now, is a less serious offense—especially if it's your first arrest. That's why you must look through us just as you would a stranger. Don't whisper to each other, look at each other knowingly, or in any way indicate that you have recognized us. But remember that to *totally* avoid looking at us is just as dead a giveaway as saying hello. Just act casually curious, but mostly uninterested, as you would with any stranger.

"Please be sure that you still have the emergency phone number that I gave you when you first signed up. If you're arrested, you'll be allowed to make one phone call, and you should call that number and say that you have an emergency message for Sheila Devin. Give the operator your working name, your exact location, and the name of the arresting officer. And then try to stay calm—because no matter how frightened you are, you must remember that I'll be working with our lawyers to get you out."

One of the new girls at that meeting was Blake, whom I had hired only the previous week. She was a slender and glamorous nineteen-year-old who was so beautiful that I had decided to make her a C girl. All she lacked was the appropriate wardrobe, so we made a date to meet at four o'clock on October 11 on the third floor of Saks. We went on a real shopping spree, and in the next two hours I helped her pick out a cashmere coat, an elegant suit, a smashing hot-pink cocktail dress, shoes, and all the other appropriate accessories. When we were done, I picked up a pair of earrings for myself to go with the outfit I had planned to wear that evening, when I had a blind date scheduled with Barry, the friend of a friend.

We moved briskly, with an eye on the clock. Although Saks stays open late on Thursdays, Blake had to leave early to study for a big test the next day. I was also in a rush because I had to go home and dress for dinner.

That night, while I was enjoying my evening with Barry down in the Village, a number of new clients called us. One man was staying at the Tudor, which wasn't on our list of hotels, so Ashley politely explained to him that we could not send anybody. Another caller was at the Penta, where the security guards have a reputation for being hard on working girls. Ashley told him, too, that she was terribly sorry, but she couldn't send any of our girls over there.

A little later on, another new client called from the Parker Meridien, which was on our approved list. Ashley suggested that he might want to see Denise or Kelly.

"Do you have anyone else?" he asked.

Suzie was on that night, and although she didn't normally see new clients, she had told Ashley that she was in desperate need of money. So Ashley described Suzie, explaining that as a C girl, she was more expensive than the others and worked on a two-hour minimum. This was no problem, the client said, and they agreed that she would be at his hotel suite at seven. Ashley then called Suzie to tell her about the booking and to reiterate our new security precautions in detail. She made a special point of reminding Suzie to ask for his plane ticket.

As soon as Suzie arrived at the Parker Meridien, she went up to room 3418, which was a luxurious two-room suite, and introduced herself to the client, a tall, dark, muscular man with a mustache. Then she asked to see his plane ticket.

"My plane ticket?" he said. "I don't have it up here with me. I left it down in the hotel safe with some other important papers." Foolishly, Suzie let the matter drop. The client then ordered champagne from room service. Suzie told me later that she had a strong premonition something was wrong and that when she went into the bathroom to freshen up, she hid her driver's license in the wastebasket. She shouldn't have been carrying ID in the first place, of course, but then Suzie was never very good about following the rules.

While they were talking and drinking champagne, Suzie repeatedly asked her host if he were a police officer. She had never asked this question before, but she was under the mistaken impression that if he really *was* a police officer and then lied about it, he wouldn't be able to arrest her. One of the girls had asked this very question at a meeting some months earlier, but Suzie had been out of town at the time.

After nearly an hour, Suzie's client asked her if she'd like to get more comfortable. She said she'd be happy to, but first she went over to the door and put on the chain—which she had also never done before. As she was undressing in the bedroom, her host got up and said that he had forgotten something back in the living room.

Suzie watched in horror as he walked to the door and took off the chain.

"What are you doing?" she cried.

Without answering, he opened the door and let in two men who had been waiting in the hall. "We're police officers," he snapped. "You're under arrest. We'll wait for you here while you get your clothes on."

Back at the office, Ashley and Claire were busy answering the phones. They were looking forward to a busy night, as the previous evening had been our biggest ever. One client alone had spent $3,000 on three girls; there had also been three dinner calls at $500 each and numerous multiple-hour calls.

At eight-thirty, Kate, who had stopped by the office to visit, left to see a client at the Halloran House. A few minutes later Sonya came in, changed into a pair of jeans, and went into the back room to settle up her account with the assistants.

She was in a cheerful mood, having just returned from a one–hour late-afternoon call that the client had decided to extend to three hours. Both she and the client had been having a wonderful time—so good, in fact, that Sonya had forgotten to call the office after the first hour, and Ashley had had to phone the client to see if he wanted her to stay longer. At that particular moment, the two of them had been enjoying a long bath together, and the client decided on the spot to keep her for two more hours. By the end of her visit, he was asking Sonya to move in with him because he had a special fondness for European women. When the three hours were up and Sonya called in to say she was leaving, Ashley asked her to pick up some potato chips on the way back.

At a few minutes before nine, the phones had grown quiet, and Ashley, Sonya, and Claire were munching potato chips and watching a PBS special on the paintings of Claude Monet. Suddenly, there was a loud knock on the door. Claire got up and looked through the peephole. When she saw a man standing there, she told Ashley.

"Who is it?" Ashley called.

"Police officer. Open up, we have a search warrant!"

Ashley immediately ran into the back room and started hiding the records. While Claire was furiously feeding papers into the shredder, Ashley and Sonya tried to push the desks back against the wall to ensure that our hiding places would be safe. (The desks had been pulled out by the man who was working on our answering machines, and nobody had thought to put them back.) But they were too heavy, so all three girls scurried back into the living room.

When it became obvious that nobody was going to open the door, the police officers started smashing it in with a sledgehammer. When they finally broke through a dozen men burst into the room. Leading the pack was Sergeant Elmo Smith, with his gun drawn.

The police snapped photographs of the office and took everything apart. One of them asked the girls to identify themselves. Sonya was first, and she didn't know what to say. Should she give her working name? Her real name? Should she say nothing?

Ashley came to the rescue. "Come on, Sonya," she

said. "Tell the man who you are." Poor Sonya was so frightened that she promptly forgot how to spell her last name.

During their search, the officers found a scrapbook that the girls had made after one of our trips to the country. There were snapshots on each page, and Jaime had written funny captions underneath each one.

One of the officers came to a picture of Ashley with her name written in below. He looked at Ashley, then back at the picture.

"So you're Ashley," he said to her.

Ashley told me later that she was dying to answer, "No shit, Sherlock." Wisely, she restrained herself and said nothing.

It took the police an hour to discover absolutely everything there was to find, after which they handcuffed the three girls and took them away. Along with the girls, they also removed the four cases of Dom Pérignon. In addition, they took our shredder, the typewriter, the telephones, and other office equipment. Among the items they confiscated—as listed in the police record—were three answering machines, five plastic file dividers, one Casio calculator, fourteen keys, two rubber stamps, six plain white notepads, one box of folder labels, forty-five white envelopes, and a Magic Marker. Left behind were two televisions, two fans, various electrical appliances, and my entire winter wardrobe, which I had stored in a closet because my apartment was so small. Over the next twenty-four hours, it all disappeared. (I later filed a claim against the city, since their negligence led to my loss. In these situations, the police are either supposed to seal the premises or leave an officer there to guard it.)

While the bust was in progress, Tess was on her way to the office to turn in a credit card slip. She was about to walk in when she noticed that the door was open and a number of men were milling about. One of them turned around and said, "Who are you?"

"Me?" said Tess. "I live downstairs. I heard a lot of commotion up here. What's going on?"

"It doesn't concern you," he replied. Tess was terrified, and she ducked into the stairway and went down to the basement, where she sat crumpled on the floor in tears. A moment later, one of the officers came down the stairs and found her there.

"What's the problem, lady?" he said.

"Can you believe it?" said Tess, making a quick recovery and rummaging through her pocketbook. "I don't have my keys. Could I ask you for a quarter so I can call my roommate at her boyfriend's?" He gave her the quarter and followed her back upstairs. Tess went outside and quickly hailed a cab.

"Drive," she said.

"Where to, lady?"

"Anywhere!"

Ashley, Sonya, and Claire were taken to a police station in Harlem, where they were fingerprinted and locked in a holding cell. Periodically, a police officer would call "Sheila" to see if anybody answered to that name. An hour or so later, Suzie was brought in, still crying. Remembering my security instructions, she introduced herself to the other girls and told them that she had been arrested for breaking and entering.

When Ashley saw Suzie, she was furious. Here was one of our ultraexpensive C girls, and she was dressed in a blue denim miniskirt and a sweat shirt to see a new client! Ashley, of course, had to pretend that she didn't know her. But later, when no officers were around, she said to Suzie, "Obviously we're no longer in business. But the last official thing I'm going to say to you is, how *dare* you go out looking like that!"

At one point, Sergeant Smith asked Ashley a few questions about the size and scope of the business, but she told him nothing. Then Elmo Smith left, and a detective named Milanesi came in to continue the interrogation.

"Don't talk to that man," he said, referring to Smith. "He's a bad person. But you can trust me."

"I can't believe you guys," said Ashley. "Do you really expect me to fall for the old good-cop bad-cop routine?"

She warned Milanesi that she wasn't going to say anything until her lawyer was on hand. But he persisted. Were any of our clients members of Congress? Did we have any secret bank accounts? Did we do business with any celebrities?

Ashley didn't say a word. But she sat there in disbelief as the detective called the newspapers to announce that a major prostitution ring had just been busted.

Eventually, each of the girls was allowed to make a phone call. Ashley called Jaime to tell her the unhappy news. Suzie and Claire called personal friends. Sonya insisted on calling the German consulate, which strikes me as just about the stupidest thing she could have done under the circumstances. But she didn't know the phone number, and she couldn't believe it when a police officer told her that if she dialed Information, it would count as her one phone call.

Finally, somebody brought in a phone book, but all of the pages for the consulates were missing. "That's all right," said the officer. "I'll call them for you later." He never did, which was just as well.

From the Harlem precinct, the girls were driven downtown in two cars to central booking. Three more cars followed as police escort. Ashley was in the first car with Detective Milanesi, and directly in front of them was a drunk driver who was swerving dangerously from side to side. The police officers were evidently convinced that these four girls represented a greater threat to society than this obviously impaired driver, for they completely ignored him.

Milanesi's phone call had apparently paid off, for on the way into central booking, the girls were greeted by a flock of news photographers. Again, they were put in a holding pen. Most of the other women in the cell were street girls, dressed in gaudy and provocative outfits. "Don't squeal on nobody," one of them told Ashley. "You're a first offender, and you'll get off easy."

"I was crying my head out," Sonya told me later in her beautifully broken English. "I cried all the tears that were in me. And I could not believe what I saw with the hookers from the street. They had hidden their cigarettes and lighters in all kinds of strange places in their bodies. One girl even had a candy bar in there! Never in my life have I seen such a thing!"

While all this was going on, I was innocently enjoying my dinner with Barry. When the doorman at my building told me that the police had been looking for me, I ran upstairs to call the office. Nobody answered, of course, so I called Risa at home. She had already heard about the bust from Denise, who had received a frantic phone call from Tess.

"Peter Fabricant is already on the case," she said, referring to the lawyer who had represented the girls during the March bust. "But it will take most of the night before the girls are processed through central booking."

Hoping to learn more, I played back the messages on my answering machine. Melody had telephoned to say that she had been trying the office but there was no answer. Joanna called to tell me that she was scheduled to see a client at nine, but that nobody had called her to confirm and there was no answer at the office. Kate had left a message that she had called the office and a man had picked up the phone.

Fearing that the police might be coming back for me, I

kept my apartment dark. Risa had advised me to go somewhere safe until we could meet in the morning and determine if there was a warrant out for my arrest, but since the police had not broken down the door earlier in the evening, I decided to take my chances. Although I knew that my line might be tapped, I spent most of the night on the phone, trying to reassure everybody I could reach. I finally got to bed around five in the morning, feeling guilty that I had a warm bed to sleep in while some of my girls were in jail.

The next day, when we finally located the girls, I was startled to learn that Suzie was with them. Ashley was the only one who knew that Suzie had been out on a call—and Ashley, of course, was behind bars.

On Friday night, bail for the three girls from the office was set at $5,000 each. I was horrified at the amount. I didn't have anything approaching $15,000, and I didn't have any way of getting it. Until I could come up with the money, the girls would be kept at Riker's Island— the city's notorious jail.

I needed to talk to somebody who could help me see my situation clearly. I called my good friend David and quickly revealed the big secret I had been holding out on him for five years. His reaction was everything I had hoped for.

"We can't let those girls stay in jail," he said. "I'll lend you the money."

Back at the court house, the three girls from the office had been sent on to Riker's Island. Suzie was processed separately, and at two-thirty on Saturday morning the lawyers called me at David's to say that her bail was set at $1,000 and if we had the money, we could come down and pick her up. Although there was probably a warrant out for my arrest, I was determined to go down there with him.

When we arrived, we found that Mel, one of our clients, was already waiting to bail out Suzie. He had read in the papers that an escort service had been busted and that one of the girls arrested was named Suzie. "I just knew that was *my* Suzie," he told me.

He had seen Suzie only three or four times, and not at all during the past year, but like several of our clients, he had become obsessed with her.

Assuming that the bail could not possibly be more than $500, he had jumped in a cab and had been down there waiting for Suzie—not even knowing it *was* Suzie— since four-thirty that afternoon. When he learned that her bail was $1,000, he was crestfallen. But when we showed up, and David provided the balance, he was immensely relieved to learn that his beloved Suzie would be set free.

When it was finally Suzie's turn to go up in front of the judge, the pimps in the courtroom went crazy when they saw what an incredible body she had.

The judge was reading from a report that had been handed to him. He looked down at Suzie and said, "I see here that you charged $250 an hour."

At which point one of the pimps called out from the back of the courtroom, "It should have been more!"

It took over an hour for the bail clerk to count the money. He counted it once, got up, walked around, and then counted it all over again. The criminal justice system moves at a painfully slow pace, but this was especially infuriating.

Mel had hoped to take Suzie home with him, but she couldn't have been less interested, so David and I brought her back to his place. David immediately went to sleep, while Suzie filled me in on the gory details of the previous night. She knew that her arrest had been her own fault, and that I was furious at her, but this clearly wasn't the time for a lecture.

A couple of hours later, a bail bondsman returned our call from the previous evening, and David went back down to criminal court to arrange bail for the three girls who were still in jail. When he returned, he rented a car and drove out to Riker's Island to bail them out and bring them back home. We agreed that Suzie would go with him so that the girls, none of whom had ever seen David before, would know that he could be trusted.

Visitors to Riker's Island must park in a special lot and take a bus to the actual prison, a mile away. When David and Suzie got there, they were told that David would be permitted to go in and collect the girls, but Suzie would have to wait for them in the reception area.

When David finally reached the right building, he was kept waiting for an hour and a half. Finally, three frightened girls emerged from a stairwell and sat down in the row of chairs behind him. David had no way of knowing whether these were the girls he had been sent to bail out, but one thing was clear: they were scared to death. Just before the girls came out, one of the guards told him that they were so terrified they weren't sure they even wanted to leave their cell.

For three long minutes, he sat there without saying a word. So did the girls. Finally he turned around and said, "I'm David."

They stared at him warily; the name meant nothing to them.

Then Sonya asked, "Did you bail us out?"

"Yes," he replied.

"Well then," she asked, "who the hell *are* you?"

"I'm a friend of Sheila's," he said.

"Really? You *are?* We're so glad you're here! We were afraid you might be a reporter."

The girls were ecstatic, and they all started talking at once and asking questions: "Did they get Sheila, too? What happened to Suzie? Were our pictures in the paper?"

To return to the main building, David and the girls climbed on the bus, which was already occupied by a couple of dozen convicts under guard. Some of these guys hadn't seen a woman in quite a while. "I had always heard women talk about men who undress them with their eyes," he told me later. "Now, for the first time, I really understood what they meant.

When they reached the main building, David went to look for Suzie, who was buying a candy bar from a vending machine. "Sorry to take so long," he said, "but I've got a little present with me."

When Suzie turned around, all four girls burst into tears and started hugging each other. Although their ordeal was far from over, at least they were out of jail and free to go home.

David brought everybody back to the city. Claire was in a particular rush: her boyfriend—who knew her secret—was the best man at his brother's wedding, which was scheduled to start in less than an hour. He waited as long as he could, but he finally had to leave for Long Island without her, not knowing when she would be released or how he would explain her absence.

Claire was determined not to let him down. If she hurried, she could still be there in time for the reception.

Chapter Thirteen

*B*y *Friday morning*, the day after the bust, Risa had learned there was a warrant out for my arrest. The charge, as expected, was promoting prostitution—a felony. I wasn't surprised, but I was angry that the authorities were making such a fuss about it all. Yes, I might have done something illegal, but I certainly hadn't done anything *bad*.

The last thing in the world Risa wanted was to have Sergeant Smith and his crew come to take me away, so she arranged to have me surrender directly to the D.A.'s office, rather than to the police. Sgt. Smith had already shown himself to be heavily involved in this case. There was an internal police department policy of not going after escort services, but this, apparently, meant nothing to Smith, who, in our view, was seeking headlines and would relish the opportunity to harass me.

If I turned myself in, however, my lawyers could maintain more control over the whole legal process and also move it along more speedily. To give me enough time to arrange for bail, the surrender was scheduled for Tuesday morning.

One factor that made everything go more smoothly was that before Risa had gone into private practice, she had been a prosecutor for the state, and her husband had once been with the police department. I assumed that because of these professional connections, Risa knew how the process worked and was able to help move it along with maximum efficiency.

Still, the police had already shown an interest in alerting the press to every move in the case, so I expected that my surrender would generate some publicity. Once the date was set, I made a list of all the people whom I wanted to tell myself before they read it in the papers.

These were not easy calls to make. "Listen," I said to each of these friends, "there's something I need to tell you that I'd rather you found out from me, rather than in the papers. I really haven't been in the accessories business for the past five years. That was just a cover for my real business. I ran an escort service. The police have arrested some of my girls, and I have to surrender to the district attorney's office on Tuesday. It's something I wanted to tell you personally."

Everybody I spoke with was remarkably understanding. Two or three of my Westhampton friends told me they already knew about my secret life, but that since I had never mentioned it, they'd thought it best not to bring it up. I was astonished that they knew, but suddenly all that didn't seem to matter anymore.

I called my brother, Andrew, and told him we had to speak about a very serious family matter. He came over to my apartment, and I revealed everything. He knew, too—from our father, who had told him two years earlier. He had only one question: "Do they know what your middle name is?"

Andrew was convinced that the press would have a field day if they learned about my family background, and I did my best to reassure him that this was unlikely. "As far as I know," I said, "they don't know my real name at all. In fact, I expect to go through the entire procedure as Sheila Devin."

I had intended to call my mother, but I just couldn't bring myself to do it. On the morning of the surrender, just before leaving my apartment, I phoned Andrew. "I know it's unfair to ask you this," I said, "but I don't have the guts to call Mom and tell her, and I don't want her to have to learn about it from the papers. Would you do it for me?" He clearly wasn't looking forward to it, but he agreed to help me out.

The only thing left to arrange was the bail, but that was no small matter. Risa told me that the D.A.'s office had been talking about a sum as high as fifty thousand dollars. I was terrified. I couldn't imagine how I could get my hands on that kind of money, and the prospect of languishing in jail until it could be raised was too horrible even to think about.

A bail bondsman was out of the question because I had nothing to put up for collateral: no home, no car, and no investments. My only alternative was to try to borrow the money from a friend.

I could think of only one friend who was in a position to lend me that much: Wes, a financier. I had met him and his wife several years earlier at the wedding of one of my girls, who had let it slip that I was a madam. Most people don't usually get to meet madams, and Wes was fascinated by my profession. He, his wife, Ellen, and I turned out to have much in common, and the three of us became good friends. On one occasion, they had invited my boyfriend and me to join them for a weekend at their vacation home in Hilton Head, South Carolina, and had us flown down in their personal jet.

Still, I was reluctant to call Wes because this was a lot to ask—even from him. And if Wes and Ellen turned me down, I didn't know what I would do. Finally I got my courage up to dial his number and ask him to help me. He needed to talk it over with Ellen and promised to call me right back. The phone rang a moment later, and they were both on the line. "Of course we'll lend you the money," Ellen said. "There's no way we would ever let you go to jail." What a relief!

The day before the surrender was scheduled, we learned that the bail was going to be "only" $7,500. In that case, I had enough money—just enough—to post my own bail, but I was warned by the bondsman who had done the girls that this would be dangerous, that I should go ahead with my plans to borrow the money. If I paid my own bail, there was always the possibility that the prosecutor could claim that the money had resulted from ill-gotten gains, in which case it could be confiscated.

The night before the surrender, I went over to Wes and Ellen's apartment on the East Side to borrow the $7,500. Ellen was out of town, and Wes had a terrible case of the flu. We were sitting in the kitchen under bright overhead lights, with poor Wes sweating profusely and dying to get some sleep. Between phone calls, I kept bringing him cups of tea.

My first call was to Risa to tell her I now had the money.

"Great," she said. "I'll need to know how to reach Wes during the day tomorrow. He may have to come down to criminal court to post the bail when your case comes up."

I handed the phone to Wes. "Wait a minute," he told Risa. "I'm happy to lend Sydney the money, but I can't afford to be publicly involved with this thing."

With time running out, I needed to find somebody who was willing to risk potential publicity. Risa advised me that it would be better to have a woman do it, because if the bail were paid by a man, the press might speculate that he was a client.

I called one of my girlfriends. At first she said yes, but then she changed her mind because her boyfriend was up for a partnership at a prestigious law firm, and she was afraid that if he were in any way connected with me, it might compromise his career. I was disappointed, of course, but this wasn't the time to argue with her.

Now it was close to midnight, and we were getting desperate. "I have an idea," said Wes. "There's an attorney I know who owes me a favor. I've sent her a number of clients, and she's the kind of person who just might do it."

He dialed her number. "Marshall? This is Wes. I need to ask you a big favor."

Marshall? The only Marshall I knew was "Joanna," one of my girls who worked days as a lawyer. It was such an unusual name for a woman that it had to be the same person.

As Wes told her the story about Sheila Devin, I started to worry: Poor Joanna. How on earth is she going to get out of this one? By the way he was talking, I could tell that she was resisting his arguments.

"Here," said Wes, handing me the phone. "She won't do it, but she wants to explain why."

I got on the line. "Does he have any idea that I work for you?" she gasped. "How much did you tell him?"

"Not at all," I said. "No, I certainly understand," I added for Wes's benefit. "I realize it's a lot to ask from somebody you've never even met. I really do understand."

I felt so guilty! Here Wes had been willing to put up fifty thousand dollars to keep me out of jail, and I was brazenly deceiving him. On the other hand, I had to protect Joanna.

By now it was one in the morning, and I was quickly running out of time. Whom could I turn to? I couldn't even consider asking David, who had already done so much for me. With his high-profile job, he could never take this kind of risk.

Finally I decided to try Jimmy Roe, my neighbor who

had brought me the disguise at Lincoln Center. He owned his own business, which gave him the freedom that wasn't available to most of my other friends. His personal preference precluded the likelihood of his being a client. My phone call woke him up, and he barely knew what he was agreeing to, but he must have heard the panic in my voice and he said he would do it.

I was tremendously relieved that I wouldn't be going to jail, and Wes was almost as happy that he wouldn't have to stay up any later. We quickly drew up an agreement by which Wes lent the money to Jimmy, and when I got back to my building I woke Jimmy up a second time and made him sign the note. I gave him my beeper so that he could be available if and when we needed him in court, and I took the $7,500 back to my apartment.

I was due at the D.A.'s office at nine-thirty in the morning. Although I didn't know it at the time, the authorities had scheduled the surrender so that their moment of triumph would be splashed across the early editions of the afternoon papers. Now that the bail was finally taken care of, I could once again breathe freely. Although I knew that the next day would be stressful and that I would be spending a few hours in jail, I felt as if I were embarking on a big adventure. In fact, paradoxically, I was actually looking forward to it. As long as I know that everything is going to turn out all right in the end, I'm willing to try almost anything.

I was too restless to sleep, so I stayed up most of the night and cleaned my apartment. At ten after seven, my buzzer rang. I assumed it was the car I had hired to take me downtown, where I was to meet with my lawyers for breakfast before walking over to the D.A.'s office.

But when I opened the door to leave my apartment, flash bulbs started popping and a photographer began snapping pictures. A man with him shouted, "Miss Devin! Miss Devin!" I slammed the door in their faces, and the air was blue with curse words. How on earth did they know where I lived?

When the taxi finally arrived and I walked out of the building, there were two other reporters in the lobby. Fortunately, they had no idea what I looked like and didn't connect me, in my demure gray suit, with their mission to find the madam. I sailed right past them, and they didn't even turn around.

Our meeting place was Ellen's, a favorite breakfast spot for lawyers and city officials. Ellen was a former Miss Subways, and the walls were decorated with photographs of her fellow winners. There was an expectant tension in the air, since none of us at the table knew exactly what the day might bring. At Risa's request, I handed the bail money to Scott, a young associate in her firm who would be there at the arraignment. Then I ate a big breakfast of juice, toast, scrambled eggs, and bacon— because I knew I might not be eating again for quite a while. Before I left, I ducked into the ladies' room to brush my teeth. I might be spending the day in jail, but at least I would go in there with a clean taste in my mouth.

After breakfast, we all walked over to the D.A.'s office at 1 Hogan Place. Here, too, a group of reporters was waiting, but they didn't recognize me and we breezed right past them into the building and up the elevator. We walked down a grimy old hall to the D.A.'s office. Several officials came out to greet us, including Dennis Wade, the assistant D.A., who was the city's prosecutor on the case. Mr. Wade shook everybody's hand except mine. I wondered whether he thought it wasn't appropriate to shake hands with a defendant or whether he was afraid of catching something.

Standing with Dennis Wade were Detective Milanesi, who was in charge of the investigation, and Lieutenant Bayer, the senior police official on the case. Elmo Smith was nowhere in sight. After the night of the bust, he seemed to have been taken off the case—presumably because of Risa's complaint. The lieutenant was talking to the lawyers, but he couldn't take his eyes off me. I imagined what he was thinking: So *this* is the prey we've been stalking for so long. Later, Risa confided that Bayer had told her that in honor of my surrender and the anticipated press coverage, Milanesi's wife had bought her husband a new Ultrasuede sports jacket for the occasion.

The actual surrender took only a few moments, and then it was time for the lawyers to leave. Risa explained that Scott would be close at hand all day to keep an eye on me and to let the authorities know that somebody was monitoring the entire procedure on my behalf. I found this enormously reassuring.

Milanesi and Bayer took me into a ramshackle office. As Milanesi laboriously typed out a succession of forms, the lieutenant kept staring at me. Whomever he had been expecting, it wasn't someone like me.

"You look so *preppy*," he finally said.

"Well, I *am*," I replied.

Both men were exceedingly polite, and when it came time to take my fingerprints, they were very concerned that I not get any ink on my clothes. The next task was to take a Polaroid shot to attach to the paperwork, and as long as they had the camera out, they couldn't resist asking me to pose with them. First, Bayer took a picture of me and Milanesi with our arms around each other. Then Milanesi took a picture of Bayer and me.

By now, I couldn't resist: "Come on, you guys, let's get one of the three of us."

"Great idea," they said. Milanesi went into the hall to find a volunteer, and we posed for a picture with me in the middle.

"Take one for me, too," I joked. "Who knows, I might be writing a book."

"No way," said Milanesi. "But if you ever need a copy, just give us a call."

Then Bayer told me, with profuse apologies, that it was time to put on the handcuffs.

"Is it really necessary?" I asked.

"I'm afraid so," he said. "If we didn't do it, we'd be breaking the law." Risa, who had thought of everything, had already arranged for me to be handcuffed in front, rather than from behind. Not only is this a more comfortable position, but it also results in a better image on the television news and in newspaper photographs. Before we left, the two officers pushed the handcuffs up under the sleeves of my jacket.

Our next stop was central booking, a short ride away. We took the elevator downstairs to go outside, but when the door opened, the place was crawling with reporters. They were crowding about and yelling, and it looked like one of those scenes after a president had been shot. It took a few moments before I realized that all these people were working themselves up into a frenzy just for me. People were shooting pictures, running TV cameras, and trying to ask me questions. The whole scene was so ridiculous that I started to laugh, which is why all the newspaper photos showed me with a huge grin on my face.

When we got outside, somebody held open the back door of a black sedan, and I climbed in for the short run over to central booking. Instinctively I moved over to make room for one of the officers, because that's how I had always seen it done on TV. But to my surprise, Milanesi and Bayer both got in the front. They didn't even bother to lock the doors.

Central Booking was invented as a way to prevent police officers from beating up on suspects in the privacy of their own precincts. These days, the place is run like a badly managed factory: police officers are everywhere, but nobody seems to be doing any work. After more tedious paperwork, my handcuffs were removed and I was asked to walk through a metal detector, which kept going off until somebody figured out that the machine was being set off by my cufflinks. I made a mental note: next time I go to jail I'll be sure to consult the special prison issue of *Vogue*.

Before they left, Bayer and Milanesi assured me that everything would be all right and advised me to be nice to the correction officers. For the long wait until the arraignment, I was taken first to a large holding pen with wooden benches on each side. Two black girls sat on one side, and on the other was a well-dressed blonde. One of the black girls was walking up and down and talking to herself; the other was sitting with a vacant look on her face. The blonde, whom I took to be a working girl, simply looked scared.

Barbara, the blond woman, wouldn't say what she was in for. One of the black women had been arrested for theft; she was eighteen and had a two-year-old son. The other woman was twenty-seven and had five children. She had been arrested because her boyfriend had filed an assault charge against her six months earlier. He had long since dropped the charges, but because of a clerical error the police had come for her in the middle of the night and hauled her off to jail. That, at least, was her version; I soon learned that nobody in jail is ever guilty of anything.

Jail is an appallingly depressing place, and this particular jail was unbelievably filthy. It was hard to imagine that there were whole departments in city buildings that nobody had been assigned to clean, and this place clearly hadn't been touched in years. I didn't exactly go in there expecting Bloomingdale's, but it was definitely the dirtiest place I have ever seen.

Yet there were the correction officers, sitting around

and doing absolutely nothing. I realize that cleaning up is not one of their jobs, but why couldn't the city have hired fewer guards and added a couple of custodians? It's inexcusable that people should be made to wait in such a dirty place before they're even officially charged with a crime.

The holding pen occupied half the room, and in front of me were tables, desks, and a black-and-white television in the far corner. I noticed that the correction officers were paying a lot more attention to a soap opera on TV than they were to us. After a while—and it's hard to know how long because you lose your sense of time in there—a girl with a clipboard came up to the holding pen and asked for our names and addresses. When I told her where I lived, she asked if there was anybody home to verify that I was telling the truth. I replied that she was welcome to discuss the matter with my answering machine.

"By the way," I said, "I notice you're all watching channel seven. Do you watch 'All My Children' at one o'clock?"

"Oh, yes," she said. "Erica's getting married to Mike today, and Adam is trying to stop her."

"No kidding," I said. "I've been watching since 1971, and I just hate to miss it."

I didn't bother to add that I had missed hundreds of episodes since my roommate at FIT had first introduced me to "All My Children." And although I really do love that show, my real problem now was that I was bored to tears, and "All My Children" represented something to focus on.

I had brought a book with me, *The Name of the Rose*, by Umberto Eco, which several of my friends had raved about. But the novel was far too complex to read in that setting. I made another mental note: next time I'll bring along some back issues of *Cosmopolitan*.

Around twelve-thirty, there appeared to be a changing of the guard, and the four of us were moved into separate cells. I didn't enjoy being alone, but what really distressed me was that I could no longer see the TV set.

As the guard was putting me in my new cell, I pleaded with her: "I realize you may have to say no to this," I said, "but is there any way that you can put me back in the holding pen so I can watch 'All My Children' at one o'clock? Erica's getting married to Mike today, and Adam is trying to stop her. I couldn't bear to miss it. Please?"

"Well, all right," she said.

By ten minutes to one, I was back in the holding pen, but not for long. Another guard came to take me to the visitor's area because Scott had come by to see how I was doing.

"Sorry," I told him, "but I can't stay. You wouldn't believe what I've had to go through to see 'All My Children.' It starts in five minutes, so please talk fast." Scott must have thought I was crazy, but suddenly "All My Children" had become the most important thing in my life.

Scott didn't have much to report, but even so, I missed the first five minutes of the show. During the commercial break, the guards brought another woman to the holding pen; incredibly, she was still working the streets at the age of fifty-four. She wanted to chat, while I, of course, was trying to watch the TV. She undoubtedly thought I was being unfriendly, but by now I had such an investment in that show that I wasn't going to let anything get in the way.

When "All My Children" was over, the guard returned me to the other cell, where I was surprised to find Barbara. We talked for a while, but I carefully avoided asking any questions about what she had done to end up here. She did, however, let me know that she was terrified of having her picture in the paper. I was feeling tired since I hadn't slept much the previous night, and in the absence of anything better to do, I decided to take a nap. I must have succeeded in dozing off, because the next thing I knew I was being awakened by the noise of a man banging on the bars with a nightstick.

"Which one of you girls is the famous one?" he asked.

I raised my hand.

"Good," he said. "I just wanted to see what the fuss was about."

Great place, jail.

At around four-thirty, Scott came back again to see how I was doing. He explained that the reason it was all taking so long was that the computer was having trouble with my fingerprints. That must have been why they had taken two more sets since I had seen him last.

By five o'clock I was no longer wondering when this tedium was going to end. Now I was starting to wonder *if*. But a few minutes later, I heard the guards opening each door in our cell block and leading the occupants away. Before long, Barbara and I were taken down a long corridor, where we joined a dozen or so women lined up against a wall. Everybody's left hand was handcuffed to a long chain, and they prepared to move us outside for the trip over to the criminal court building, where we would eventually be arraigned.

I was the last one on line, and as the guard was about to attach my handcuff, I asked her if I would have access to a bathroom where we were going.

"No," she said, "you better take care of it here. Go back into that last cell, and make it snappy." I did as she instructed, and just as I was finishing, I looked up and was disgusted to see that a male guard had been watching me.

When I came back, the last cuff was occupied and I

was brought up to the front of the line. They were obviously not ready to move us, because we were allowed to sit down on a bench in one of the cells, from which I could see three other cells, all filled with girls chained up just as we were. They all looked like stereotypical hookers with short skirts, elaborate hairdos, and plenty of makeup.

After a good hour of waiting, we were finally ready to be moved. Knowing that there would probably be photographers waiting outside and that Barbara was afraid of being exposed, I urged her to take my sunglasses and to hold my book over her face. The guards kept telling me to hurry, but behind me the girls were walking so slowly that I couldn't move any faster. As we walked through the halls, whole groups of police officers were lined up, staring at us. When we got outside, a veritable pack of news photographers started shouting and snapping pictures.

We were loaded into the back of a van, and as the first one in, I was all the way in the far corner. There were too many girls to fit in the vehicle, so when all the seats were occupied, more girls piled in and sat on the other girls' laps. When all the lap space was occupied, the rest simply sat on the floor, as if this were the most natural thing in the world.

The doors were closed, and we were completely in the dark. This is a stupid way to do it, I thought. Somebody could get hurt in here and nobody would know.

The girls, for whom this was evidently a routine experience, were all trying to figure out why the press photographers had been there. They soon guessed that it was because of me, which made everybody want to know who I was and what I had done. It was a ludicrous scene, being interviewed by twenty-five or thirty street girls, all of whom were shouting questions at me in the dark.

Because their voices were all reverberating around the metal truck, I couldn't make out exactly what they were asking. I started feeling a little uneasy. I didn't want them to think I was being snobbish or rude, but everybody was shouting at once and there was no way to hold a conversation in there.

Finally, one of the girls yelled for everyone else to shut up and that she would ask the questions.

"What are you in for?"

"Promoting prostitution."

"First time?"

"Yes."

"Don't worry, honey, you'll be out in no time."

"That's good."

"What are all those newspaper dudes doing here?"

"I ran an escort service, and they think it's a big deal."

"You mean you ran some kind of *house*?"

"Sort of." I tried to explain that we were an outcall service, but none of them understood what that was. Finally, I told them I was a madam.

"What?"

Out of the dark came a voice. "That's a female pimp, fool!" This got everybody laughing. Then I was barraged with questions: How much did we charge? How did it work? Did I have a pimp?

In the midst of this group interview, I realized that the van had not moved in several minutes. As long as we were just sitting around, some of the girls decided that this would be the perfect moment to light up a cigarette. There was no ventilation in the van, and I thought I was going to die of asphyxiation. Some of the girls yelled about getting some light, and I started yelling for air. When nothing happened, they started banging on the metal walls of the van, and between the pounding and the screaming, the noise was deafening. Together with the smoke and the darkness, it made for an unnerving few minutes.

In the basement of the courthouse, we were once again lined up against a wall. After our handcuffs were removed, we had to empty our bags and our pockets and take off our shoes to show them the soles of our feet. The guards conducted a quick body search of all the girls except me, a courtesy that I certainly appreciated. I guess they didn't consider me dangerous.

At this point, the guards passed out some bologna-and-cheese sandwiches, along with little packets of mustard for our sandwiches and sugar for our tea. After the bust in March, Denise, Kelly, and Corinne had joked endlessly about those terrible sandwiches. So had Suzie, who had been busted just five days ago.

The tea was served in Styrofoam cups. It had been sitting around for so long that it was barely warm, but it felt wonderful.

Clutching our sandwiches and cups, we were taken into a large holding pen. The scene was like a grand reunion, as many of the girls knew each other from previous arrests. They milled around, calling greetings and gossiping about their friends and their pimps. Instead of using names, everybody was called "girlfren'" or "ho"—for whore.

One of the girls kept asking everybody for sugar, and we all gave her our little packets. I didn't understand what she was doing until the girl next to me explained that sugar provided some relief for heroin addicts.

It had been hours since my big breakfast at Ellen's, and although bologna and cheese are not my favorite foods, I was so hungry that I wolfed the sandwich right down. After this forgettable experience in fine dining, I decided that a little after-dinner conversation was in order. As long as I was there, I wanted to learn as much as I could about these girls and their world. After all, we were, at least theoretically, in the same business.

I was amazed when they told me that they counted on being arrested twice a week and that this was simply part of the cost of doing business. When I found out later that it costs the city three thousand dollars per arrest, the whole thing seemed even more ludicrous. What a waste of taxpayers' money! If only the city would give that three thousand dollars directly to the girls, they'd probably stay off the streets for a month!

During the next couple of hours, I received a crash course in street prostitution. As somebody who had always worked on the management side of the business, I was especially interested in the role of the pimp. What, exactly, did he do for the girls in return for all their money? I had always assumed that the pimp's role was to protect the girls from the clients, but the real story, I soon learned, was that he protects them from other pimps. A girl without a pimp is considered a renegade, and to prevent her from working, the other girls' pimps harass her by following her around and making it impossible for a client to approach her.

I was incredulous: "And for this you give them *all* your money?"

The girls didn't see it that way. Their pimps did a lot, they said. They divided up the territory among the various girls, and they bailed them out whenever they were arrested. The pimps also bought them clothes, gave them a small allowance, and handled all their money.

To my surprise, and despite the one heroin addict, drugs did not seem to play much of a role in these girls' lives. This was not the case with the pimps, however, and those girls whose pimps didn't have a "habit" would brag about it to me and the other girls. There seemed to be a caste system, and the girls whose pimps had habits occupied a lower rung than those whose managers may have preferred other vices.

As we talked, more and more girls were brought in. I

noticed that before they sat down on the floor—the bench space had long since been occupied—they took off their clothes, turned them inside out, and put them back on again. After watching a number of girls go through this bizarre ritual, I asked one of my cellmates what it was all about. It made perfect sense to her; they did this so that their outfits wouldn't get dirty from sitting on the floor.

I was also curious to learn how the girls had been arrested in the first place. After all these years, you'd have thought that they would have recognized the officers who kept bringing them in. I was dumbfounded when they told me that the police would pull up to the curb in a large van and simply motion for everybody to pile in.

I knew I was being naive, but I still had to ask: "Why don't you simply run away?"

They told me that any girl who tries to run away is chased and beaten up, and that it was much easier and more convenient for them to cooperate. That way, at least, nobody got hurt.

Two of the women in our cell were obviously not working girls. They just happened to be legitimately walking down the street when the roundup was taking place, and despite their protests, they had been forced into the van. This, I learned later, was not uncommon. Several years ago, the city of New York paid a large out-of-court settlement to a free-lance writer who had been arrested for "loitering with intent to solicit." In reality, she happened to be standing on a street corner waiting to meet a friend. Apparently, she had chosen the wrong corner.

Given the flamboyant and imaginative outfits most of the working girls had on, it was hard to believe that the police were too blind to recognize the two outsiders for what they were—or weren't. For the working girls, spandex seemed to be the fabric of choice, presumably because it's so tight and shiny. Because spandex tights are not the easiest things to get in and out of, I was puzzled as to why these girls were all wearing them.

"Honey," said one of the girls, "we don't sleep with these guys." Oral gratification was the name of the game on the street—at least the streets where these girls had been picked up. In other parts of town, the girls were more likely to take their customers to a nearby hotel.

Naturally, the girls were also curious about me, because in my dress-for-success wool suit and silk blouse I looked very different from everybody else in there. Normally, it's not the sort of outfit that makes you stand out in a crowd, but then again, this wasn't exactly my usual crowd.

At around nine o'clock, one of the newest arrivals brought in that day's *New York Post,* which carried the story of the surrender earlier in the day and a picture of me leaving the D.A.'s office. This inspired a replay of the scene in the paddy wagon, with everybody shouting questions all at once.

Every now and then a guard would come by to take a few of the girls upstairs for arraignment, where they would be formally charged. Every time a guard would approach the holding pen, the noise level would rise. But the guard just stood there, refusing to raise her voice. Finally one girl would call out, "Shut up! Shut up! She ain't gonna *yell!*" Then everybody would quiet down so the names could be called.

It was nine-thirty before they finally got to me. I told Barbara to keep the book, and I wished her luck. Then I said good-bye to the group of girls with whom I had been talking. As I left the cell, everybody started shouting and cheering me on. "Go get 'em, girlfren'!"

I left with mixed emotions. These girls had been so

nice to me, and so open and interesting, that my brief experience in jail was far more positive than I could have imagined. Although I was delighted to be getting out of there, the street girls had become real to me, and it saddened and angered me that they would soon be back here again. And again. And again.

It was a long walk up the stairs and through the corridors. Suddenly a door opened—and there was the courtroom, full of people. I was seated on a bench on the far right, the same place Suzie had been sitting a few days earlier. I looked around and finally spotted Risa.

The courtroom was a scene of mass confusion. It was a very large room with dark brown paneling, which had probably been nice many years ago but had long since fallen into disrepair. The benches were made of wood; the floor was green-and-black linoleum. I guess I had been expecting the kind of courtroom I was used to from television, which was small, clean, and orderly, but this was another world.

The chaos was so vivid it took a few moments before I realized that cases were actually being adjudicated. People were walking in and out, and several groups were talking near the judge's bench. I couldn't imagine how anything was being accomplished.

They took me right away, even though there were other people before me, some of whom had probably been waiting a long time. A court officer brought me up to the table at the front, where Risa was waiting for me. He pointed out a little white arrow that was painted on the table, indicating where the defendant is supposed to stand.

A prosecutor from the D.A.'s office started reading the charges, using accusatory and inflammatory language and talking about a "million-dollar call girl ring." Risa and Peter kept objecting, saying that the district attorney would have ample time to try the case in court.

Then the prosecutor started talking about all the "paraphernalia" that was found in the office, as though the police had seized sex toys or whips instead of record books. This made me furious, and I called out an objection. Risa told me to keep quiet.

Finally, it came time for the judge to ask the big question: "How do you plead?"

I looked him straight in the eye. "Not guilty, Your Honor."

The bail was officially set at $7,500, as we had expected. When we left the courtroom for the bail clerk's office, there were more photographers and reporters waiting for me than I had ever seen in one place. We had to shove our way through the horde.

Scott handed over the money, and nobody asked us to prove that it wasn't mine. Then he, Risa, and Peter formed a triangle around me as we once again prepared to face the press.

We opened the door, and there they were again. This time, the place was so thick with reporters and photographers that we could hardly move. They were yelling at me, screaming their questions, sticking their microphones in my face. "Miss Devin! Miss Devin!" Somehow we pushed past and made it out the door.

There was yet another group of photographers waiting for us as we walked down the steps of the building.

"Which one is her?" somebody yelled.

"In the gray suit," somebody shouted back. I realized with some amusement that he didn't know whether to take a picture of me or of Risa.

We walked two long blocks, trailed by a pack of reporters, before we finally found a cab. We ended up in a restaurant in the Village, where I ordered carrot soup and a chicken sandwich while Risa, Peter, and I sat and talked until nearly midnight. I filled them in on everything that had happened, and they explained how they intended to carry out my defense over the next few months.

When I finally got home, Jimmy Roe and two other men I was friendly with on our floor were waiting up for me, and we all got together in Jimmy's apartment. He had taped the eleven o'clock news, and as he played the scene of me leaving the D.A.'s office earlier that morning—it seemed like a week ago—I provided a running commentary on what had really happened. It was a terrific story, and I gave them a dramatic and comic rendition of all that had happened. I told them everything: how Lieutenant Bayer had said I looked so preppy; how the girls had asked me questions in the back of the van; what it was like trying to dodge all those reporters. I acted out all the parts and mimicked many of the characters, leaving my tiny audience in stitches.

"You know, Sydney," one of them said, "you really ought to keep notes on everything that happens to you. After all, you might want to write a book about it all."

At that moment, writing a book was the last thing on my mind. But the next day, when David came over to hear all the details of my brief time in the slammer, I turned on the tape recorder before I started the performance. I realized I would never remember all these details, and although I wasn't planning to write a book, who could tell how things would turn out? Only a week ago I was living my regular life and my secret had been safe. And now, suddenly, the business had been shut down, I had been charged with a crime, and every journalist in New York was dying to talk to me. But even though I knew my ordeal was far from over, I hadn't the faintest idea that all hell was about to break loose.

Chapter Fourteen

*T*he *morning after* the surrender, I was front-page news. MILLION DOLLAR MADAM FREED ON BAIL, read one headline. According to the article, "The alleged 'Million Dollar Madam' of the swankiest brothel in town was freed last night after paying $7,500 bail in crisp $100 bills." Not bad, I thought: three errors in the first sentence alone!

The following morning, on my way back from the gym, I stopped at my local newsstand to see whether the papers had anything to add about my case. I glanced at the *Post* first and was relieved to see that I was no longer on page one. Instead, the large black headline described another alleged call-girl operation run by someone known as the "Mayflower Madam."

I turned to the *Daily News,* whose headline read, COPS HUNT BACKER OF POSH SEX RING! That was more like it! I bought both papers, along with a copy of the *Times,* which I read every morning, but for whom news about madams was evidently not fit to print. Since the newsstand was only a block from my apartment, I took the papers home, poured myself a glass of juice, and sat down at the dining room table to read them.

I was nervous about the story in the *Daily News,* because I was afraid that one of my clients or friends would be falsely named. Fortunately, nobody was. The story claimed that in 1982, a mystery man had given me hundreds of thousands of dollars, and immediately after this infusion of cash, our volume of calls had quadrupled. This, of course, was a complete fabrication, but somehow it didn't surprise me. I was, however, contemptuous of the paper's defective logic: even if somebody *had* put a lot of money into the business, how did it follow that four times the number of men would suddenly be calling us?

Only then did I notice a second, smaller article—this one revealing my true name and identity! And when I turned to the *Post*, I realized with a shock that the "Mayflower Madam" was actually *me*. To back up its claim, the paper had even gone to the trouble of putting together my family tree.

I was stunned. It was one thing to be written about as the pseudonymous Sheila Devin, the Million Dollar Madam. But now, suddenly, I was Sydney Biddle Barrows, the Mayflower Madam. Being exposed had always been my greatest fear, and I had imagined that if it ever came to this, I would never recover. But now it had happened; it was *real*, and I had no choice but to accept it. Okay, I decided philosophically, it could be worse. At least "Mayflower Madam" sounds pretty intriguing.

Although both papers had conducted their own investigation into my real identity, the confirmation had come from Steve Rozansky, my long-ago boyfriend. On the night of the surrender, he had evidently recognized me on the television news and had contacted both the *Post* and the *News* to tell them who I really was. "The last time I saw her," he was quoted as saying, "she was an executive with a little briefcase and a suit, out to make a success of herself. Commercial sex had to be the furthest thing from her mind." In fact, the last time he had seen me was almost eleven years earlier, when I hadn't even owned a briefcase. Otherwise, his description was accurate.

He was also quoted as saying, "I knew that whatever she chose to do she would definitely be successful—and it would be done with taste and class."

I certainly couldn't say the same for him. He now claimed to be a blackjack dealer at a Bronx social club—not the sort of thing most people would brag about. (I snidely wondered why *he* hadn't been arrested, for I couldn't recall any news items to the effect that gambling had been declared legal in the Bronx.) It was also clear that he had approached the *Post* with more than mere information. He had evidently brought along those nude photographs of me that he had taken in Amsterdam eleven years earlier—the same pictures he claimed to have "lost" when I had asked for them back after we returned from Europe.

The *Post* informed its readers that while it had, indeed, obtained these photographs, "it was decided they were not suitable for publication in a family newspaper." Considering what *is* deemed suitable for publication in the *New York Post,* that was quite an indictment.

The next day, however, the *Daily News* printed one of the Amsterdam pictures. And surprise—so did the *Post,* which devoted half a page to a photograph that only a day earlier had been deemed "unsuitable." It's amazing what competition can do to your values.

I was devastated. I could live with being called the Mayflower Madam, and I could even tolerate having my real name known. But now nude photographs of me were being splashed across two of the largest newspapers in the country! I couldn't believe that Rozansky had so shamelessly betrayed me, and I was disgusted that I had ever given him the time of day.

Thank God for Risa, who promptly arranged for a temporary restraining order so that Rozansky couldn't sell any more pictures. This was around the time the infamous photographs of Vanessa Williams, the former Miss America, had appeared in *Penthouse,* resulting in enormous publicity for the magazine. And although Rozansky's pictures of me were tastefully done and not at all explicit, there were rumors that *Playboy* was interested in publishing them.

Several weeks later, we argued the case in front of a judge. Rozansky's lawyer contended that I was a public figure and that he was free to sell the pictures to anyone he wished. We countered that the photographs had been taken in the capacity of a friend taking snapshots of another friend, with the full expectation of privacy, and that I was in no way a public figure. Eleven years ago, there had been no reason for either of us to believe that these pictures would ever be of public interest; if there had, I never would have allowed them to be taken.

We also pointed out that I had never signed a release. That had been Vanessa Williams's undoing: because she *had* signed one, *Penthouse* had a legal right to publish her photographs.

Despite these arguments, the judge threw out the temporary restraining order. In his decision, he noted that while Rozansky had certainly betrayed my trust, there was nothing in the law to prevent him from selling the pictures.

This was on a Friday, and although we expected to get another restraining order on Monday, Risa and I were afraid that Rozansky might try to sell the pictures over the weekend. To head off this possibility, we sent telegrams to all the men's magazines, warning that anyone who published these pictures could expect a massive lawsuit. Presumably, our threat was credible because that was the last we heard of the matter. Later, another judge granted a permanent injunction against the sale of the photographs.

Still, the publication of these photos in the *Post* and the *News* was a real nightmare. I had always known that a bust was possible, but who could have imagined that a few photographs from a foolish hour in the summer of 1973 would ever return to haunt me? Yet if there's one thing I remember clearly from that day, it's that even amidst the giddy haze of youth and summer sun, I knew I was making a mistake.

Unfortunately, the nude shots were not the only troublesome photographs in the press that I had to contend with that week. The day they were published, the late afternoon edition of the *Post* ran a front-page group photograph of the people in my summer house with the headline caption, THE HAPPY MADAM.

Now this, too, was no ordinary snapshot. Every summer, our house in Westhampton would sponsor a BLT party—which stands for black tie, toga, and lingerie; guests were required to wear one of these three outfits or any combination thereof. For some reason, preppies get a real kick out of dressing up in silly outfits, with straitlaced, dignified young bankers and lawyers showing up in boxer shorts, sneakers, and tuxedo jackets. These parties were completely innocent, and the costumes were invariably loony rather than sexy or revealing.

Although nobody in the photograph was indecently exposed, several members of the group were wearing ridiculous getups, and one man, who had a prominent position on Wall Street, was dressed in a ludicrous toga. Moreover, the paper made clear that these smiling, upright people were somehow linked to me and implied that they might have been part of all kinds of wild goings-on involving that notorious sex queen, the Mayflower Madam.

I learned of the picture through a frantic phone call from one of the men who ran the summer house. Apparently, one of the members had left work early and had seen the photograph at a newsstand. Within minutes, telephones were buzzing all over town. Everybody was in an uproar, and an emergency meeting of all house members had been called for that night. I had been spending the day at Risa's office, dealing frantically with the Rozansky pictures, but I knew I had to be at that meeting to reassure my friends that the police would not come knocking on their doors in the middle of the night.

I knew these people well, and I could imagine how frightened they must be. Some were responsible for multimillion-dollar accounts, and to be exposed on the front page of the paper in their underwear must have been a terrifying proposition—even without the link to the Mayflower Madam. The men were afraid of being thought of as my clients, and the women worried that people might think they worked for me.

The emergency meeting was held in the East Side apartment of one of the women in the house—the same one, incidentally, who worked in the handbag business and who, I had feared, would discover that my accessories business was a charade. When I walked in, people hugged and kissed me and were extremely supportive. When they settled down, I tried to reassure the group that the publication of this photograph did not mark the end of the world—or even of their careers.

"I can certainly understand how upset you all must be," I began. "After all, it's very disconcerting to suddenly find yourself on the front page of the newspaper, especially if you're not completely dressed. Speaking as one who has just appeared in the papers not at all dressed, you really do have my sympathy."

It was a good opener, and everybody laughed. I went on to explain that the only reason the picture had been printed in the *New York Post* was because I was in it. I stressed that nobody was interested in further invading their privacy and that it was most unlikely that the *Post* or anyone else was going to explore my connection with the summer house in greater detail.

When I finished, there was some speculation as to how the newspaper had obtained the photograph. It had been taken a year and a half earlier, and everybody in the house had been given a copy. Obviouly, one of the members—or former members—had given his or her copy to the *Post*. But who had betrayed us? There was even talk of bringing suit against the paper and forcing them to reveal their source.

Some people were afraid that the *Post* was going to print their names and addresses, but I had already asked Risa about this possibility, and she thought it most unlikely. "They're not going to print your names," I said. "You haven't done anything wrong."

"Are we in any danger of being arrested?" someone asked.

"None at all," I said. "I'm the one who may have broken the law. You people didn't really know anything about it."

"Will we be asked to testify at the trial?"

"That's most unlikely. It's not as if you have any valuable information to offer about me."

Gradually, I was able to reassure everybody that no other shoe was about to drop. I had expected people to be in a hurry to leave, but most of them had already canceled their Friday-night plans and wanted to continue talking. Despite the group's initial anxiety—or perhaps because of it—there was a sense of excitement about the evening. Now that people felt less threatened, they were eager to learn more about my case, and the focus of their questions shifted from their own situation to mine.

"Did you ever realize you could be busted?"

"Sure. I always knew that the police could close us down. But the worst scenario I could imagine was the routine kind of bust that's very common among escort services. You close down for a few weeks, and then you open again with business as usual. That's what happened to us back in March, when the police arrested three of our girls. Normally, it's just a form of harassment. I never imagined we'd be in the headlines."

"Will you have to go to jail?"

"I spent one day in there, and believe me, I'm not eager to go back! My lawyer assures me that this is extremely unlikely, especially for a first-time offender."

"Why do you think they singled you out? Did you forget to pay off the cops?"

"No. As far as I'm aware, escort services don't pay off anybody. Maybe houses do, but not escort services. Certainly I never did, and nobody ever asked me for money. The only contact I had with the police was when somebody called us to ask for a donation to the police retirement fund. As to why they singled me out, our best guess is that there was some cop who thought he was going to get a promotion if he busted me. I think my landlord had convinced him that we were the biggest and most prestigious operation in the city."

"What did you do about taxes?"

"I paid them. I was running a legitimate business, and I paid taxes on what I made."

"Has the Mafia ever been in touch with you?"

"No. We were much too small to interest the Mafia."

"Why didn't you put all your client records on a computer? You could have wiped them out in two seconds."

"It was hard enough to find good assistants without also having to look for people with computer experience. Besides, a computer would only recognize the exact spelling of a name, and with all the foreigners on our list, that would have been a nightmare."

One of the veteran members stood up and said, "Sydney, I don't have a question, but I do want to say something. From everything I've read, you ran an honorable business. Maybe you operated outside the law, but I'm disgusted that the police spent taxpayers' money to go after someone like you. When my mother was mugged outside of her building, it took the police almost an hour to get to her apartment. New York is a dangerous city. There are murderers and rapists walking the streets. Why did they bother with you? If they thought that your business represented a public danger, then they have some pretty screwed-up priorities."

This was greeted by prolonged applause. "Thank you," I said with a smile. "I'm glad I'm not the only one who feels that way." But almost everybody, it seemed, had a similar story to tell, about the police being unavailable or late when they were really needed.

"Sydney," somebody else asked, "what do you think about this whole thing?"

"I think it stinks," I said. "If the police really wanted to get rid of the negative consequences of prostitution, they certainly chose a funny way to go about it. Obviously, I don't believe that escort services should be illegal in the first place, but if you're going to close one of them down, why pick on the only one that represents a clear alternative to all the others? When they shut us down, the police drove hundreds of clients and dozens of girls back into the hands of the sleazy operators. And take it from me, there are some pretty shady characters in this business."

This statement, too, was greeted by applause. I had always been well thought of in this group, but who could have predicted how my friends would react when they learned that I had been less than honest with them over the years? But if this evening was any indication—and it was—then I had been blessed with some very good friends.

The only sour note of the evening came after we broke for pizza, when one of the newer members, a woman I barely knew, took me aside.

"Sydney, why?" she asked. "How could you do such an awful thing?"

"What do you mean?" I replied. "What did I do? Did I murder anyone? Was I dealing drugs? Did I abuse children? I never forced anybody to call me, and I never forced anyone to work for me. As a matter of fact, both my clients and my girls considered themselves exceptionally fortunate to have found somebody like me."

She walked away, disgusted with my answer. She obviously had been hoping for an expression of remorse, but I didn't feel any.

Fortunately, my reassurances to the group proved to be correct, and the press did not pursue the summer house connection any further. After a few days, the house members began to treat the whole incident as a joke. That was a good strategy, because after the picture had appeared in the paper, they had to put up with a great deal of teasing on the part of their friends. By the summer, somebody had made up a bunch of T-shirts with a red logo: *Post*-Busters.

I wish that I, too, could have been so light-hearted, but during the weeks that followed, my mood alternated between righteous anger and depression. At least I was busy. I was in constant touch with the girls, keeping them informed of recent developments and talking with them about the case. Then there were my friends, who called to offer support and to learn the latest news. My phone didn't stop ringing for weeks.

People were dying to know what had happened to me during the bust and the surrender, and I told them everything. These repeat performances soon became tedious, but I wanted to get the story right each time because you can't expect people to support you if they don't have the information they need to understand your predicament. In describing the details again and again, I felt like an actress who presents the identical performance a dozen times a day; each time she goes on stage, she has to give it her best. I often wished I could have told my story on tape, so that my friends could have called a special Dial-a-Story number and listened to it at their convenience.

My doorbell rang almost as often as the phone. For weeks after the bust, reporters were camped outside the building, in the lobby, and even outside my door. Jimmy Roe and my other neighbors were constantly shooing them away or asking the doorman to get them to leave. One fellow from ABC-TV made a daily pilgrimage to my doorstep, arriving around six each evening. He would attempt to talk to me through the closed door, and I would repeatedly ask him to go away. When I wouldn't open the door, he and his colleagues would slip notes under it, begging me to talk to them and promising to present my side of the story. But for legal reasons, I was under strict orders not to talk to *anybody*.

My silence, however, did not seem to cool the enormous public interest in my story, and now that I was "famous," people looked at me and saw dollar signs. Throughout the weeks and months after the bust, Risa was hearing from literary agents, book publishers, magazine editors, and movie producers. But all of them had their own agendas, and many of them wanted a piece of the action. We were even contacted by a group of California gynecologists who offered to contribute fifty thousand dollars to my living expenses in return for 10 percent of all my future earnings. I was so broke that I was tempted to accept, but Risa wouldn't hear of it.

When I wasn't angry about what had happened, I felt depressed about my situation and worried about the future. At least I wasn't alone. I was spending most of my time at Risa's office, where she and her colleagues involved me in every stage of their thinking and planning. I also remained in close touch with the girls. Although the business was closed forever, I had not stopped caring about them. If anything, the events of October 11 had drawn us closer together.

Throughout October and November, I had thirty frightened girls calling me, each worried that she might soon be facing legal charges and that her real name and address would appear in the papers just as mine had. The police had begun to leak some of the clients', names to the press, and because they had seized all our records in the bust, there could be no guarantee that the girls' identities were safe. I was dying to reassure them that their anonymity would be protected, but there was evidently an open channel between the police and the press. If nude pictures of me could appear in the newspapers, how could I be sure that the girls' names wouldn't be next?

As it turned out, their names never did appear in the papers. But the daily anxiety they experienced over this dreadful prospect was overwhelming. The girls also suffered in smaller ways. Because they had all kinds of questions that I couldn't answer, I directed them to a lawyer who would represent them. But whenever one of the girls came to see him, everybody in the office would come out to stare. Later, when the Internal Revenue Service went after some of the girls—they must have learned their names from the police—there were further indignities. One accountant leered at Tricia and asked if she had any garter belts or lingerie that she wanted to write off as a business expense. Others shamelessly pressed the girls for graphic details about their experiences with the clients.

With Cachet no longer in business, most of the girls were soon experiencing serious financial problems. When you're used to earning a good income, you begin to arrange your life around it. Some girls had settled into beautiful apartments with high rents, and others had quit their regular jobs. None of them had counted on the possibility that everything we had built up could all come tumbling down.

Previously, when the girls had work-related or money problems, I had usually been able to help them. This time, however, I was powerless. I felt terrible, because although the girls had all joined up voluntarily, they were now suffering on my account. If I hadn't been the Mayflower Madam, this would have been just a routine bust.

Ever since we had opened, I had been a mother figure for the girls. Some of them were still in college or graduate school, and most were new to Manhattan. They were constantly coming to me or calling me up with questions:

"Sheila, can you recommend a good dentist?"

"Sheila, can you help me find an apartment?"

"Sheila, where should I go to buy a coat?"

"Sheila, can I talk to you about my boyfriend?"

I loved having the girls call me and being able to help them out, and now that I was no longer in the business, it was one of the things I missed the most.

The only way for the girls to make anywhere near what they had been making with me was to sign on with another escort service. But in addition to the money, they had also grown accustomed to our way of doing things. They knew in theory that our agency was different from the others, but those girls who started working again were in for a rude shock. In their new jobs, they were expected to go to second-rate hotels at three in the morning to see clients who hadn't been properly screened and about whom they had no information. And if it was a credit card call, they might not be paid for weeks.

I spent hours on the phone listening to them gripe about their new employers and trying to help them out with the problems. "With you it was fun," Melody said. "But now I hate it. The clients just aren't the same as the men we used to see."

Tricia told me about a call with a man who had spent the first hour with her at the hotel bar. Later, he called the agency and complained about having to pay for that time, which was "merely" social. Amazingly, the owner agreed to let it go. "I guess the clients matter more to her than we do," said Tricia.

I guess you're right, I thought.

Poor Denise was sent on a call to the Howard Johnson, which had not been on our approved list, to see a Japanese businessman who spoke almost no English. Fifteen minutes into her visit, when she and the client were still in the talking stage, two security guards knocked on the door.

"We're going to take you to the police," they said.

"Please don't," Denise begged. Having been arrested back in March, she now had a record.

"I'll tell you what," said one of the guards. "We'll let you finish the call, if you'll give us all the money."

Considering the alternative, Denise quickly agreed. When she returned to the client's room he was too frightened to continue the call, so he paid her and sent her back out again. The two guards were waiting in the hall. They led Denise to an empty room, where they took her money and then forced her to have oral sex with them.

When this story got around, several girls went as a group to one of the better agencies and more or less dictated their own terms. This particular service was so delighted to have some of "Sheila's girls" that the owner permitted them to veto any hotels that weren't on our list. They were even allowed to collect the money at the end of the call, which was an unprecedented concession.

During the weeks after the bust, the girls did enjoy one advantage for which I envied them: whenever my case was discussed, they had the luxury of remaining anonymous. Because my arrest was the talk of the town, just about every girl who had worked for me overheard or participated in at least one discussion about the Mayflower Madam.

Jeanette and Cameron were having a drink in a restaurant one evening when two men came over to flirt with them. When one of the men noticed that Cameron was carrying a newspaper with my picture on the front page, he started bragging that he knew all about our operation.

"I've been to her brothel, you know."

"You *have?*" said Cameron. "That's amazing. What's it like?"

This was all the encouragement he needed. "Now you girls have to understand that this is one of the poshest bordellos in the city. The richest men in New York go there. They charge you a flat fee of a thousand dollars, which includes a gourmet steak dinner with caviar and champagne. For dessert, they send you upstairs with the girl of your choice."

"That's unbelievable," said Jeanette. "Who would have guessed that something like that could exist right in our own neighborhood!"

"Amazing," added Cameron. "I guess we're just not very hip to what's going on in this town."

One night, about a month after the bust, Jaime was invited to an elegant dinner party on Park Avenue. Across the table sat a man whose name she recognized from our client list. As soon as the group was seated, people started talking about the Mayflower Madam.

"You know what bugs me?" said the client's wife. "They're making the girls take all the heat. These kids are having their lives ruined, while the men are getting off scot-free. I hope they publish that client list!"

Jaime stole a look at the husband and noticed a wan smile on his face.

A few weeks later, Jaime was working as a hostess at a trade show when she recognized the name of the man at a corner booth. She wasn't sure whether or not to introduce herself, but finally she went up to him and said, "Peter?"

"Yes?"

"Do the names Sheila and Cachet mean anything to you?"

Peter just froze.

"It's all right," she said. "You see, I'm Jaime."

Peter looked terrified.

"Really, it's okay," she said. "I'm not going to tell anybody. I just wanted to introduce myself."

Once he realized that he was in no danger of being exposed, he started to relax. "*You're* Jaime?" he said, grinning. "I want to hear *everything*." They went out for coffee, and he sat there entranced as she told him all about us.

The day after the bust, Jaime had flown up to Boston to see her boyfriend, a graduate student at Brandeis University. She was hoping to escape from the nightmare, but en route to his house they stopped at a drugstore to pick up some aspirin and there, staring her in the face, was a front-page story about me in the Boston *Herald*. Until now, Jaime hadn't told her boyfriend about her job as an assistant at Cachet. But seeing my picture in Boston was the final straw. She felt so alone and so terrible about what had happened that she told him everything.

Five minutes later, she wished she could have taken it all back. He was outraged and refused to believe that her job was restricted to administrative duties. Before the day was over, they broke up over it. It's too late now, of course, but I hope he reads this book so he'll finally know that Jaime was telling him the truth.

*   *   *

Not long after the arraignment, the prosecution decided to convene a grand jury for the purpose of collecting evidence to determine whether a crime had been committed that warranted prosecution as a felony. About a dozen of the girls were required to appear as witnesses, and all of them were granted immunity in return for their testimony. Sunny was subpoenaed first when two police officers came to her door at seven in the morning. In Joanna's case, the police marched right into her office at the downtown law firm where she worked, which terrified her. Arden wasn't home when the officers arrived, and they proceeded to tell her roommate the whole story. The other girl hadn't known a thing about Arden's secret life, and as soon as Arden came home, she demanded that Arden move out at once. Colby heard the news when she received a phone call during breakfast at her parents' house. Her mother answered the phone, but Colby somehow managed to take down the relevant details without incriminating herself in front of her family.

Although the grand jury proceedings themselves were secret, the girls were terrified that reporters might be waiting for them outside the building. Ginny suggested, mostly as a joke, that they all disguise themselves as nuns, and for two or three days there was considerable enthusiasm for that idea. In the end, however, nobody was prepared to carry it out.

It didn't matter, though, because no reporters were there. But Jaime insisted on arriving in disguise anyway, showing up once as a fat lady and another time as a Hasidic matron. The other girls dressed appropriately and were properly intimidated by all the legal trappings of the grand jury, but for Jaime this was guerrilla theater, and she seized the lead role.

Moreover, she insisted on playing it as a comedy. As

the transcripts of the proceedings showed, Jaime was often funny and sarcastic in her testimony, and on more than one occasion she had the grand jury in stitches—which infuriated the prosecutor. At other times, she didn't hesitate to express her anger, especially at the prosecutor's tendency to focus on the sleazy side of the story.

At one point, the prosecutor asked her to explain a code that he had found on a client card:

Q. What's "L.P."?
A. Well endowed.
Q. Well, I mean—we are all adults. Would L.P. mean large prick?
A. No.
Q. What would it mean?
A. Long penis. No. I'm making a joke. It means well endowed, and that's all it means.
Q. Well endowed in what sense?
A. You like this topic, don't you?

Jaime's comments must have flustered him, for shortly afterward he asked Jaime to identify a piece of evidence. Although it was labeled "Exhibit C," the prosecutor mistakenly referred to it as "Exhibit LP," to which Jaime responded, "I guess this is very much on your mind."

Later in the proceedings, the prosecutor asked Jaime about a memo in which I had warned the girls about an increase in police activity during an election year:

Q. What does that refer to?
A. That refers to the fact that police seem to think that there are things more important than murder and robbery, that they have nothing better to do than rent three-hundred-dollar suites at the Parker

Meridien, waste taxpayers' money, drink champagne, and have call girls over.
Q. Are you finished making your speech?
A. Maybe, but I'm not sure.

Jaime told me later that the women on the grand jury seemed considerably more antagonistic than the men. "They obviously hated who we were," she said. "And the feeling was mutual. They struck me as exactly the severe and moralistic types whose husbands would need to call us."

At one point, Jaime addressed the jurors directly:

The Witness. Are you all allowed to talk to me?
Juror. Oh, yeah.
The Witness. You can? Are you bored, or is this stuff pretty interesting?
Q. Miss Johnson, please do not make any comments, and do not ask any questions.
A. Oh, all right. But they all look so bored that I felt sorry for them.

I myself did not testify before the grand jury, because the prosecution was not about to grant me immunity. Nor did I hear any of the testimony. But months later, when I finally read through the court transcript, one brief exchange, with Sunny as the witness, stood out in bold relief:

Q. Now, when you went out for one hour to a hotel or a residence, what did you expect?
A. I expected to meet a gentleman and be treated like a lady.

Well done, Sunny. I couldn't think of a better way to summarize what we were all about it.

Chapter Fifteen

At Thanksgiving, six weeks after the bust, I went home as usual to be with my family in New Jersey. By now, of course, they knew all about what had happened—and about the real nature of my "accessories" business.

I had finally called my mother the day after the surrender. "I know," she said as soon as she heard my voice. "I learned about it from Andrew. I'm so sorry." Although she certainly didn't approve of what I had done, she was very supportive and deeply concerned about what would happen next. To my enormous relief, she resisted any temptation she might have felt to lecture me or criticize me. Instead, she wanted to know if I had a good lawyer. How was I bearing up? Was there any danger of my being sent to jail?

"Why don't you speak to your attorney about getting a bodyguard?" she said. "With all those crazy people in New York, how can you be sure that somebody won't try to throw acid in your face?"

My stepfather thought my arrest was an act of idiocy on the part of the authorities. He comes from Austria, where this sort of thing is legal in specific areas and with certain restrictions, much as gambling is permitted in America through lotteries, off-track betting, and casinos. He had once been mugged in New York, and like my friends from the summer house, he was angry that the police had gone after me when there were so many more important—and more dangerous—fish to fry.

He also told me that he had recently had a visit from a New York police officer who wanted to know if the small, nonprofit music school that he ran out of their house wan't really a money-laundering operation for my business.

Furious at this insult, my stepfather took the man into his office, showed him several years' worth of tax returns, gave him a lecture about respecting peoples' privacy, and sent him right back to New York.

As we were all sitting down to dinner, my stepfather said, "Sydney, I almost forgot. Mother has an interesting story to tell you about the Social Register."

"What happened?" I asked, turning to her.

"Well, they certainly do work fast," she replied ruefully. "Our new copy arrived on Tuesday, and we're already out of it." It was true: they had eliminated my name and that of my mother, my stepfather, and my father and his wife. But they hadn't touched any of my grandparents; I guess they didn't dare fiddle with the Biddles.

Although being listed in the Social Register had never been terribly important to my mother, she was indignant at the unfair way our family had been treated. She felt that the same criteria ought to apply to everybody, and she knew that I wasn't the first person in the register to have been arrested. If one of the Rockefeller girls or one of the Vanderbilts had been running an escort service, would her parents have been dropped? Over the years, the sons and daughters of many prominent people had been convicted of dealing drugs and other serious offenses, and their names were still in. I, on the other hand, hadn't even been indicted yet.

I shared her indignation. Why should my mother be punished for what I had allegedly done?

"Maybe *they* don't want me," I said, "but you'll never guess who does. Barbara Walters sent me a personal letter saying that whenever I was ready, she was interested in talking to me."

I had been pleased to hear from Barbara Walters because an interview with her was the best forum I could imagine for presenting my side of the story. As long as I was being arrested, I might as well go out with a splash. Perhaps I was naive, but I took her interest as a professional compliment.

When I mentioned Barbara Walters, my mother looked a little alarmed. Not surprisingly, she hoped the whole business would fade away without any further publicity, and watching me talk about my escort service on national television wasn't something she looked forward to. I assured her that it would be quite a while before I would be allowed to talk to anybody from the press—assuming I even wanted to.

Shortly before Christmas, the grand jury concluded its deliberations and handed down a one-count indictment, charging me with promoting prostitution in the third degree. They could have cited me for each booking over the five and a half years, but then they would have had to specify not only the dates and places, but also the names of the men, which they were clearly unwilling to do. They also could have named the police officers from the two busts, but they claimed I was running a million-dollar business, so mentioning only those men would have looked like a cover-up. The gist of the one-count indictment was that while they were sure some acts of prostitution had taken place between 1979 and October of 1984, they were unwilling or unable to specify exactly who had done what and to whom.

The indictment came as no surprise, as grand juries

are often controlled by the prosecution. When Bernhard Goetz, the so-called subway vigilante, was indicted, Barry Slotnick, his attorney, told the press: "If the district attorney wanted, a grand jury would indict a ham sandwich."

Which brings us, finally, to the legal side of the story. The details of my case are varied and complicated, and to describe them in their entirety would fill another book. Instead, I'm going to hit a few of the highlights.

Or lowlights, as the case may be. I knew I had entered the twilight zone when, during the first few days after my surrender, several prominent lawyers whom I had never met each began to spread the word that he was representing me. I was astonished, but apparently this sort of thing goes on all the time in high-profile cases: big-name lawyers issue these announcements in the hope that their statements become a self-fulfilling prophecy.

Risa, of course, headed the defense team. But for the first few days, the prosecutor at the D.A.'s office wouldn't speak to her, presumably because she was a woman. Instead, he dealt only with the male lawyers who were working on the case under her direction.

"You're Sydney's friend," he told Risa, "so we'll talk to you on that level."

"I may be her friend," she answered, "but I'm also her attorney."

Only after Risa instructed the other members of the defense team to refer all calls to her did the prosecution begin to treat her with respect. Apparently, this wasn't easy. When Dennis Wade, the assistant D.A. who handled my case, finally met her, one of the first things he asked was, "Why doesn't Sydney Barrows have a regular whore lawyer?"

Later, presumably because of Risa, and perhaps because the judge assigned to the case was also a woman, the prosecution added a woman to its team. At one

point, during a very heated argument about what constituted an appropriate punishment, she said to Risa, "We
feel that Sydney Barrows must go to jail."

"I don't think that's bad enough," said Risa, her
voice dripping with sarcasm. "I think she should get a
lethal injection!"

Next to Risa, the most important member of our team
was Mark Denbeaux, a professor of law at Seton Hall
University School of Law in Newark, New Jersey. Mark
had already argued the Rozansky case, and Risa asked
him to serve as the trial lawyer and to take an active role
in my criminal defense. Unlike many defense lawyers in
the New York area, Mark isn't part of the old-boy
network of ex-prosecutors from the district attorney's
office, which makes him more independent and less
predictable. And unlike many of his colleagues who
invariably negotiate a plea for their clients, he isn't
afraid of going to trial.

At first, Mark wasn't interested in working on what
seemed to be a routine prostitution case. But when he
saw that the D.A.'s office seemed interested in prosecuting and harassing only the women, and had no intention of involving any of the clients, he was outraged at
this blatant double standard. Although this point was
rarely mentioned in the press and is often ignored by
both the public and the police, prostitution is a crime not
only for the women who practice it, but also for the men
who patronize these women. For Mark, and for many
other observers, the prosecution's interest in going after
the women while ignoring the men was both discrimina-
tory and hypocritical, and he was determined to make a
constitutional issue of it.

From the very beginning, Dennis Wade of the D.A.'s
office was pressuring me to take a plea—which meant
that I would plead guilty in return for a reduced penalty.
But the prosecution's idea of a reduced penalty was still

a substantial fine—something in the neighborhood of fifty thousand dollars.

At a meeting with Risa and Mark in Risa's office on East Twenty-first Street, we discussed the pros and cons of accepting their offer.

"If you take the plea," said Risa, "it will all be over. If you don't take it, we can go all the way to trial. In theory, you could end up in jail. But because there was only a one-count indictment and you have no previous record, I can't imagine how that could happen, especially since no other owner of an escort service has had to serve time."

"Let's look at both scenarios," I said. "What happens if I take the plea?"

We made a list: first, the sooner I took the plea, the sooner the whole legal battle would be over, and the less debt I would be incurring for legal bills. Second, taking the plea meant that I would know in advance what the penalties were; there would be no unpleasant surprises. And then there were the girls: although I was sorely tempted to fight this case in a trial, it would mean a serious risk of public exposure for the girls, who would undoubtedly be called as witnesses. The clients, too, might be called, and their names would also be made public. Finally, there was the remote possibility of jail.

On the other hand, taking the plea would have meant that I was giving up without a fight. I felt strongly that I had run an ethical business, and to the extent that I may have violated any laws, it was those laws that should have been on trial. I wasn't ashamed of what I had done, and I was more than willing to defend my actions in court.

It wasn't an easy decision. "How soon do I have to make up my mind?" I asked.

"That's the good part," said Mark. "You can take a plea at any point in the process. If you ever get to the point where you want to throw in the towel, just let us know. Until then, we'll fight this all the way.''

He continued, "The whole business of a plea is a kind of legal street game. Whatever your real intentions are—and we know you haven't made your decision yet—Risa and I will try to persuade the prosecution that you will never plead, and that you actually look forward to a trial. The more they believe you're serious about going to trial, the better the terms they'll offer you. But we've got to be convincing. If they think we're bluffing, the terms they offer won't be nearly as good."

A few weeks later, Mark told me that he had talked to Dennis Wade.

"I told him that since you had three thousand clients—"

"Wait a minute," I interrupted. "Where did you come up with that number?"

"I extrapolated from the client books."

"Three *thousand*?"

"Think about it," he said. "Didn't you have a lot of clients who called you only once?"

"Sure."

"And you kept records on everybody?"

"Faithfully. For five and a half years."

"And didn't you have a couple of new clients every night?"

"Absolutely. Some nights we had as many as eight."

"Well then, three thousand clients means that you averaged two new clients a night. Does that sound right?"

"When you put it that way, three thousand sounds low. Okay, go on."

"Anyway, I told Dennis Wade that when we go to trial, I intend to start the process of selecting a jury by reading the names and addresses of all three thousand clients to the prospective jurors, just to be sure they don't know any of these men."

"Hold it," I said. "If you did that, what would prevent the press from taking it all down and then publishing the names?''

Mark smiled. "Nothing at all," he said.

"Are you kidding?" I said. "I promised these men confidentiality, and I don't intend to go back on my word.''

"Don't worry," Mark replied. "I can assure you that the D.A.'s office will like the idea even less. But if they want to portray you as having three thousand clients, then they've got to believe that we're prepared to call them in to testify. At any rate, I told Dennis Wade that my best estimate is that three hundred and forty of your clients were lawyers practicing in New York City, and that I would start by calling them all in as witnesses. Some of these guys are very prominent, and all of them would have to hire other lawyers to represent them. This would lead to a real circus, because even if the prosecutor granted them immunity, there's still a good possibility that they could be disbarred for committing a crime. And if any of these men paid for the company of the girls with their business credit cards, there would also be some nice little tax problems. Believe me—there's *nothing* the D.A. would less rather do than to publicly embarrass all these lawyers.''

"But what if you're wrong?" I asked. "What if they do call the men?''

"Just to reassure you," said Mark, "let's take it one step further. If the men actually came to testify, I don't see how you could lose. If they claimed that they didn't pay money for sex, but that they were somehow able to charm these girls into sleeping with them, then you would be acquitted because that's clearly not prostitution. But even if they said that they did pay money for sex, which is a crime—and remember, they will have immunity—it's hard to imagine that any jury would let you be the scapegoat while the men got off. And in the unlikely event that a jury *did* convict you, it would be even more unlikely that a judge would give you anything more than a slap on the wrist."

This argument formed the cornerstone of the defense—that it was ludicrous for the prosecution to claim that I ran an escort service where prosperous men paid considerable sums of money for sex, while at the same time pretending that our clients were innocent of any criminal wrongdoing. If the men were innocent of patronizing prostitutes, then I had to be innocent of promoting it.

There was nothing new about this double standard. When it comes to prostitution and the law, it has always been this way: women pay for the crime while the men go free. Back in 1979, Mayor Koch tried to change all that with a controversial new idea: a radio broadcast called the "John Hour," where announcers on WNYC, the city-owned radio station, read the names of men who had been convicted of patronizing prostitutes. But the public outcry was enormous, and the experiment was abandoned a few days later. So, too, was the policy of arresting men for patronizing prostitution. In 1983-84, for example, 5,409 women were arrested in Manhattan for prostitution—a figure that doesn't include the more than 10,000 others who were arrested for "loitering with intent to solicit"—but only 196 men were arrested for patronizing them: a ratio of over twenty-seven to one.

We also pointed out that selective prosecution applied equally to promoting prostitution. Despite their visibility on the streets and in the courts, where they show up to bail out the girls, the pimps—in other words, the *men* who promote prostitution—are almost never arrested. In 1984, for example, only three men were arrested for "felony promoting," as opposed to fifty-one women. If the police were really going after the sellers of prostitution, how could they justify arresting women, who constitute only a fraction of the promoters, yet virtually ignoring the male pimps?

Finally, the defense pointed out that the authorities had devoted far more time, money, and energy to closing us down than they had ever spent on any other escort service. And all this for an operation they themselves acknowledged publicly did not involve any drugs, any violence, any police corruption, any organized crime.

Our other main line of argument was that I ran an escort agency, not a prostitution service. Running an escort business is not a crime, and evidence that I was running one does not inevitably prove that I acted to promote prostitution. The law defines prostitution as having sex for money—or merely agreeing to have sex for money. But our clients didn't pay us for sex, or even the promise of sex. They paid us for the girl's time.

And no matter what did or didn't take place during that time, the price was exactly the same. If we had charged $100 an hour when no sexual activity took place, and $200 an hour when it did, that would be a very different matter. But in our case—and most escort services operate this way—the price was the same for each and every hour. And as the girls stressed repeatedly to the grand jury, they never *had* to sleep with a client; it was always their decision.

According to the letter of the law, prostitution does not occur merely because sex takes place and money changes hands. It's only prostitution if the client is actually paying *for* sex. The question, then, is whether we *intended* to sell sex for money, and we claimed that I did not.

In order to substantiate its case against me, the prosecution had to show that the client books seized by the police on October 11 had indeed been written by me—at least in part. Accordingly, they called for a handwriting analysis, whose results would be shown to the grand jury.

It so happens that Mark Denbeaux is one of a tiny but growing number of lawyers who believe that the validity of handwriting analyses has never been proved. According to Mark, even if every person really does have unique handwriting, it doesn't necessarily follow that those features can be quantifiably measured and scientifically judged—especially when one handwriting sample is judged against only one other sample.

The analogy he likes to offer is the difference between a showup and a lineup. In a mugging, if the police bring in a suspect and the victim says, "Yes, that's him," this is known as a show-up, and because it's unduly suggestive it does not constitute legal evidence. In a lineup, however, the police bring in half a dozen people and the victim is asked to identify the one who committed the crime. Obviously, a lineup constitutes a higher order of proof.

In my case, Mark offered to provide a sample of my handwriting together with that of ten other people; only if the "expert" could pick out mine, he contended, would that person have the right to be taken seriously. If handwriting analysis were really a scientific skill, our test would not be overly difficult.

While all of this was being argued, the prosecution's star handwriting analyst suddenly dropped out of the case when he ran into a rather embarrassing conflict of interests: after looking through the client books, he found that he recognized the names of too many lawyers who were also *his* clients! In the end, an employee of the police department carried out the handwriting analysis.

The test consisted of having me write over and over again certain phrases that appeared in our client records. During the test, I was seated at an old wooden table that was full of pockmarks and blisters, and I carefully positioned my paper over the biggest blister patch I could find. And although I normally hold my pen between my index and my middle finger, I decided that this might look suspicious, so for the first time in my life I tried to write in the "normal" position. The test went on for five hours and was thought to have been the longest such exercise ever conducted in the state of New York.

Mark had been unable to prevent my taking the handwriting test, but he did succeed in convincing the judge to allow us to test the prosecution's expert if the case ever came to trial by having him pick out my handwriting from a group of other samples in open court. If he failed, of course, the jury could not be expected to believe his earlier opinion. After that ruling, the second handwriting expert declared that he was unable to conclude that the handwriting on the documents in question had been done by the same person who wrote the samples. Presumably, having his expertise tested in court was not an ordeal he looked forward to.

Having won a small victory, we moved on to the next front. On the night of the bust, the police had seized all our client records and other documents. Under the law, they had a right to take that material. But the law also includes a provision called "discovery," under which the defendant has the right to copies of any documents that the prosecution is going to offer as evidence. Accordingly, we asked to have the client books returned to us.

From the start, however, the prosecution refused to let us have them. They argued that the client books represented the records of an illegal business and that I might sell them to another escort service. They also argued that the material fell into the category of "the instrumentality of the crime," a phrase normally used to describe such evidence as a gun or narcotics. When I heard that one, I felt like Alice trying to defend herself before the Red Queen.

"What do we do now?" I asked Risa.

"We go back to court to get them," she said. "The law is very clear on this point; they've got to hand over the books."

"What do you think is their real motivation in holding on to them?" I asked.

"They're probably worried about the confidentiality of the clients."

That's what I thought, too. Some of our clients were fairly powerful, and I wondered if some of them might not have called the D.A.'s office to urge that this case be handled as discreetly as possible. If we had the books in our possession, the prosecution could no longer guarantee their confidentiality.

"What an insult!" I said. "We kept those names confidential for five and a half years. I'm sure that most of our clients would rather have us holding those names than the D.A.'s office." (This was more true than I knew at the time, for later we learned on good authority that the names of our foreign clients had been given over to the CIA, presumably for use as possible blackmail.)

"Don't worry," Risa said. "Sooner or later they'll have to release them."

When it came to retrieving the client books, the judge agreed with us that there were only two possibilities: either these men were indeed our clients, which meant they were also potential witnesses to the case and we might wish to call them or they were innocent people whose privacy should be protected. But if *that* were true, then no crime had been committed and the entire case should be dismissed.

Under orders from the bench, the prosecutor reluctantly permitted us to make copies of the client books.

There was also a struggle over which side would pay for the photocopying—and at what price.

I ended up being charged for photocopying the client books during a period when my own financial situation was quickly becoming precarious. The lawyers were spending an incredible amount of time on my case, and I had long ago run out of money to pay them. Because of my legal needs, they were devoting fewer hours to other, more solvent clients. And as Risa pointed out, defending yourself can be extremely expensive when the government goes all out to get you with its unlimited funds.

One morning in February I was talking to David about my financial problems when he mentioned having read somewhere that John De Lorean had thrown a fund-raising party to help pay for his defense. "How about doing something like that?" he said.

It sounded like a good idea. I was receiving a lot of supportive mail from strangers, and people were always stopping me on the street to say they wanted me to win. "We could probably get a lot of people to show up," I said.

"I think so, too. Besides, it's a lot better than the plan my sister came up with."

"Which was?"

"She was joking, but I'll tell you anyway. She says that now that you have the client records, you should write to each man on the list to say that you're thinking of writing a book, and that in return for a modest donation you'd be more than happy not to mention his name."

I laughed. "A little extortion, huh? You know I'm not that kind of girl."

The plan we settled on was considerably more respectable: a big fund-raising party in April for the Mayflower Defense Fund at the Limelight, a Manhattan disco in an old, renovated Episcopal church. Tickets would cost forty dollars, which would include a buffet supper and live entertainment.

Our first task was to send out invitations. I began by calling all the girls, as well as all my friends, and asking everybody to put together a list of their friends whom they thought might be interested in attending such an event. The assistants made up a list of some of our favorite clients, and we invited them, too. As soon as the invitations were ready, I asked the girls to come to my apartment to help stuff and address the envelopes. We worked for three evenings and got about two thousand pieces into the mail.

We printed up a formal invitation that read as follows:

The Friends of Sydney Biddle Barrows
request the pleasure of your company
at
The Mayflower Defense Fund Ball
on Tuesday evening, April 30th
at The Limelight
Avenue of the Americas at Twentieth Street

Guests are asked to arrive between
7:00 P.M. and 7:15 P.M. for receiving line.
Buffet will be served at 9:00 P.M.
Dancing will commence thereafter.

Black tie optional.
Uniforms for serving officers.
Ladies need not wear tiaras.

The last line—about the tiaras—was included as a joke, although I learned later that some of my friends weren't altogether certain of that. But I had once seen the phrase on an invitation to a party at the British embassy, and I thought it might be fun to use it here.

One guest—Ana Biddle from Philadelphia—really did show up in a tiara. (Although we had never met before, we are undoubtedly related.) Because she was an authentic Biddle wearing an authentic tiara, there was a big picture of her on the front page of the *Daily News* the next morning.

Not everybody was thrilled about the idea of a Mayflower Defense Fund Ball. "The Mayflower doesn't need defending," claimed a member of the Mayflower Society. And I'm told a number of lawyers were furious that, in their view, we were treating the problem of my legal bills as though it were a charitable cause. There were also some sniffs from the charity ball crowd, many of whom evidently felt that our event might give their parties a bad name.

I was looking forward to the party, but I didn't have a thing to wear. The Mayflower Defense Fund Ball would have been the perfect occasion for my fabulous black taffeta showstopper, but it was among the items stolen from the office immediately after the bust. Knowing that I had few options, a friend of mine who worked for Tracy Mills, the prominent dress designer and manufacturer, offered to ask Mr. Mills if he would let me wear one of his dresses in exchange for the publicity. He agreed, and I was delighted.

As the party drew nearer, the *Daily News* and the *New York Post* were each clamoring for an exclusive angle. My attitude toward both papers had changed markedly since October, when their stories about me and the business were full of misinformation. Now that my story was primarily a legal one, the papers were working closely with Risa and Mark to make sure they had their facts right. In addition, they had always treated me well. Readers were obviously intrigued by the idea of a high-class madam, so both the *News* and the *Post* went out of their way to stress that angle.

We decided that the *Post* would be given an advance shot of the dress—a pink taffeta strapless gown that I wore with a pearl-and-diamond choker and the same white elbow-length kid gloves that I had worn as a debutante fourteen years earlier. In return, we promised the *News* an exclusive photo at the party of me with my escort—about whom there had been considerable speculation.

The party began with a receiving line. Risa had insisted that most people were coming because they wanted to meet the Mayflower Madam, and I decided that a receiving line seemed like the most expeditious way of going about it. As each guest approached the line, his or her name was announced—like the procedure at a very formal ball. Mark Denbeaux was the first to greet the guests; he would present them to me, and I would introduce them to Risa.

A number of my out-of-town friends were there that evening, in addition to a great many strangers and at least a hundred journalists from all over the country. Among the guests were book publishers, movie producers (several of whom flew in from California just for the occasion), friends of friends, curiosity seekers, and the owners of three other escort services, who had come to show their solidarity. There were even a few clients, and although not all gave their real names, I had spoken to them on the phone so often that in some cases I recognized their voices.

Many of my personal friends were dying to come but were simply afraid, for the usual reasons: the women because people might take them to be one of the girls, and the men because they might be regarded as clients. My summer house crowd stayed away in droves. Appearing in one picture with me was hard enough to live down; having it happen again would be considerably more difficult to explain.

A group of my cousins came in from Vermont and New Jersey, carrying a bunch of balloons with a sign reading, "We don't approve, but we're still family." Three of my friends flew in from Los Angeles, another from Dallas, and two more from Florida, just for the ball.

All night long, people kept coming up to me with kind and supportive remarks: "You look beautiful." (Risa had thoughtfully arranged for me to have my hair and makeup done professionally.) "We really admire you." "We were talking about you at work, and we're all behind you." Several men asked me to dance, but the moment we reached the dance floor, I was surrounded by people who wanted to talk. It was an elevating and magical experience to be the guest of honor at a party where hundreds of people—most of them complete strangers—had turned out to support me.

Toward the end of the evening, Richard Currier, a composer and singer, performed a song called "Mayflower Maiden," which he and lyricist Jim Piazza had written especially for the occasion, and whose refrain went like this:

> You're a woman, you're a headline
> You're a media event;
> We rise to your descent,
> You're a media event.
> And how are things inside
> Those eyes that never cry
> Those smiles that seem a million miles away?
> Has something in you died,
> Or does the girl survive,
> The girl next door you were just yesterday?

After the song, I got up and publicly thanked my lawyers, my friends, the girls, and everybody else who had stood by me over the past six months.

The party received extensive press coverage all over the country. My favorite line was the lead from the story in *Newsday:* "Sydney Biddle Barrows turned out last night to press the flesh. And people paid to do it—exactly the sort of activity that got her in trouble in the first place."

The article ended with a quote from a member of the Social Register Committee, who said that I was "the first Biddle in generations who knew how to make any money."

Because so many of the guests were members of the press, who were admitted free, we didn't raise as much money as we had anticipated. But that turned out to be secondary; from a public relations standpoint, the party was an unqualified success. Typically, the prosecution tries to present the defendant as a heinous character who must be put away, but after the party and all of the press it generated, it became even more difficult to portray me as a criminal. In a very real sense, we had succeeded in trivializing the case.

For me, in sharp contrast to the dreariness of the long legal struggle, the Mayflower Defense Fund Ball was the most fun I've ever had. I had always grown up with the idea that my wedding would be the high point of my life, but it's difficult to imagine anything that could top this.

Chapter Sixteen

I *have* *always* been a regular reader of the *New York Times* and the *Wall Street Journal,* but until the bust, I paid little attention to New York's two major tabloids, the *Daily News* and the *New York Post.* While I had often glanced at their huge black headlines as I passed by my local newsstand, I had never actually read the *News* and had bought the *Post* only once—years earlier, the day the Son of Sam murderer was caught.

At first, it was disconcerting that the *Times* and the *Journal,* the papers that our clients read and in which their business activities were often detailed, all but ignored the bust while the tabloids couldn't get enough of me. But when I thought about it, I realized it was hardly surprising: here was a young Manhattan madam of prominent ancestry, whose well-dressed and elegant girls visited wealthy, powerful men for "immoral" purposes and whose career ended abruptly with a dramatic police raid. It's for stories like this that the tabloids exist.

Even so, nothing could have prepared me for the extent of the coverage that Cachet and I received in the weeks following the bust. At one point, we were on the front page of the *Post* and the *News* every day for two weeks—with the exception of a three-day interval when Indira Gandhi was assassinated.

Every time I went to court, there would be twenty or thirty reporters waiting by the entrance and I would be on the first page again. I would be walking with Mark or Risa, sometimes both of them, and they would repeatedly say, "No comment," as the questions were shouted out. (I wasn't even allowed to say *that*.) In front of us, walking backward, press and TV photographers would be shooting pictures. Every now and then one of them would fall over or bump into a lamppost, adding an element of slapstick to the scene.

Over at the *Times*, Russell Baker wrote a column lamenting the fact that his own newspaper was ignoring the hottest story in town. "At the *New York Times*," he observed, "we are not supposed to be interested in Mayflower Madams, but don't let the starchy façade fool you. Behind it lurk masses of newspeople seething with just as much delight in prurient-interest stories as the people over at the *Daily News* and the *Post*."

And a few paragraphs later, "I envy the people at the *Post* and the *News*. This is a story, and there is nothing a newspaperman loves more than a story, except Friday night at the pay window."

Tabloids feed on scandal—or the appearance of scandal—and in the period immediately following the bust, the papers gave us such classic headlines as COPS SAY DEMURE BLONDE RAN SWANK BORDELLO *(Post)* and TOUCH OF CLASS, RING'S GIRLS ALL HAD IT, PROSTY SAYS *(News)*. Both papers made frequent references to the "brothel" and the "bordello" and continued the practice long after it had become clear that the only men to ever set foot on the premises were telephone repairmen and delivery boys. But they were simply unable to refer to our headquarters as an office.

For some reason, I wasn't really offended by the coverage in the tabloids. I read the stories with interest, but I didn't take them personally. I always had the feeling that they were about somebody else.

At first, the press focused on the size and reputation of the operation. As the *News* wrote after my surrender, "A demure blond 'executive' whom police called 'the most professional madam we've ever come across' turned herself in yesterday to face charges she headed a millionaire call girl ring that catered to company presidents and Arab sheiks from around the world."

Later on, one of the papers published the names of several celebrities, claiming they had appeared in our client records. I didn't recognize these particular names, but this was dangerous territory, and I was worried about what might come next. Lieutenant Bayer had given me his card, and I called him to register my alarm.

It was Elmo Smith who answered the phone. "Sergeant Smith here.

"May I please speak to Lieutenant Bayer?"

"He's busy. What's it about?"

"It's about the Mayflower Madam," I said. This was not the time to identify myself.

"Oh, well, you can tell *me* about it.

"No," I said, "I have to speak to the lieutenant."

"Why don't you speak to me?" he said. "I'm the main man on this case. I'm the one who got her."

"I'm *terribly* sorry," I said in my most haughty WASPy tone of voice. "But I've never heard of you. Besides, you're only a sergeant and he's a lieutenant. I couldn't possibly talk to anyone but *him*."

"What do you mean?" he said. "Didn't you see my name in the papers?"

Eventually he put me through to the lieutenant. "This is Sheila Devin," I said. "It's one thing to arrest me and to splash my name all over the papers, but who gave you the right to ruin the lives of my clients? That's despicable, and I can't believe it's not illegal!"

Bayer seemed genuinely apologetic. He said he had no idea how something like this could have happened, and he assured me that his department, too, was concerned about the problem. I believed him, and it wouldn't have surprised me to learn that he had received some angry phone calls from City Hall. Knowing some of our clients, I'm sure that these "disclosures" in the press made them nervous enough to call in their chips from friends in high places.

Throughout the first few weeks, there was enormous press interest in the client books. The *Post* claimed that "the books contain the names and sexual preferences of the alleged clients of the blueblood Mayflower descendant accused of controlling high-class hookers for thousands of high-rolling men." The reference to the "sexual preferences" of our clients was rather misleading, as our notes were limited to the type of girl a client preferred and, in some cases, an indication that he occasionally liked to play bridge.

Alas, the paper was unable to reveal any of these names, although it did hold out the hope that if readers would only stay tuned, they might yet learn the juicy details: "The identities of the celebrities and playboys who allegedly paid for sex with beautiful escort girls remained a closely guarded secret—but may yet come out during the trial."

Inevitably, there were several references to the indisputable fact that the disclosure of our clients' names would lead to widespread domestic embarrassment—a prospect that certainly had me worried, although it delighted the press. One of the papers ran a cartoon that portrayed a woman sitting in the living room and reading the paper. Her back is to the kitchen, where we can see her husband kneeling—with his head in the oven. "Wow," the wife is saying. "Those Mayflower johns may have to testify in court. Won't that be fun, hon?"

Another cartoon showed a well-dressed man who was hiding a newspaper behind his back. We can just barely make out the headline, which reads, WHO'S WHO IN MADAM'S BOOK?

"What's that, dear?" he's saying to his wife. "The paper, dear? It didn't arrive again, dear!"

Another major theme in the tabloids was the way I dressed for my various appearances in court. In its coverage of the surrender, the *Post* had described me, rather cleverly, I thought, as "a slender 5-foot-7 blonde . . . impeccably dressed in a gray suit, gray pumps, and a beige silk blouse demurely buttoned to the neck—her chic outfit spoiled only by government-issue matching steel bracelets."

Even the much respected Murray Kempton, who generally has weightier matters on his mind, felt moved to comment on the fashion show. Writing in *Newsday*, he observed that at one of my court appearances, "Miss Barrows was wearing a suit of what a wise woman in attendance identified as 'periwinkle blue,' and she would have been altogether fetching if the shoulders had not been built up in the fashion that we associate with Jeanne Kirkpatrick and that make it clear that the wearer, whether madamish or not, is undeniably managerial."

It soon became clear that in New York City the story of the Mayflower Madam was a battle between two competing newspapers, the *Post* and the *News*. For the most part, I preferred the coverage in the *Post*, whose articles were generally more accurate. Although the *Post* certainly made its share of mistakes, there were times when I was convinced that the *News* was really in the business of reporting fiction.

At one point, a reporter from the *News* showed up at my apartment.

"Who is it?" I asked.

She identified herself. "I'm very sorry," I called out from behind the door. "I have no comment."

When I didn't hear her leave, I looked out the peephole and saw that she was still standing there. I continued to go about my business, and when I checked a couple of minutes later, she was still there. Feeling sorry for her, I opened the door and repeated, as politely as I could, that I was not able to speak to her.

She asked me a few questions anyway, but I told her again that I wasn't going to answer them. "I realize you're only trying to do your job," I said. "But my lawyers have absolutely forbidden me to talk to anybody. I'm paying a lot of money for their advice, and I feel that I ought to take it." Just then the phone rang, and I ran back inside to answer it, closing the door behind me.

But I had forgotten that the acoustics in my apartment were such that anybody who stood outside my door could hear virtually everything that was said inside. The following day, the *News* ran a front-page headline: EXCLUSIVE INTERVIEW WITH MAYFLOWER 'MADAM'.

Naturally, the reporters at the *Post* were furious at the possibility that I had given an interview to the competition, until Risa explained to them that the alleged interview never actually took place. The next day, the *Post* ran its own story, charging that the report in the *News* of an "exclusive interview" with the Mayflower Madam was a lie.

A day or two later, the *News* ran a banner headline: A PRINCE, MADAM, AND A WILD PARTY; SAUDI BATHED WOMEN IN CHAMPAGNE. According to the article, which was a complete fabrication, several of the girls and I had once attended a party at the Waldorf Towers, where the host, an unnamed Saudi prince, had given a number of the girls a champagne bath.

The following day, the *Post* struck back: WALDORF:

PRINCE'S PARTY NEWS TO US. Two days later, the *News* stuck by its guns: THE PRINCE'S BUBBLY BATH? IT WASHES.

For most news events, the weekly newsmagazines are considerably more accurate than the daily papers. Because they don't feel the pressure of a daily deadline, they have the luxury of covering a story more slowly and thoroughly—which generally means more accurately.

That's why I was particularly annoyed at the full-page article in *Time,* whose headline, A BLUEBLOOD'S BORDELLO IS BUSTED, showed no greater concern for the facts than did the tabloids. *Time* ran a photograph of the brownstone where our office was located; it was captioned "Barrows' Bordello." (Just for the record, my dictionary defines "bordello" as "a house of prostitution; a brothel.") Here, too, there was great interest in the names of the clients, with "a list so rich with executives, athletes, Arab sheiks, foreign officials, movie stars, and prominent society figures that one awed officer called it a *Who's Who.*" The magazine also reported that "each patron's pet vices were neatly inked next to his name."

Newsweek's article was far better researched, and kinder, too: "To a field overrun by pimps in garish Cadillacs, she apparently brought the upper-class virtues of decorum, good taste, and hygiene." The magazine even quoted Sergeant Elmo Smith, who said, "You couldn't help but be impressed."

My favorite article of all was written by Gigi Mahon for *Barron's,* the financial weekly, which ran the piece in its prominent, frontpage column, "Up & Down Wall Street."

"You really have to admire a well-run company, no matter what field it's in," the story began. After noting that "Sydney was one heck of a businessperson," and that I ran the place "with a benevolent yet firm hand," Ms. Mahon went on to provide an unusual and amusing commentary on my "crime" and its appropriate punishment:

"Now, we're not one to interfere with the lawful pursuit of justice, but it *does* seem to us that this business is just the kind of thing that the Reagan administration and all those supply-siders have in mind when they tell us that entrepreneurs are the lifeblood of American business and should be encouraged with tax cuts and the like.

"After all, think what Ms. Barrows was doing for the economy and our capitalist society. Men of means were paying money for a service, and that money was then flowing out all through the system. . . . The girls were making money, which means that Bloomingdale's was probably making money. Heaven knows the top New York hotels, which now charge 220 bucks a night for one of their *lesser* rooms, were making money.

"So, not that we hold any sway in these matters, we would urge that the alleged madam, if convicted, be sentenced to public service work. And we would even go so far as to cross the boundary into the cruel and unusual by suggesting something *really* unpleasant. That is, that Ms. Barrows be forced to teach a semester at the Harvard Business School, or maybe even go through the training program at McKinsey & Co. Surely then she would learn the lesson that crime doesn't pay, even while unlearning the lessons she's learned about good mangement."

I liked the *Barron's* article not only because it was complimentary, but because our business was finally being written about *as a business*. They accepted us for what we were and weren't trying to pass any moral judgments or make us seem titillating or scandalous. Given the number of men from the financial world who used to call us, this is where our story really belonged.

On December 10, *New York* magazine ran a long

cover story entitled "The Story of the 'Mayflower Madam.'" I still wasn't allowed to give any interviews, but I agreed to pose for the cover when the editors promised to fact-check the article with me before it ran.

Among other topics, the article touched on the Mayflower Madam's surprising primness: "Sheila seemed to abhor the usual vocabulary of the trade—'johns,' 'tricks,' 'repeats,' and 'regulars' were all called clients—and she was highly fastidious in her approach to sexual matters." Whoever their source was, I'm glad that she resisted any temptation to make our operation seem more salacious than it actually was.

For me, the most interesting quote in the article was a statement by Robert Morgenthau, the district attorney of Manhattan: "We didn't make a big deal out of this case. The press made a big deal out of it. We didn't know that we were arresting the Mayflower Madam."

This was, to our knowledge, his first public comment on the whole affair. And it confirmed what we suspected: that the district attorney was highly embarrassed by my case and wished it would go away. Bernhard Goetz had recently been arrested for attempted murder, and there had been several other highly publicized acts of violence and police brutality. Everyone could see that the police had better—albeit less titillating—things to do than chase a bunch of high-class call girls. It was they who brought in the press, and now they were paying the price.

Two weeks after the article appeared, *New York* magazine ran several letters to the editor. "I can now walk safer streets and enjoy sounder aleep," wrote one reader, "knowing that the notorious 'Mayflower Madam' will soon be brought to justice. With the arrest of hardened criminals like Sydney Biddle Barrows, maybe our law-enforcement agents can go to work on less serious offenders, such as murderers, rapists, and armed robbers."

Another reader, Gloria Hoffman Rice, wrote to say that she had recently received her copy of the B'nai B'rith *Star*. "And guess who advertised in this square, upright publication? Chutzpa has no bounds!"

Not so fast, Gloria. You might be surprised to learn that the hardworking sales staff at the B'nai B'rith *Star* called *me* to solicit that ad. I got a real kick out of the whole thing and was pleased that they treated us like any other business.

It did occur to me, of course, that the man from the *Star* didn't really understand what we were all about. "You realize that we're an escort service," I told him, "with all the ramifications that this implies."

"I understand," he said.

I was delighted because advertising in this publication could have opened up a whole new market for us. Unfortunately, we never got a chance to find out, as we were busted before the ad appeared.

I have always found it more than a little disingenuous when famous people complain about the negative side of their celebrity status. But now, suddenly, I understood what they were talking about. Fame, as I soon learned, is a very mixed blessing.

Now I'm aware that my experience of fame was somewhat unusual. Unlike most people who suddenly become famous, I hadn't exactly been looking for attention. I hadn't expected it, wished for it, or worked to get it. In fact, I had worked extremely hard to avoid it.

Whenever a celebrity talks about the high price of fame, people tend to say, "Oh, sure. I bet she's crying all the way to the bank." I certainly wish that had been true in my case. Some people become famous and trade up from taxis to limousines, but in my case, fame led right down to the subway.

Fame has different dimensions, of course, and being

known and being recognized are not the same thing. Although it wasn't much of a consolation for being put out of business, it did make life a little easier to know that millions of people were now aware that the notorious Mayflower Madam was also an exemplary businesswoman.

But being *recognized* was something else again. It was one thing to be recognized at parties, in restaurants, and on other occasions when I was looking my best. But I was unprepared and disconcerted to discover that people recognized me even when I was wearing my glasses, no makeup, and sweat clothes. In a city of strangers, I was often picked out of a crowd on the subway, in the supermarket, or just walking down the street.

I suppose I shouldn't have been surprised. In addition to the constant exposure on the local television news, my face had been on the front cover of the tabloids day after day. Even if you don't read these publications, you can't avoid seeing *other* people reading them, especially on buses and subways. Walking in Manhattan, you'd pass a newsstand every three minutes—and there I was again! No wonder some of my friends started teasing me that they were growing tired of seeing my face. But business is business, and the first rule of journalism is to make a profit. "I always knew when you were in the paper," one friend told me, "because when I got to the newsstand, all the copies of the *Post* had already been sold."

When people recognize me on the street, they usually give a knowing smile and continue on their way. But some people stare, and if I'm in a store or on the subway, they often come up to ask if I am, indeed, the Mayflower Madam. It seems, though, that this kind of inquiry has its own etiquette. Apparently it's considered gauche to come right out and ask, "Are you the Mayflower Madam?" Instead, people tend to say, "Excuse me, but did anyone ever tell you that you bear a striking resemblance to Sydney Biddle Barrows?''

Often, especially for the two or three months following the bust, people would come up and say things like ''Good for you!'' and ''We're behind you!'' and ''Fight them all the way!'' Drivers would shout out encouragements from car windows. And some people just wanted to shake my hand to let me know they were with me.

One day it hit me: I now had a public. Previously, the idea of ''having a public'' had always struck me as ludicrous. The phrase itself reminds me of Erica Kane, the chief villainess on ''All My Children.'' In the fifteen years I've been watching the show, Erica has been, among other things, a model, a businesswoman, the wife of the richest man in the world, and a magazine editor. But regardless of her occupation, her overwhelming concern is always her ''public,'' in whose name she justifies all sorts of selfish and dastardly deeds.

Now, for the first time, I was beginning to understand that people in high-profile situations really *do* have a public. When I thought about it, I had to admit that I was interested in certain celebrities, which meant that I constituted part of their public. And to some extent, at least, everybody who followed my story in the papers was part of mine.

Being recognized was sometimes awkward, but not being recognized could be equally difficult. One evening, at a friend's wedding reception, everybody at my table, except for one woman, knew who I was.

''So what do you do?'' she asked.

''I'm between jobs right now,'' I replied.

''And before that?''

''I was in the entertainment business.''

She kept talking and asking me questions, and I continued to keep the conversation vague. The other people at the table got a big kick out of the whole thing, but I could hardly come right out and say, "Well, actually, I'm the Mayflower Madam."

Another thing that happens when you're famous is that people write you letters. I received a great deal of mail, most of it as a result of the stories in the tabloids. My favorite letter, from a man in Philadelphia, included these comments:

"The first thing I want to say is: Keep you head held high as you have done. You can't possibly know how many people are on your side, both consciously and subconsciously. Second, this thing will blow over very soon, and will be a footnote in society's history. Sure, it will be a talking point, but as time goes by, more of amusement than ridicule.

"The truth is that the men who don't eat quiche wish they knew you, and the women who have any gender are jealous or titillated. So I say, carry on."

And from a *Mayflower* descendant in Westchester:

"I have been following the papers these past few weeks, and I have come to believe that *you* are now the victim in what is believed to be a victimless 'crime.' Plus, by violating your privacy, making fun of you, and revealing your address, the authorities have tried to make you fair game for anyone. I want you to know that I'm 100% behind you."

"Fight them all the way!" wrote a physician from Suffern, New York, on his prescription pad.

"This is a note to express my admiration," wrote a Manhattan man. "Don't let the bastards grind you down!"

"Above all," wrote another supporter, "why should you be punished for providing a service for people who are willing to pull out the credit card rather than go through the hell of a singles bar?"

To my delight, only four of the hundreds of letters I received were negative. Of these, my favorite came from an outraged, anonymous citizen who was evidently confused by whether I was Sheila Devin or Sydney Barrows:

"Dear Miss Whatever Your Name Is," the letter began. "A whore is a whore is a whore. You've broken the law, harlot. Do you really think the law should give you a medal? Culture or not, jail is too good for you!! Do you know that derelicts, prisoners, and bums came over on the *Mayflower*? So don't toot your own horn, pig!"

Throughout my ordeal, I had one regular correspondent: a man from Brooklyn who signed his letters, "Big Frankie, your bodyguard forever until I die." His letters were kind, supportive, and full of assurances that God was on my side and that everything would turn out all right. After my case was finally resolved, Big Frankie finally revealed his last name and address, whereupon I immediately called to thank him for his support. Later, when he read in the papers that a film was going to be made, Frankie wrote me one more letter, enclosing a picture, which he asked me to forward to the producer in the hope that he could play a "klint"—a client—in the movie.

It's always difficult to know what the other side is thinking, but as spring moved into summer and I had still shown no interest in taking a plea, it became apparent that the prosecution was growing increasingly nervous over the possibility that we might actually go to trial. On June 4, matters became even more difficult for the prosecution when Justice Brenda Soloff notified them that they would have to file a more complete bill of particulars. In other words, they not only had to provide details for *each* alleged act of prostitution—including the date, time, place, girl, and patron—but they also had to connect each of these acts to me.

Risa and Mark, meanwhile, were trying to get the case

dismissed. They had demanded a bill of particulars from the beginning, arguing that the prosecution had failed to show any evidence to justify its claims. "Your Honor," Mark told the judge, "there has never been a case where a bigger mountain has been made out of a smaller molehill. People in the rest of the country can't even imagine why this case is being prosecuted. But people in New York can understand it, because all New Yorkers can recognize a good landlord-tenant dispute when they see one."

With an election campaign on the horizon and the prospect of a highly embarrassing trial before them, the D.A.'s office finally made me an offer I could hardly refuse: I could plead guilty to the misdemeanor of promoting prostitution in the third degree and pay a fine of five thousand dollars. I would also be granted a certificate of relief from all civil disabilities, which was a proclamation from the court stating that although I had admitted wrongdoing, my "crimes" were judged so minor that I was to suffer no civil penalties, and no employment opportunities should be denied me because of my criminal record.

By this time, the judge was eager to call it quits. In describing my options, she had warned me that if the case went to trial, and if I were found guilty, I could conceivably end up with "one year in prison and a period of three years' prostitution—I mean probation."

On July 19, a Friday, I returned to court for the last time, along with a number of the girls, Jimmy Roe, David, and various other friends. At the arraignment back in November, I had pleaded not guilty, and now I was back to plead guilty.

"Miss Barrows," said the judge, "have you changed your plea?"

"Reluctantly, Your Honor," I replied. Now that the moment was upon me, I was in a foul mood. Giving up was difficult enough; I had no interest in giving up graciously.

The judge was willing to grant me an "unconditional discharge," provided that I pay the fine that very day. (A "conditional discharge," even if the only condition is the payment of bail, just doesn't sound as good.) Once more, David came to the rescue by going right to his bank to arrange for a certified check. What a friend.

The previous night, when the *Post* had asked Risa what we were looking for, she replied, "A kiss on the wrist." The phrase appeared in the morning paper and soon entered the legal lexicon. Despite the guilty plea— and my mood—we all felt that we had won a significant victory, and Risa and Mark made a point of choreographing the rest of the day as though we had received an acquittal. We started the day with breakfast at Ellen's, and after the plea we took a limousine to Wood's, an elegant restaurant, where we held a combined press conference and champagne victory party. This was followed by a victory lunch at Forlini's, where defendants traditionally go after they are acquitted because it's a favorite lunch spot for people in the district attorney's office and for criminal and Supreme Court judges.

Everyone was celebrating, but I was still bitter at having been forced to give up the fight. Although I wanted to protect the girls and the clients, I had also looked forward to the opportunity of confronting my accusers and discovering just what Elmo Smith was up to. According to Mark and Risa, the prosecution's case was very weak, for in addition to insufficient evidence and our charge of selective prosecution, there was the strong possibility of illegal wiretaps, a badly designed search warrant, and other governmental misconduct. They had no cards to play, and we knew it. I had smelled a victory, for which a kiss on the wrist was no substitute.

In the middle of an elaborate Italian lunch, I suddenly

found tears rolling down my cheeks. I excused myself and went home: I was upset at having given up the fight, and I needed some time alone.

That night, we held a last-minute party in a private room at the Limelight. Although this one was much smaller than the Mayflower Defense Fund Ball, there was almost as much press coverage. All the assistants showed up, as did many of the girls, including some who had worked for me years ago. Kate used the opportunity to resurface after months in hiding. Right after the bust, she had disappeared off the face of the earth, and I learned at the party that she had been living in California at the house of one of our clients, who had told her to call if she was ever in trouble.

At midnight, I left the party with Susan and Tom Eley, two old friends who had invited me to spend the weekend at their summer house upstate. (It was Susan who had set up my blind date on that fateful night in October.) We spent a glorious, peaceful weekend by the shore of the lake, lying around and soaking up the sun. We were completely isolated; there were no reporters, no flash bulbs, no ringing telephones. My long ordeal was finally over—or so I thought.

For some time, I had been thinking about writing a book about my experiences. Actually, I had thought of writing one even before the bust, although it would have had to be published anonymously. But I thought that the business was fascinating and that some of our stories were pretty good, and I was confident that a good number of readers would think so, too. I even had a title in mind: *We Are Three at the Waldorf*, which was how some of our Arab clients used to begin their telephone inquiries.

In the weeks following the bust, Risa and Mark had heard from a number of writers, publishers, and agents who were interested in my story. But each of these people had his or her own agenda, and although I was eager to get started, selecting a coauthor and a publisher was not a decision that I wanted to rush.

In the spring, a friend of Risa's in Boston recommended William Novak, the Boston writer who had collaborated with Lee Iacocca on his best-selling autobiography. After the unprecedented success of *Iacocca*, Novak had been besieged by offers and was currently talking with Tip O'Neill's people about writing a book with the Speaker of the House. Bill came to New York to meet with Risa and me, and as I told him my story, he immediately zeroed in on what was important and unique about the business I had run. "If people think the car business was interesting," he told me, "wait until they read about *this*."

A number of publishers were interested in signing up my book, but two were especially serious: one was a large company that I'll call Type & Hype; the other was Arbor House, a relatively small company that was on the rise. Before making any commitments, both publishers wanted to meet me.

The editors at Type & Hype asked me to join them at a fancy Chinese restaurant. As soon as Risa and I walked in—for until the case was over, I went nowhere without a lawyer—two high-powered men started firing questions at me. Within a few minutes, it became clear that the book they had in mind for me was far more salacious than the one I was planning—or able—to write. I couldn't wait to get out of there, and I told Bill and Steve Axelrod, our agent, that no matter how much Type & Hype offered, I wasn't prepared to do that kind of book.

My meeting with the Arbor House people took place in their conference room. As I walked in, I noticed that the table had been set with champagne glasses.

"I see you guys like to celebrate early," I said.

But the joke was on me, as they brought out Perrier—and Pepperidge Farm cookies.

Although the Arbor House group asked some tough questions, I could see that they took my business seriously *as a business*. And although they certainly wanted a story that was both amusing and forthright, it was clear from the outset that a dirty book was the farthest thing from their minds.

Bill Novak and I agreed that it would be important for him to interview the girls. Although I could certainly supply enough information about the business side of our operation, they were the ones who knew all the good stories.

At first, most of the girls were reluctant to meet with him, because after reading all the stories about us in the tabloids, they were afraid the book would sensationalize our business and distort what we were all about. But when I assured them that I intended to tell the story as it really happened, and that as the co-author of *Iacocca*, Bill, too, had a reputation to protect, they soon changed their minds.

Throughout the spring and summer of 1985, Bill made a number of trips to New York to interview both the girls and me. When his friends learned what he was up to, they all volunteered to help out. "Are you *sure* you don't need a research assistant?" they would ask.

Each time he came to town, I would invite a few girls over to my apartment for an evening of wine and conversation. In addition to helping us on the book, these group interviews served as a way for the girls to stay in touch with each other and to talk about old times. Our business had ended so abruptly that we hadn't ever had the luxury of sitting down and talking about what the whole experience had meant to us. We had only recently started calling each other by our real names, which was a painful admission that the good old days were really over.

Because I had been their boss, and because I wanted the girls to speak to Bill without any inhibitions, I usually found some pretext to leave the room for most of the evening. But believe me, it wasn't easy to walk out on these conversations as the girls described the business from their own perspective, telling Bill how they first came to Cachet, what it was like to work for me, and how much they missed the camaraderie we all had.

I was there for part of these discussions, however, and a few of their comments have stayed with me. There was Tricia: "Look at me. I'm nice, I'm pretty, I'm sweet. I was president of my senior class in high school. If my friends found out I was a call girl, they'd die."

And Melody: "You can have millions of dollars, and some of our clients did, but if you don't have anyone to share it with, what's the point? Some men try to buy that companionship. I'm not saying it's as good as the real thing, but it beats the hell out of being alone. Besides, sometimes the real thing isn't that good, either."

And Sunny: "At first, it didn't thrill me to see all these married men fooling around. But then I started looking at it from their perspective. For most of our clients, who were hard-driven, hardworking men, an evening with one of us was an extraspecial treat they looked forward to every now and then, just as I sometimes reward myself for a month of strenuous dieting by going out for a hot-fudge sundae."

And Liza: "It was wonderful to be in the office on a night when the phones were ringing and business was humming. The girls were happy to be going out, and the clients were happy to be seeing them. Although sex was certainly part of the package we were selling, I knew all along that we weren't really in the sex business. And then one night it hit me: we were in the happiness business. The Constitution guarantees the right to life, liberty, and the pursuit of happiness, and all we were doing was helping people pursue a little happiness."

As soon as the book was contracted for with Arbor House, we were besieged by offers from production companies wanting to buy the film rights for a TV movie. I met with a number of film people, all of whom assured me with great sincerity that they would make the kind of movie I really wanted. In the end, we struck a deal with Robert Halmi, a respected film producer in Manhattan, a European gentleman who just couldn't believe that New York's criminal justice system would waste its time and energy prosecuting somebody like me.

As I write these words, the TV movie has not yet gone into production. Shortly after the deal was signed, however, I was distressed to learn that the network that plans to show the movie informed the screenwriter that he was not allowed to portray the fun we had or the camaraderie that existed among the girls. Apparently, advertisers were afraid that Moral Majority types would object that we were making prostitution look too appealing. In other words, because of the nature of their work, the girls who worked for me could not be depicted as happy or healthy people. It may be perfectly fine to glorify war and violence and police work, but call girls must not be portrayed in a favorable light.

I was exasperated to discover that television operates under such severe restrictions and tends to cater to a small minority whose sensibilities are so easily offended. I don't see why television programs can't be assigned ratings just like movies, so that viewers can make their own judgments. Commercial television is bad enough without also having to regulate everything down to the lowest common denominator.

My long legal case had ended on a Friday. The following Monday, as soon as I had returned from that relaxing weekend in the country, I had to contend with a whole new set of problems. Risa had been contacted by the New York State Crime Victims Board, which asked to see copies of all contracts that book publishers and movie producers had entered into with me.

To understand this development, we have to go back to 1977. When David Berkowitz, the so-called Son of Sam murderer, signed a contract for a book about his life and crimes, the state of New York passed legislation providing that any money a person convicted of a crime receives from a book or movie project that tells the story of the crime is to be placed into a special escrow account for five years. During that time, any victims of crimes committed by the guilty party may sue for compensation from that special account. If there are no victims, or if the victims are unsuccessful in their claim, in five years the money reverts back to the perpetrator.

The purpose of the Son of Sam law is clearly admirable, and for many kinds of crime it's a good law. But in a prostitution case, who are the victims? Neither clients nor girls could make a claim, of course, because they were participants in the crime. My indictment didn't name any victims, and the D.A. couldn't find any, either. That's not surprising, of course, because prostitution is the ultimate victimless crime. Even the chairman of the victims board told a reporter that "the law was not really intended to cover this kind of situation."

To date, only one self-described "victim" has come forward. In a letter dated August 29, 1989 (!), an ex-Manhattan woman wrote to the board as follows:

> Gentlemen:
> Crime has paid for Sydney Biddle Barrows, the Mayflower Madam.
> On doctor's orders I was forced to leave our

apartment home of 19 years because of Ms. Barrows' all-night bordello operating full scale next door to me. I am in [the place was omitted in the copy of the letter forwarded to us by the board] recuperating from the drug-related sex screams and crimes on my life I had to endure.

My temporary relocation and medical expenses have been excessive, I miss New York City.

May I file a claim with you, as I remain under medical care after a year?

On July 19, when I walked out of court, I was told that I was now a free woman. I had pleaded guilty to a misdemeanor, and I had paid a nominal fine. But to my enormous disappointment, the misdirected energy and the waste of taxpayers' money continued. Just as the police department took its officers off serious cases and the district attorney tied up city prosecutors and court time to pursue me, now the New York State Crime Victims Board was ignoring countless victims of real crimes while it was off on a wild-goose chase looking for victims who did not—could not—exist.

Once again, the press had a field day. A cartoon in the *Post* showed a group of lawyers in the office of the victims board cross-examining a group of men whose arms and legs are covered with casts and bandages. One man, who is bandaged from head to toe, is standing before the judge, who is asking him, "And just when did your wife discover that you were featured in the Biddle Barrows Black Book?"

Like their counterparts in the other helping professions, our girls brought tenderness and comfort into our clients' lives. We were *there* for them. We listened to them. We made them feel better. We gave to them emotionally, and we gave to them physically. Sex may be its own reward, but touching and hugging are the most healing and life-enhancing activities in the world.

Our society still needs to learn to tolerate the idea of women making a living by being intimate with men. Some people say that prostitution is degrading. Certainly it can be, but not in the agency I operated. I can think of a lot of jobs that are considerably more degrading than sharing an enjoyable evening with an attractive, successful man who is delighted to have you there and is willing to pay top dollar for your company.

But because prostitution is still illegal, the management side has attracted some fairly disgusting people. And whenever society makes a certain conduct illegal, it creates ancillary crimes as well. As everyone knows, the illegality of prostitution makes it an attractive operating ground for gambling, drugs, violence, and even organized crime.

American cities spend appalling amounts of money to combat prostitution. And how do they go about achieving this noble purpose? By rounding up large numbers of women, putting them in jail, and then dumping them out again the next day. Meanwhile, of course, the clients and the pimps are left alone.

Under our current system, undercover police officers trick women into offering them a good time just so they can arrest them. Do these women really represent such a danger to society that the police should be spending their time in this way? Of course not. The sooner these laws are reformed, the healthier our society will be.

I sometimes wonder what my Mayflower ancestors would have made of my situation. Granted, they were not exactly famous for their enlightened sexual attitudes. On the other hand, having escaped from religious persecution, they were genuinely passionate on the subject of freedom. Had they lived in a more enlightened era, they would have understood that the private behavior of consenting adults is not the business of the state. And they surely would have known that there have always been men who were willing to pay for the company and the favors of the opposite sex. It's not called the oldest profession for nothing.

Acknowledgments

*T*here are *so* many people whose love, time, understanding, and support have made both this book and the last year and a half of my life possible, that I want to take this opportunity to thank them.

—Bill Novak, for his infinite patience and amazing ability to turn hundreds of hours of tape recordings into this comparatively short book! It was fun and it was sad, it was interesting and it was dull, we were silly and we were serious; and it ended up being a wonderful experience. Linda Novak's insightful questions and comments were as welcome as her gracious hospitality.

—Risa Dickstein, who did far more than simply head up the defense team; my admiration of her professional skills, imaginative legal work, and an ability to turn defeats into victories is equal to my gratitude for the endless hours she devoted to all the other more personal aspects of the case. Rarely does such friendship and affection spring from a professional relationship and I am but one of many whose life has been touched by her natural exuberance and deep personal concern and caring; she is a person who truly adds to the quality of life of those around her.

—Mark Denbeaux, whose spirit, enthusiasm and brilliant strategy made this case far more than just the typical obfuscation of justice. His disdain of the "old boy network," his willingness (more like eagerness, really) to go to trial, his uncompromising principles and standards of fairness, and his relish for challenging the status quo made what could have been a harrowing ordeal into a great deal of fun.

—Peter Fabricant, for his selfless concern, hard work, long hours, and shrewd legal work.

—Scott Felcher, for all the long hours, lost weekends, hard work, "Sydney-sitting," and irrepressible good humor.

—Barbara Dixon, for her indefatigable energy, staunch commitment, and hard work.

—George Brooks, for all those late nights, long weekends, and good cheer—we miss you.

—Renee Scotland, whose energy, organization, devotion, high standards, and hard work pulled it all together.

—Michael Zimmer, Ahmed Bubulia, Charles Sullivan, Michael Reisinger, and Neil Cohen, who realized the importance of the constitutional issues involved, and despite the fact that many people were hostile to them for supporting my cause, worked many long hours developing new theories and legal defenses for this case. The high quality of their scholarly work and their warmth, sympathy, and emotional support meant more to me than words could ever convey.

—Steve Axelrod, who has put in more work on this book than he ever imagined possible and whose clear head, sound judgment, and endless patience kept me in line through the long struggle.

—Larry Goldmen and Jay Goldberg, for representing and taking such good care of my girls.

—Steve Hyman and Wayne Brody, for their hard work, long late hours, and calming influence.

—Ken Warner, for making an exception and helping me when I needed it.

—Tony Speisman for his time, concern, and little green rubber ball.

—"David," whose caring, generosity, and unwavering support leaves me at a loss for a way to ever thank him enough, and to whom I will always be indebted. I love you more than anyone in the world.

—Susan Davis-Eley and her husband Tom, two of the most supportive and special friends anyone could ever have.

—Wendy Weiler Chappell and her husband Donald, whose love and wonderful little dinners meant so much to me.

—Jimmy Roe, whose friendship, courage, and positive energy helped me make it through.

—Jim Black and Jim Tracy, who always had the time to listen, to talk, to care, and to help.

—Larry West, for his sympathetic ear, sound advice, and unwavering support.

—Paul Schaye and Bob Behr, for all the trips to the country, fun dinners, and time, energy, and thoughtful advice.

—L.S.C., for putting up with the tears and the mood-swings. I thank you for being there.

—John Ryan, who always had the time to listen, to care, to help, and to be there.

—Nancy Bonwit, Jay Fraze, and all of those 32 Beach "Post Busters" who have stood by me in spite of the fact that no one will ever let them forget that front-page "exposure" in their underwear!

—"Wes" for his caring, generosity and friendship.

—Gael Love, the first person who took a chance and gave me the opportunity to do the *Interview* layout.

—Jackie Burnham and Ed Callaghan, for their many hours of hard work, their genuine concern and support, and all their other kindnesses.

—Louis Licari, for making me beautiful so often.

—Marion Sunshine, for all her help and friendship.

—David Cobell and Jennifer Lawrence, who made me glamorous beyond my wildest dreams.

—Richard Currier, for all his kindness, support, and friendship.

—Dallas Boesendahl, for all his help, concern, and hard work.

—C.J. Blanda, for the lovely reception and supper he gave for all my friends after the ball.

—Adam Beal, Tracy Mills, Tony Chase, and Michael Katz for their beautiful clothes.

—Zeus Goldberg, for the champagne press conference at his restaurant, Woods.

—The Limelight, for the Victory Party and the Mayflower Defense Fund Ball.

—Judy Horon, for her friendship, support, and belief in me.

—Dr. Steven Lamm, Dr. Gary Sherman, Dr. Hugh Melnick, Dr. Robert Schweitzer, Dr. Patricia Saunders, and Dr. Noble Endicott, who took care of me when I needed it.

—Claudette, Tricia, Melody, Jamie, Liza, Ashley, Joanna, Shelley, and Vicki, for all of their time and their stories that went into the making of this book.

—Claudette, Melody, Tricia, Jamie, Liza, Sunny, Cameron, and Sonya, for all their time and their stories which unfortunately never made it into the movie.

—Those unnamed clients who took the time to work with us on this book so that we could have a more complete view of their side of the story.

—All of my friends, too numerous to name, who have stood by me, encouraged me, been there for me, stood up for me, listened to me, cared for me, helped me, and gave me advice. I thank you all from the bottom of my heart.

—Above all, my family, who have stood by me and have been caring, supportive, generous, and understanding far beyond the call of duty—and especially my mother, to whom I hope to make it all up some day.

I may have been the person who organized the business, but the girls are really the ones who should get the credit for its dazzling success. I always thought of them as "my babies" and loved them and cared about them and hoped for their success in life with all of my heart. I would like to take this opportunity to thank them individually (by their working names) and to wish all of them, wherever they are, every happiness.

Adrienne	Brittain	Danielle
Alanna	Brooke I	Darlene
Alexandra	Brooke II	Debbie
Alexis	Cameron	Debra
Allison	Camille	DeeDee
Amanda	Carey	Deidre
Amy	Carla	Denise
Angela	Carole	Devin
Anne	Carolyn	Diane
Annette	Cathy	Didi
Anya	Cecelia	Donna
Arden	Celia	Dominique
Ariana	Chantal	Dorian
Arlene	Charlotte	Dory
Ashley	Cheryl	Elaine
Audrey	Chris	Eileen
Avery	Christy	Elise
Barbara	Claire	Elizabeth
Bianca	Clarissa	Emily
Blaine	Claudette	Erica
Blake	Colby	Gabriella
Bobbi	Corinne	Gina
Brea	Dale	Ginger
Brent	Dana	Heather I

Heather II	Lonnie	Robin
Helena	Lorraine	Sally
Irene	Louise	Sandy
Jade	Lynne	Severine
Jaime	Maggie	Sharon
Jane	Margot	Shawna
Janine	Marguerita	Shelby
Jeanette	Mariko	Shelley
Jeannie	Marisa	Shari
Jennifer I	Megan	Sherry
Jennifer II	Mei	Shevaun
Jenny	Melanie	Sonya
Jessica	Melissa I	Sophia
Jerri	Melissa II	Stacey
Joanna	Michelle	Sunny
Jody	Mila	Susan
Judy	Mitzi	Susie
Julia	Miya	Sylvia
Julie	Monica	Tara
Karen	Montgomery	Taylor
Katherine	Nancy	Tess
Katy	Natalia	Terry
Kelly I	Natalie	Tina
Kelly II	Natasha	Tracey
Kerry	Nicole	Tricia
Kristen	Nina	Trish
Kristine	Pamela	Valerie
Laura	Patty	Vanessa
Laurie	Paula	Veronica
Lee	Penny	Vicki
Leigh	Polly	Victoria
Lena	Raviana	Wren
Lindsay	Rebecca	
Lisa	Roberta	

I would like to express my admiration and gratitude

once again to the assistants, those hardworking and conscientious Superwomen who held the girls, the clients, and the business together.

Ashley
Claire
Connie
Jaime
Liza
Lorraine
Rebecca
Veronica